D0807358

Astros and Asterisks

Terry and Jan Todd Series on Physical Culture and Sports
Edited by Sarah K. Fields, Thomas Hunt, Daniel A. Nathan,
and Patricia Vertinsky

Also in the series:

Astros and Asterisks

Houston's Sign-Stealing Scandal Explained

EDITED BY JONATHAN SILVERMAN

University of Texas Press ⟡ Austin

Copyright © 2023 by the University of Texas Press
All rights reserved
Printed in the United States of America
First edition, 2023

Requests for permission to reproduce material from this work should be sent to:
Permissions
University of Texas Press
P.O. Box 7819
Austin, TX 78713-7819
utpress.utexas.edu/rp-form

♾ The paper used in this book meets the minimum requirements of
ANSI/NISO Z39.48-1992 (R1997) (Permanence of Paper).

Library of Congress Cataloging-in-Publication Data
Names: Silverman, Jonathan, 1965– editor.
Title: Astros and asterisks : Houston's sign-stealing scandal explained / edited by
    Jonathan Silverman.
Description: First edition. | Austin : University of Texas Press, 2023. | Series: Terry
    and Jan Todd series on physical culture and sports | Includes bibliographical
    references and index.
Identifiers:
    LCCN 2022048798
    ISBN 978-1-4773-2742-5 (cloth)
    ISBN 978-1-4773-2743-2 (paperback)
    ISBN 978-1-4773-2744-9 (PDF)
    ISBN 978-1-4773-2745-6 (ePub)
Subjects: LCSH: Houston Astros (Baseball team)—Corrupt practices. | World Series
    (Baseball) (2017) | Baseball—Corrupt practices—History. | Sports—Corrupt
    practices—Moral and ethical aspects. | BISAC: SPORTS & RECREATION /
    Baseball / History | LCGFT: Essays.
Classification: LCC GV875.H64 A88 2023 | DDC 796.357/64097641411—dc23/eng/20221017
LC record available at https://lccn.loc.gov/2022048798

doi:10.7560/327425

Contents

Acknowledgments

The Astros cheating scandal broke in the late fall of 2019, after the World Series and before COVID began to devastate the world a few months later. In a short period of time, the scandal gathered momentum as its weirdness became apparent and its particulars ensnared what was becoming baseball royalty: the manager, coaches, and players of the 2017 World Series champion Houston Astros, who seemed to have perfected what Michael Lewis termed Moneyball and Ben Reiter called Astroball. They were fired just two months before COVID shut down spring training. At about that time, I pitched the idea of a type of contextual snapshot of the Astros scandal to one of the editors of the Todd series in sports for the University of Texas Press. My idea was to find writers who could put this weird scandal in perspective in a lively and thoughtful way.

The reader will judge how well this succeeds, but I could not be more thrilled with the result. In putting together an edited collection, editors rely on the work and talent of their contributors. So my first duty is to thank them, the contributors who wrote for the collection directly and others who graciously allowed me to reprint their work.

Publishing any book is impossible without editorial support, and everyone involved with the University of Texas Press has been enormously supportive. Robert Devens supported the proposal from the beginning, and Dawn Durante has advocated for the work at every step of the editorial process, mixing support with insightful and necessary critique. Peggy Gough, Robert Kimzey, Sarah McGavick, and Mia Uribe Kozlovsky were invaluable as well in answering questions and otherwise engaging the manuscript's production. Gregory McNamee provided smart and thoughtful copyediting.

I also thank the anonymous reviewers who made the book so much better with suggestions on the micro and macro level. I also want to thank Brooks Varni from *The Athletic* for giving permission for Evan Drellich's column.

Without Dan Nathan suggesting authors, I would not have been able to pursue this book. Sarah Fields, like Dan a series editor, was also supportive of this work.

UMass Lowell supported my work directly through providing funds for the images in this book. Karen Morin and Richard Serna helped me negotiate support for image processing. Luis Falcon, Sue Kim, Wael Kamal, and Joe Hartman also provided support.

I find my deepest support and connection among my colleagues. They help produce an atmosphere that encourages both collegiality and scholarship, as well as a deep commitment to teaching. Special thanks go out to Todd Tietchen and Jacky Ledoux. Librarian Rose Patton was invaluable getting all sorts of materials through interlibrary loan. A special shout out to Faculty Writing Spaces and my co-fellow, Natalie Houston, for encouraging writing at the university, and Anne Maglia, Eric Si, and Paulette Brooks for supporting Writing Spaces. I wrote much of this book in timed writing sessions with Natalie and the wonderful patrons of the London Writers Salon, an online writing accountability group based in London but experienced everywhere.

NASSH members were enthusiastic about the book from its conception, and many of its members are in the book. At a relatively late time in my scholarly career, I'm delighted I've found a community to call my own.

I would like to thank my mom, Beverly Silverman; my brothers, Jason and Joel; my sister, Alba; and my nephews Noah and Theo for their support.

And a final thanks to all my fellow graduate students in American Studies at University of Texas at Austin. Our department culture always seemed to focus on how to make books out of subjects, a process I have continued to participate in with colleagues, students, and publishers since I've graduated. That this became a book largely follows from that speculative process, trying to imagine a book out of an idea. What you have before you is exactly that.

Introduction

On November 12, 2019, Ken Rosenthal and Evan Drellich published a shocking story on the website *The Athletic*: during the World Series, the Houston Astros had stolen signs from the opposing team using a camera that transmitted them to a monitor near the dugout, where players hit a trash can to let their teammates know what was coming: no bangs for a fastball and bangs for breaking balls and off-speed pitches. What followed was outrage from numerous corners of the sports world and beyond. Commentators, fans, and players still talk about the scandal, which has now morphed into a cautionary tale of hubris and given opposing fans a long, perhaps lifetime, cudgel to batter Astros supporters.[1]

In a baseball game, a catcher, or sometimes a coach in a dugout, usually communicates to the pitcher the type of pitch they think the pitcher should throw, usually with a hand gesture recognizable to the pitcher. But fairly regularly over time, baseball players have tried to decode these signs and convey them to the batter. Typically, after cracking the signs, players convey these stolen signals while on base to a player at bat. That seems like a game within a game, one of many, perhaps questionable but within the spirit of baseball, a game with its share of deception.

However, the Houston Astros crossed a line that has long been considered unethical—taking advantage of new technologies to decode and communicate the signs. Recent work suggests that one of the most famous home runs of all time, Bobby Thomson's pennant-winning homer in 1951 off Ralph Branca to deliver victory to the New York Giants over the Brooklyn Dodgers, may be attributed in part to sign stealing using a telescope and buzzer.[2] The recent hard turn toward analytical analysis using a combination of traditional and new methods of measurement required more cameras in many different places, which led to two storied Major League Baseball (MLB) clubs' being exposed for using outside means to convey signals. In recent years, the league punished the Boston Red Sox for using Apple watches to tell batters what pitches were coming and the New York Yankees for using dugout phones illegally. Indeed, one of the Astros' defenses is that they were reacting to others' cheating by cheating themselves.

The process in the resulting scandal unfolded like this: As part of the game's rapid evolution in statistical analysis, MLB allowed teams to use cameras all over the stadium and to install replay rooms where footage could be reviewed in real time. Astros personnel stationed one of the cameras at Minute Maid Park (formerly Enron Field) in the outfield, where it was perfectly situated to capture the catcher's signs from the opposing team. That footage played on a video monitor in the Astros dugout, near the aforementioned trash can. Previous knowledge of opposing pitchers' signs aided the effort; Astros personnel collected signs on a spreadsheet called "Codebreaker," developed late in the 2016 season, which allowed the players to quickly interpret which pitches were coming.[3] As Tony Adams writes in this volume, the process lasted all summer at home games—even when the team was way ahead—until September 21, 2017, late in the season, when White Sox pitcher Danny Farquhar figured out that the Astros knew his signals and were using them to guess his pitches correctly. The banging stopped for a while, but according to Commissioner Rob Manfred, citing player testimony, it continued during the playoffs, though Adams says later in this book that cheating during the playoffs was hard to confirm. The Astros beat the Red Sox in the American League divisional series and the Yankees in the championship series. The Astros won the World Series, beating the Los Angeles Dodgers in seven games.

The Astros did not repeat their World Series success in 2018 and 2019 but advanced to the ALCS in 2018 before losing to the Red Sox. In 2019, they returned to the World Series, ultimately losing to the Washington Nationals. A few months later came *The Athletic* exposé: by way of an interview with Mike Fiers, then of the Oakland A's but a pitcher for the Astros in 2017, Rosenthal and Drellich revealed the signal-stealing scheme to the world. The outrage came from sports talk hosts, columnists, Twitter denizens, and casual fans alike. Many MLB players—especially those for the Los Angeles Dodgers, who lost to the Astros in a close World Series, and the New York Yankees, who lost to Houston in the American League Championship Series—seemed particularly upset. After the story broke, MLB conducted an investigation, and it suspended Houston general manager Jeff Luhnow and manager A. J. Hinch, as well as Boston Red Sox manager Alex Cora, who had been a Houston bench coach in 2017. Their clubs fired all three men (Cora and the Red Sox "parted ways") as well, and former Astro Carlos Beltrán, considered a ringleader of the scheme, was fired (parted ways) as a newly hired manager of the New York Mets after serving less than three months in the position. Cora was later rehired by the Red Sox and Hinch hired by the Detroit Tigers, and Beltrán worked part-time for the New York Yankees as a broadcaster in 2022. Manfred did not punish individual players, giving them immunity from punishment if they cooperated with the investigation. Most controversial of all, he allowed the Astros to keep their 2017 title, and he did not punish a single player. Commentators broadly speculated that Manfred chose to give the players immunity in hopes of avoiding conflict with the powerful Major League Baseball Players Association.

We are left with a situation that may be unprecedented—confessed cheaters who are going unpunished, at least officially. Some might argue that these cheaters have actually been rewarded. When Olympic athletes are caught cheating, they are stripped of their medals and sometimes their world records. Recruiting violations have caused college basketball teams to retroactively forfeit games. Here Major League Baseball confirmed that the 2017 World Series winner cheated, and yet the record will show that the 2017 Astros were the World Series champions.

In 2020, the sporting world braced for a season of retribution. Commentators speculated that this might include beanballs by opposing pitchers, protests by fans, and tense series between the Astros and Dodgers and the Astros and Yankees. There were only a few games in spring training, and informally the Astros did have a few more beanballs, and fans booed and held up derisory signs. Then COVID-19 hit and postponed the season. The protests continued online, with angry fans and Astros troll accounts on social media, but it wasn't the same as being in the park and booing or banging on trash cans or holding up punning signs about trash cans.

Like everyone else in the world, I had plans that were scuttled by the pandemic, and these plans included doing in-person research for this book. I wanted to go to Houston to talk to fans of the Astros. I wanted to go to opposing stadiums to see what fans would do and say. I wanted to see the reaction to the scandal in a stadium. But the pandemic muffled any chance of an in-person response, leaving many fans unsatisfied with the scandal on multiple levels. As my friend Abi Cooper said, "I wanted booing." At the end of 2020, the Los Angeles Dodgers won the World Series, which seemed to lower the intensity of the Astros scandal, though the Astros' appearance in the 2021 World Series against the Atlanta Braves brought a slew of reminder pieces about the scandal. The Astros lost. When they won the World Series in 2022, many observers brought up the cheating again.

The echoes of actual trash can banging remain, simply because there has been no cultural resolution. This unresolved controversy propels *Astros and Asterisks*, which approaches and analyzes the controversy from a variety of angles. We explore this subject in five sections:

- "Histories of Cheating in Baseball," which covers the period before the scandal came to light;
- "The Scandal Unfolds," which tells the story of the cheating scheme itself;
- "Fans and the Scandal," which covers both how the fans reacted and why they reacted as they did;
- "The Scandal and Its Ethical Dilemmas," which explores some of the ethical issues attached to the scandal; and
- "Technology and the Scandal," which explains the implications of using technological and informational means to cheat.

The approach is loosely chronological and parallels the way we often process big events, by recounting the story of the event, getting close to the people who experienced it, and then providing multiple contexts in which to understand it. A baseball sign-stealing scandal is a small event in the scheme of things, but it provides a window into so many elements of societal interest: what constitutes cheating and why do people do it, the strange symbols that pop up into our cultural consciousness, and the way Big Data and technological innovations have become entwined in our everyday lives.

History

The complications from the scandal largely arise from a historically imprecise response to cheating in baseball over time. As Steven Gietschier explains in his history of cheating in baseball, there has long been a dance of sorts between pitchers, batters, umpires, and the baseball establishment over rules that are often selectively enforced. For every stolen sign it seems like there is a spitball, and sorting out who ultimately has the advantage depends on when you look at baseball history. George Gmelch, now an anthropologist, uses his experience as a former professional ballplayer to show that attitudes about cheating are contingent and complicated. He writes that the lines between gamesmanship and cheating are clearer to nonfans—except when it comes to the way the Astros used the tools for scouting in ways that were unintended.

Until fall 2019, the public was unaware of the sign-stealing scandal, but there was a significant scandal in 2018 and 2019 before it came to light. That scandal occurred *after* the sign stealing but before it was revealed. In 2018, the Astros acquired from the Toronto Blue Jays relief pitcher Roberto Osuna, a top-shelf reliever who had been suspended for seventy-five games for violating the league's domestic abuse rules by committing acts of violence against his girlfriend, the mother of his child, drawing considerable criticism. When the Astros won the league championship series against the New York Yankees the next year, assistant general manager Brandon Taubman, in front of three female reporters including Stephanie Apstein from *Sports Illustrated*, repeatedly said, "Thank god we got Osuna. I'm so fucking glad we got Osuna." According to the journalists there, including Apstein, who had written about this problematic pickup, Taubman's repeated utterance was menacing. While most of the attention has been focused on the sign-stealing scandal, Katherine Murray considers the way the Astros apparently chose to pursue a championship over common decency. In her chapter, she asks larger questions about what this choice by the Astros says about gender and baseball. She argues that although it remains relatively unknown, it is every bit the scandal that the sign stealing was.

While observers agree that the Astros cheated, not everyone projected the same amount of outrage about their shenanigans. Delving into multiple contexts in which to examine cheating both in and out baseball, historian Richard Crepeau explains that cheating has been so prevalent that the reaction to the Astros may well be an overreaction.

Taken as a whole, these pieces show how the past is intertwined with the present, with precedent and context necessary components for understanding the cheating scandal.

The Scandal Unfolds

As the scandal emerged in late 2019, the reaction was a mix of outrage and amusement, perhaps because the elements of it were so unusual: not only was it team oriented, but there was also a mix of high and low tech; the camera and the garbage can make an odd pair. Because of the scandal's unusual components, high stakes for baseball fans but low stakes otherwise, Will Leitch argues the scandal is "fun" in his explanation of its context, which we have printed as it appeared soon after the sign-stealing scheme was uncovered. It wasn't steroids, and it was a Rube Goldbergian setup that, if you were not involved with those teams and players who might have been directly affected by the Astros' cheating, seems ingenious, if underhanded and wrong.

Then there is the trash can itself. In the midst of public happenings, unlikely symbols often emerge—think of the hanging chad in the 2000 election. In the Astros scandal, the trash can itself became a strange and powerful symbol, one that Roberta J. Newman examines. The fallout unfolded in a variety of ways. Evan Drellich, writing for the website *The Athletic*, notes that the blame did not rest solely in the hands of the players; he lists more than a dozen reasons why the scandal occurred.

Fans Respond

A large majority of non–Astros fans were predictably outraged by the scandal, but Astros fans had a more complicated response. Some renounced the team, but many didn't. Tony Adams, a longtime Astros supporter, chose to find out what actually happened; as he noted, the commissioner's report did not have a lot of detail. Adams tracked down game footage and charted the bangs. He writes about his process and the complex reactions he has had to seeing the Astros' first championship rhetorically overturned. Matthew Klugman examines the fan response from a historical perspective, then turns his attention to the way Astros fans reacted when confronted about their loyalty in the face of the scandal. Then two European baseball fans, Michael Hinds, an Irish literature professor, and his colleague at Dublin City University, philosophy professor Joseph Rivera, put the scandal in global perspective through a dialogue that explores the relationship between bad behavior, national identity, and sports.

The Ethics

The "what" of the scandal was compelling enough, but its complexity as group behavior also leads to questions about the ethical aspects of the scandal. Even the players involved seem not to be sure why it went on for so long. In *The Athletic*'s "755 Is Real" podcast in April 2020, Evan Gattis, a catcher for the Astros during the 2017 season, mused that people participated because of a pack mentality. "It got out of fucking control," he said. "I'm glad the objective truth is out there. It was not right, and it was wrong." He described the excitement of winning and what it meant to Houston after the devastation of Hurricane Harvey in August 2017, which claimed more than a hundred lives and caused more than $100 billion in damage. "But now it's kind of different. It's like, 'That happened, and we cheated.'"[4] The shocking part, law professor Mitchell Nathanson notes, is that it came out at all, given baseball's disgust for truth tellers, recounting that at least some of the initial response came from former players who lambasted Fiers for revealing clubhouse secrets. In addressing the tension between individual participation and team guilt, Allison R. Levin and Matthew Staker cover the way a team dynamic helps keep secrets like cheating within a clubhouse. Erin C. Tarver explains the way individual behavior is contextualized within collective responsibility, why the official and public responses to the Astros scandal have seemed so inadequate, and why it reverberates beyond baseball.

Technology

The details about the way the scandal worked emerged more gradually over the months following *The Athletic*'s revelation in late 2019, particularly the way technology was involved. Sports studies scholars Dain TePoel and Eileen Narcotta-Welp explain how technological developments, especially in the growth of Big Data, have put players further at the mercy of neoliberal political and economic pressures and increased surveillance. Later we learned that the Astros front office had documented its sign stealing in a program called "Codebreaker." So, like the video itself, spreadsheets were used to aid sign stealing and document the Astros' transgressions. I write about that and its relationship to the growth of analytics, why the two different games being played—one on the field and one on the spreadsheets—led inexorably to this scandal, and why it violates our idea of baseball as a pastoral game.

The Appendix

In handing down his suspensions, Rob Manfred issued a report that provided an account of the scandal and explanation of the investigation process, as well as detailing the punishments. The commissioner's report reflects not only MLB's needs but also the way it anticipates the public's response to the document. The report is a type of public legal document—Manfred is a lawyer, after all—and perhaps it is unsurprising that the scandal also led to actual legal action. Former Blue Jays pitcher Mike Bolsinger, whose terrible outing against the Astros in 2017 was his last in the majors, sued the Astros. I have included his lawsuit in this volume, for it aptly chronicles the issues in his case and scandal. His lawsuit was dismissed in California and refiled in slightly altered form in Texas, but he voluntarily dropped the case in 2021. But the lawsuit is an interesting document because it captures some of the drama and what was at stake in the scandal. Of course, the venue in which most of the judgments are coming to bear is the court of public opinion, and while the verdict seems to be settled, we are still understanding the scandal.

This Book

The lineup here is a mix of journalism, commentary, and academic analysis. My aim in providing this blend, besides helping us understand the scandal from a variety of perspectives, was also to suggest that different forms of analysis and examination can provide a more nuanced perspective. Looking at a cultural phenomenon means having complicated reactions to it, sometimes all at once, sometimes over time, sometimes filled with amusement and sometimes with anger. The writers begin with the same off-speed, weirdo story—the Astros cheated by stealing signs through a camera and conveyed them banging on a trash can—and really get their (metaphorical) swings in.

Notes

1. The following sources were very useful in composing the introduction: Ken Rosenthal and Evan Drellich, "The Astros Stole Signs Electronically in 2017—Part of a Much Broader Issue for Major League Baseball," *The Athletic*, November 12, 2019, https://theathletic.com/1363451/2019/11/12; Dayn Perry, "Astros, Red Sox Sign-Stealing Timeline: Everything We Know about MLB Scandals," CBS Sports, November 24, 2020, https://www.cbssports.com/mlb/news/astros-red-sox-sign-stealing -timeline-everything-we-know-about-mlb-scandals/; and Jacob Bogage, "What Is Sign Stealing? Making Sense of Major League Baseball's Latest Scandal," *Washington Post*, February 14, 2020, https://www.washingtonpost.com/sports/2020/01/14/ what-is-sign-stealing-baseball/.

2. Tom Jackman, "Baseball's Cheating History Includes Its Most Famous Home Run, the 'Shot Heard 'Round the World,'" *Washington Post*, February 13, 2020, https:// www.washingtonpost.com/history/2020/02/13/giants-cheating-home-run-1951/.

3. Jackman, "Baseball's Cheating History."

4. "The Tale of Evan Gattis, Part 2," 755 Is Real (podcast), *The Athletic*, April 2, 2020, https://podcasts.apple.com/us/podcast/the-tale-of-evan-gattis-pt-2/id147915 0771?i=1000470284872.

The Houston Astros Timeline

Before Major League Baseball

1888: Houston Buffaloes, a minor league team, formed.
1920: Formation of Texas Negro League and Houston Black Buffalos.
1949: Newark Eagles of American Negro League moved to Houston.

The Founding and the Early Years

1960: Houston Colt '45s franchise approved by MLB; becomes Houston
   Sports Association, led by Judge Roy Hofheinz, who eventually becomes
   sole owner.
1962: First MLB season.
1964: Name changed to Astros.
1965: Astrodome built.
1965: First two-million-attendance year (and first million-attendance year).
1969: Astros finish 81–81, first time at .500.
1972: First winning season, finish 84–69.
1975: Hofheinz turns control of Astros over to creditor.
1979: John McMullen purchases team.
1980: First NL West title and playoff berth; lose to Philadelphia Phillies 3–2
   (games) in National League Division Series (NLDS).
1986: First National League final, lose to New York Mets 4–3 in National
   League Championship Series (NLCS).
   Mike Scott wins NL Cy Young.
   Mike Scott wins NLCS MVP.
   Hal Lanier wins NL Manager of the Year.
1991: Jeff Bagwell wins NL Rookie of the Year.

The Drayton McLane Era

1993: Drayton McLane buys Astros for $115 million.

1994: Jeff Bagwell wins NL MVP.

1998: Larry Dierker wins NL Manager of the Year.

2000: Enron Field opens.

   First three-million-attendance year.

2002: Enron Park changed to Minute Maid Park after Enron goes bankrupt.

2004: Roger Clemens named NL Cy Young winner.

2005: First World Series appearance, lose to Chicago White Sox, 4–0. Beat Atlanta Braves 3–1 in NLDS and St. Louis 4–2 in NLCS.

   Roy Oswalt named NLCS MVP.

2007: Craig Biggio wins Roberto Clemente Award.

The Crane/Luhnow Era

2011: Jim Crane buys Astros for $680 million.

   Jeff Luhnow named GM.

2013: Astros move to AL West.

2015: First playoffs since 2005. Beat New York Yankees in Wild Card; lose to Kansas City Royals 3–2 in ALDS.

   Dallas Keuchel wins AL Cy Young Award.

   Carlos Correa wins AL Rookie of the Year.

2017: Astros win World Series 4–3 over Los Angeles Dodgers, and George Springer wins World Series MVP.

   Hurricane Harvey hits Houston.

   José Altuve wins AL MVP.

   Justin Verlander wins ALCS MVP.

2018: Astros beat Cleveland Indians in ALDS 3–1; lose to Boston Red Sox 4–1 in ALCS.

   Alex Bregman wins All-Star Game MVP.

   José Altuve wins AL Hank Aaron Award.

2019: Astros beat Tampa Bay Rays 3–2 in ALDS; beat New York Yankees 4–2 in ALCS; lose to Washington Nationals in World Series 4–3.

   Justin Verlander wins AL Cy Young Award.

   Yordan Alvarez wins AL Rookie of the Year.

   José Altuve wins ALCS MVP.

The Scandal Timeline

Fall 2016: Codebreaker, a website to keep track of opponent signs from
catcher to pitcher, concocted by Astros personnel.

Spring 2017: Astros begin using sign-stealing system.

May 28, 2017: First game with more than twenty bangs.

September 21, 2017: White Sox pitcher Danny Farquhar realizes Astros are
stealing signs.

September 22, 2017: Astros dismantle equipment (possibly temporarily).

October 5, 2017: Astros beat Boston Red Sox 3–1 in ALDS.

October 21, 2017: Astros beat New York Yankees 4–3 in ALCS.

November 1, 2017: Astros win World Series, beating Los Angeles
Dodgers 4–3.

July 30, 2018: Roberto Osuna, fresh off an MLB seventy-five-game suspension for physically abusing his girlfriend and mother of his child, traded
to Astros.

October 19, 2019: Brandon Taubman, an Astros executive, says, "Thank God
we got Osuna" to a group of female sportswriters, including Stephanie
Apstein of *Sports Illustrated*, who was wearing a domestic violence
awareness bracelet.

October 21, 2019: Apstein publishes story about incident on SI.com; Astros
deny it.

October 24, 2019: Astros fire Taubman.

November 12, 2019: Ken Rosenthal and Evan Drellich run story in *The
Athletic* detailing the accusations of former Astros pitcher Mike Fiers
that the Astros stole signs.

November 12, 2019: Jimmy O'Brien, nicknamed Jomboy, posts first video
breaking down how Astros stole signs.

January 13, 2020: Commissioner Rob Manfred issues report and takes
action:

Suspends Astros GM Jeff Luhnow, Astros manager A. J. Hinch, Red Sox
manager Alex Cora, and Astros assistant GM Brandon Taubman, all
for one year. Astros owner Jim Crane announces firing of Luhnow
and Hinch (Taubman had been fired the previous year).

January 14, 2020: Alex Cora and Red Sox agree to "part ways."

January 16, 2020: Manager Carlos Beltrán, a supposed ringleader of the
sign-stealing scandal, and the New York Mets agree to "part ways."

January 29, 2020: Astros fan Tony Adams posts signstealingscandal.com
after having listened to more than eight thousand balls and finding more
than one thousand bangs.

February 22, 2020: Astros booed at first spring training game with Washington Nationals.

March 13, 2020: Major League Baseball suspends spring training.

November 5, 2022: Astros win World Series, beating Philadelphia Phillies 4–2.

After Revelation of the Scandal

2020: Astros beat Oakland A's in ALDS 3–1; lose to Tampa Rays 4–3 in ALCS.

2021: Astros beat Chicago White Sox in ALDS 3–1; beat Boston Red Sox in ALCS 4–2; lose to Atlanta Braves in World Series 4–2.
Yordan Alvarez wins ALCS MVP.

Sources

Adams, Tony. Signstealingscandal.com.

"Buffs to 'Stros History of Houston Baseball. ABC 13. November 2, 2017. https://abc13.com/astros-mlb-houston-colt-45s/2545230/.

Fink, Rob. "Houston Eagles." *Texas State Handbook.* July 17, 2007.

"Houston Astros Team History & Encyclopedia." Baseball Reference. https://www.baseball-reference.com/teams/HOU/index.shtml.

"MLB Team History—Houston Astros Awards." ESPN.com. https://www.espn.com/mlb/history/teams/_/team/Hou/history/awards.

Perry, Dayn, "Astros, Red Sox Sign-Stealing Timeline: Everything We Know about MLB Scandals." CBS Sports, November 24, 2020. https://www.cbssports.com/mlb/news/astros-red-sox-sign-stealing-timeline-everything-we-know-about-mlb-scandals/.

Presswood, Mark. "The Negro Leagues in Texas." *Texas Almanac* 2008–2009. https://www.texasalmanac.com/articles/the-negro-leagues-in-texas.

"World Series and Postseason." Baseball Reference. https://www.baseball-reference.com/postseason/.

Astros and Asterisks

PART I

HISTORIES OF CHEATING IN BASEBALL

Bobby Thomson of the New York Giants hits a home run at the Polo Grounds against the Brooklyn Dodgers in the playoff game of October 3, 1951. Ralph Branca is the Dodgers pitcher delivering his home run ball. This incident shows how prevalent cheating has been in baseball history. (AP Photo)

CHAPTER 1

Baseball, Hot Dogs, Apple Pie, and Cheating: Blame It on the Pitchers

STEVEN GIETSCHIER

During the sometimes raucous interval between the top half of the eighth inning and the bottom half at Boston's Fenway Park, baseball fans have the chance to listen to, or sing along with, a recording of Neil Diamond's "Sweet Caroline." The first verse of this song starts with these words: "Where it began, I can't begin to knowing." Diamond is singing about a love affair, of course, but his lyric could easily be borrowed to preface the long history of cheating in baseball. Where it began, we can't begin to knowing.[1]

Cheating is as hallowed as playing the game itself. Even before baseball evolved from an amateur sport to a professional business and going back perhaps to the game's folk origins, it is not hard to imagine players taking liberties with whatever habits or rules were in place to press their advantage. Certainly, by the emergence of professionalism in the 1860s, ballplayers had determined that cheating could help them win.[2]

Baseball, spelled "base ball" throughout most of the nineteenth century, was a gentlemanly recreation when amateur clubs in New York and Brooklyn, then two separate cities, began playing it in the decades before the Civil War. The focus of the early game was far different from today's confrontation between pitcher and batter, and winning was supposed to be immaterial. Some of the fun came from hitting the ball, that is true, but more than that, "base ball" was an opportunity for fielders to display their prowess. That's what made the game worth playing. Pitchers pitched the ball so that batters could hit it so that fielders could exhibit their skill. Catch the ball, either on the fly or on one bounce, and the batter would be out. Fail to catch the ball cleanly, and a fielder could still put the batter out by tagging him or the base or by throwing the ball at him and hitting him, a premodern practice called "plugging" or "soaking." These are the talents that fielders sought to demonstrate, even as nonplayers began to show up to watch.[3]

Amateur "base ball" had an umpire, but not in the modern sense. The earliest surviving rules, those of the Knickerbocker Base Ball Club in 1845, stated that there shall be "an umpire, who shall keep the game in a book provided for that purpose," and that "all disputes and differences relative to a game, [are] to be decided by the umpire, from which there is no appeal." Thus, the early umpire acted as scorekeeper and as adjudicator if the two clubs could not agree on a safe/out call. These disputes were supposed to occur only occasionally since those playing the game regarded arguing as beneath their status as gentlemen.[4]

How did this change? How did an amateur activity intended for recreation and fellowship turn into a competitive sport played for money? Students of the early game point to the proliferation of matches between clubs, replacing intramural games, as the seedbed for change and to the evolution of the pitcher's role as the proximate cause. Matches between clubs upped the ante. They introduced a new kind of competition, an "us vs. them" interaction with victory, not camaraderie, as the goal. Clubs so engaged began to look for ways to win, and pitchers led the way when they began to alter how they pitched to gain an edge.[5]

Early pitchers delivered the ball underhand—like pitching horseshoes—and let the batter hit it. That started the fun. But once matches became competitive, pitchers who could get batters to hit the ball weakly or even strike out by swinging and missing three times could give their clubs an advantage. "Swift pitching," that is, pitching the ball fast, along with its counterpoint, what modern fans call the changeup, became the new standard.[6]

Pitchers who could vary speeds to confuse batters earned plaudits, but batters could rebel against swift pitching by refusing to swing. There were no called strikes at the time, so pitchers trying to strike out batters needed to trick them into swinging at pitches they thought they could hit. And with this attempt to deceive came, inevitably, the opportunity to cheat.

Enter Jim Creighton, a teenaged New Yorker who pitched the ball fast. He lowered his release point so that the pitched ball appeared to be rising, and he probably twisted his wrist just a bit, putting some spin and movement on the ball that made it harder to hit. This first pitching revolution, to borrow researcher Richard Hershberger's phrase, changed the game irrevocably. It altered the very nature of the activity, shifting its focus from fielder against runner to pitcher versus batter. Swift pitching also led to a series of rule changes, including called strikes and called balls and, over time, increasing the distance between the pitcher's plate, today's pitching rubber, and home base, today's home plate.[7]

Innovation was not necessarily cheating, but pitchers were still not satisfied. In what Hershberger calls the second pitching revolution, they pushed the edge of the envelope in two additional ways: first, by gradually adjusting the angle of their delivery, raising their arm from underhand to sidearm and eventually to overhand throwing, and second, by twisting their wrists even more than Creighton did and delivering what came to be called a curveball. Deception became everything.[8] Warren Spahn would not pitch until the middle of the twentieth century, but his mantra could have been theirs too. "Hitting is timing," he said, and "pitching is upsetting timing."[9]

Hershberger's two pitching revolutions gave rise to the modern umpire, whose job it was to pass judgment on every play, indeed on every pitch. The umpire's responsibilities increased gradually, but by the 1880s, he had moved from a passive position in foul territory somewhere near the first-base line to an active position behind the catcher so that he could call balls and strikes while also being ready every time the batter hit the ball to call plays in the field and at every base. The assumption undergirding the umpire's larger role was that players were no longer gentlemen, that they could no longer be relied upon to play by the rules unless they were watched.[10]

The umpire's job was difficult, made more so as play became rowdier and more cutthroat. Besides, pitchers were not the only ones putting umpires to the test. Any situation where a player might gain an advantage knowing that the game's sole umpire could not see what he was doing was ripe for subterfuge. In a maneuver so common that it had a name, the skip play, a base runner might cut a corner as he rounded second or third base. An outfielder might claim he had caught a ball on the fly and not trapped it. An infielder might insist that he tagged a runner or stepped on a base when in fact he had not. A fielder might impede a runner's progress by grabbing his belt. Even more seriously, a player or manager might argue with an umpire, threaten him, or encourage fans to do the same as a matter of sheer intimidation. Umpires earned the right to eject players and managers from a game, and league presidents could discipline offenders, but the umpire's profession remained one fraught with peril.[11]

An obvious strategy to combat these shenanigans was to assign more than one umpire to a game, but this did not happen for quite a while. The two major leagues did not require two umpires per game until 1912. By the mid-1920s, about half of all games had three umpires, but this did not become standard until 1944, and only in 1953 did the four-man crew become the rule.[12]

Another opportunity for skullduggery arose after teams began using signs that opponents could attempt to steal and decipher. Evidence suggests that the first uses of signs may have involved catchers positioning fielders in anticipation of a batter's hitting a ball in a certain direction. In 1860, a newspaper account praised the catcher for the Excelsiors, a Brooklyn club, "for the manner in which he would telegraph advantages to be gained, or the direction as to which one of the fielders should take a 'fly.'" The 1869 Cincinnati Red Stockings, baseball's first openly all-professional club, were lauded for employing two sets of signs, one flashed by centerfielder and captain Harry Wright to direct "the movements of the fielders" and a second by catcher Doug Allison, "who indicates by signs to the pitcher and base keepers the proper thing to do at the right moment."[13]

Signs that positioned fielders need not have been given in ways that stressed secrecy, but early on, players learned that they could use concealed signs to gain an advantage in certain situations. Newspaperman Henry Chadwick, who explored in print the intricacies of baseball so thoroughly and so passionately for so long that he earned the nickname "Father Baseball," wrote in 1874 that "when a catcher sees an opportunity to catch a player napping off a base, a certain signal should be given by which the pitcher may understand that he is to throw to the base promptly." Chadwick also explained the principal use to which defensive signals would be put. "If the pitcher is familiar with a certain habit of the batsman before him of hitting at a favourite [sic] ball," he wrote, "he should give the catcher a sign informing him that he is going to send in a slower or swifter ball or a higher or lower one than ordinarily is pitched."[14]

No one knows which battery first used signals to indicate what the next pitch should be, but the practice gained currency once pitchers began "swift pitching" and accelerated during the 1870s with the introduction of the curveball because catchers had to know what pitch was coming. Nor is it clear how many pitchers gave these signals to catchers and how many catchers indicated which pitch they would like pitchers to throw. Chadwick wrote in 1874 that calling the pitch was the pitcher's responsibility. Candy Cummings, one of the pitchers credited with inventing the curveball, said in 1878 that he signaled to his catcher. *Sporting Life*, a weekly newspaper founded in 1883, said that giving signs "is not the catcher's office." Pitcher Hoss Radbourn did "all the signaling himself." Bill Hutchison did so, too, although he sometimes shook his head "yes" or "no," pretending the catcher was calling them. New York Giants pitcher Christy Mathewson said that during the 1911 World Series he gave his signs to catcher Chief Meyers because they thought their opponents, the Philadelphia Athletics, were stealing them.[15]

Other sources, though, testify that pitchers' giving signs was far from universal. Larry Corcoran, who won forty-three games in 1880, may have had his catcher move a wad of tobacco to one side of his mouth to signal for a fastball and to the other for a curve. Another account says it was catcher Silver Flint who devised the tobacco sign, and a third had catcher King Kelly using one finger for a fastball and two for a curve. An 1886 article in the *Boston Globe* suggested that having the catcher give the signs "is a better plan when the catcher is a cool and experienced man." John Montgomery Ward, a college graduate who played several positions, wrote in 1888 that "until within a few years this sign was always given by the pitcher, but now it is almost the universal practice for the catcher to give it to the pitcher, and if the latter doesn't want to pitch the ball asked for he changes the sign by a shake of the head."[16]

As giving signs became standard and important, the chance arose for the other team to try to steal them. Figuring out an opponent's signs has never been against the rules, and batters quickly understood the advantage to be gained by such spycraft. Know what pitch is coming, and the chance of hitting it well jumps. Longtime New York Yankees coach Art Fletcher said, "A good sign stealer can always get a job." A team whose signs are so obvious that the opponent can detect and decipher them easily opens itself to this sort of surveillance. "The fault is not with the people stealing the signs," said Hall of Fame outfielder and broadcaster Ralph Kiner, "but with the people giving them." There are limits to the propriety of this espionage, however. A base runner on second is free to watch the catcher flash signs and learn what he can. A batter, on the other hand, who surreptitiously glances back at the catcher as he is calling pitches is liable to suffer consequences.[17]

When the Brooklyn Dodgers won two major league pennants in a row, 1889 in the American Association and 1890 in the National League, pitcher Germany Smith credited "our studying and learning the signs of the opposing pitchers." He explained that [Cincinnati catcher] Jim Keenan "would crouch down close to the ground in giving the sign and would use two fingers. The players in the base lines couldn't see him give it, but a man on the base could detect it. He would give the coacher a hand signal, who would in turn 'tip' the batter."[18]

The 1889 California League was the scene of a similar escapade, explained by Oakland Colonels captain Norris O'Neill. "Pop Swett was catching for San Francisco," he said, "and when Pop wiggled his right hand, that meant that he wanted a straight ball. When he moved left, a curve." When the catcher signaled for a fastball, a coach would let the batter know by yelling to a base runner, "Cover a little ground." When a curve was coming, the tell would be "Take a good start."[19]

Teams attempting to steal signs in this fashion fell within the rules and customs of the game, but adopting the use of mechanical, electrical, or technological assistance seemed, at least to some, to cross a certain line. Speaking for himself and implicitly for many others, longtime coach and manager Don Zimmer said, "If you're getting signs from a scoreboard, bullpen, using glasses, to me that's cheating." Yet, breaching this protocol goes back a long way, perhaps to 1876, the National League's first year, when opposing teams accused the Hartford Blues of stealing signs from a shack located just outside their ballpark.[20]

A more notorious case arose in 1900 when the Philadelphia Phillies, a third-place team, played particularly well at home because of a ruse concocted by Petey Chiles, a reserve who usually coached third base, and catcher Morgan Murphy, who played in only eleven games but hardly ever sat in the dugout. Chiles often stood in a puddle in the corner of the coach's box and twitched his legs oddly, while Murphy's preferred game-time perch was the clubhouse beyond the centerfield fence. Visiting teams long suspected that something was up. During a doubleheader against Cincinnati on September 17, Reds shortstop Tommy Corcoran watched Chiles gyrate and rushed to the coach's box. He began scratching the ground with his spikes precisely where Chiles stood. Buried just beneath the mud, Corcoran uncovered a small wooden box with an electrical buzzer inside and wires protruding. The gambit was that Murphy used a spyglass to see the catcher's signs from the clubhouse and pressed a button that sent a small shock to Chiles, who would relay the information to the batter.[21]

Umpire Tim Hurst dismissed the commotion and resumed the game, but a couple of days later, the Reds claimed to have found the push button in the clubhouse and wires leading to the Phillies dugout. Two weeks later, the Reds exposed a simpler spying system in Pittsburgh. They found a hole cut into the center of a large letter "O" painted on the centerfield fence. Through the hole protruded a metal rod that could be turned like the hand of a clock. "12 o'clock" meant a fastball, "9 o'clock" an outside curve, and "3 o'clock" an inside curve, said the Reds. The Pittsburgh club offered no denial.[22]

Apparently, both the Philadelphia and Pittsburgh clubs knew about each other's trickery and pledged not to cheat against each other. Phillies owner John Rogers admitted that his club did use opera glasses, but he claimed that the wooden box and wires were left over from an amusement company that had rented the ballpark in July. Sportswriter Charles Dryden scoffed at this denial, revealing that Chiles had hatched the idea while using field glasses at a New Orleans racetrack the year before and seeing a ballfield in the distance. At first, Chiles's accomplice had used rolled paper as a signaling device. When other teams complained, he got more inventive after recalling that he had once been shocked by stepping on an exposed live wire.[23]

A decade later, George Stallings, manager of the New York Highlanders, today's Yankees, put a spotter in an apartment outside the team's ballpark, Hilltop Grounds. From there, the spy could see home plate through field glasses and relay the catcher's signs using sunlight bouncing off a mirror. On cloudy days, the snoop manipulated the crossbar in the letter "H" in an advertising sign. A white crossbar meant a breaking ball and a black crossbar a fastball. The 1948 Cleveland Indians did something similar by employing a telescope that pitcher Bob Feller had used as a naval gunnery officer during World War II. They put the telescope in the scoreboard and relayed the catcher's signals to the batter from there. "Hey," said Feller, "all's fair in love and war and when you're trying to win a pennant," which the Indians did.[24]

Mechanical and electronic malfeasance has not soiled baseball's quest for integrity very often, but cheating in all its forms is one of the bass lines that supports the rhythm of the game. In particular, pitchers have never stopped looking for ways to subvert the rules and get away with it. Russell Ford, who pitched in the majors from 1909 through 1915, may hold the dubious honor of inventing the first pitch to be banned, the emery ball. When he threw a wild warmup pitch that hit a wooden upright behind the plate, the ball got scuffed and thereafter behaved erratically. Ford experimented with his find, used a broken bottle to replicate his discovery, and then settled on a piece of emery cloth that he could conceal in his glove. Opponents eventually caught on, and rule makers outlawed it in 1915.[25]

More famous than the emery ball, and more ubiquitous, was the spitball. No one knows what amateur physicist first spit on a baseball, threw it, and watched it break sharply, but Jack Chesbro brought fame to the pitch when he used it to win forty-one games for the 1904 New York Highlanders. The pitch became popular, so much so that the *Sporting News* called 1905 "the spit ball year." Even though batters were not sure how it would break, there was little push to outlaw it. In fact, Brooklyn manager Ned Hanlon said in 1905 that "the 'spit ball' is one of the scientific evolutions of the game, and as such I suppose it ought to be encouraged."[26]

Nevertheless, the spitball was banned along with all other means of doctoring the baseball in 1920,[27] even though sportswriter Hugh Fullerton argued that "an examination of the records of the spit ball pitchers over the last eight years shows them losers." Pitchers must not have agreed with Fullerton because they took prohibition as a challenge to devise new ways to deceive batters without being caught. The spitball did not disappear even after the careers of those allowed to continue using it came to an end. Famous alleged practitioners have included Nels Potter, Preacher Roe, Lew Burdette, and Gaylord Perry, who once had a catcher admonish him, "Reduce the load of juice, Gaylord. [Home plate umpire Ed] Sudol is getting suspicious of that splashing sound in my mitt."[28]

How could batters retaliate for these flagrant abuses of the code? One way was to return to what the Phillies had done in 1900. Half a century later, electronics again played a role in the most notorious sign-stealing escapade in baseball history. The Giants and Dodgers had been locked in a long, intense rivalry that mirrored the competition between New York and Brooklyn, separate cities until 1898. The Giants began play in the National League in 1883. The Dodgers started in the American Association, then a major league, a year later and switched leagues in 1890. Most of the time, the Giants had the upper hand, lording it over the Dodgers as New York looked down its nose at Brooklyn. But in the 1940s, Larry MacPhail and Branch Rickey transformed the Dodgers into perpetual contenders. Brooklyn won the National League pennant in 1941, 1947, and 1949. They dropped a two-of-three playoff in 1946 and lost the 1950 pennant on the season's last day. Meanwhile, the Giants, after winning the pennant in 1933, 1936, and 1937, had trouble finishing in the first division.[29]

The year 1951 appeared to be no different. In mid-August, the Dodgers built a thirteen-and-a-half-game lead over their rivals, but the Giants won thirty-seven of their final forty-four games to force a playoff that they won on "the shot heard 'round the world," Bobby Thomson's three-run home run in the bottom of the ninth inning in game three. Years later, the truth came out. The Giants had cheated. Rumors circulated for years, abetted by an Associated Press story in 1962, but not until 2001 did some of the surviving Giants admit that, beginning in July, the team had used a telescope in the centerfield clubhouse to read the catcher's signs and a buzzer system to relay them to the bullpen and the dugout. "Every hitter knew what was coming," said pitcher Al Gettel. "Made a big difference."[30]

Even without electronics, hand-operated scoreboards continued to provide a roost for sign stealers. In 1956, the Baltimore Orioles accused the Chicago White Sox of positioning someone with a telescope in the scoreboard at Comiskey Park. American League president Will Harridge replied that there was no rule against stealing signs, and the White Sox kept doing it. The Milwaukee Braves gave binoculars to a bullpen coach and later allowed two pitchers carrying binoculars and wearing overalls and hats as disguises to sit in the stands at Chicago's Wrigley Field. When New York Mets pitcher Jay Hook admitted in 1962 that the 1961 Cincinnati Reds, for whom he played, had used sign stealing to win the pennant, the uproar was substantial.[31]

All along, even with emery paper and spitballs outlawed, pitchers continued to find ways to nick the surface of the ball or otherwise adulterate it. Cardinals shortstop Leo Durocher sharpened his belt buckle and used it to scuff the ball for Dizzy Dean. Whitey Ford had a jeweler make a ring with a small rasp welded onto it. "I had my own tool bench out there with me," he said. Catcher Elston Howard filed a buckle on his shin guard for Jim Bouton. Rick Honeycutt was once caught with a small piece of sandpaper and a thumbtack taped to his index finger. In 1987, umpires visited the mound after Joe Niekro threw a slider that broke inordinately. They found a piece of sandpaper and an emery board that popped out of his pocket. A week later, Kevin Gross was caught with sandpaper in his glove. In 1999, umpires discovered that Brian Moehler also had sandpaper taped to his thumb.[32]

More recently, pitchers have pushed to see what rules 3.01 and 6.02(c) really mean. Rule 3.01 states that "no player shall intentionally discolor or damage the ball by rubbing it with soil, rosin, paraffin, licorice, sand-paper, emery-paper or other foreign substance," and 6.02(c) says, in part, that the pitcher shall not "apply a foreign substance of any kind to the ball" or "deface the ball in any manner." Yankees pitcher Michael Pineda was caught with a tacky substance on the heel of his pitching hand in 2014. He was not ejected because he was not alone. Former pitcher Al Leiter told the *New York Times* that "a lot of guys used" a substance he recalled as True Grip, "or they would use something else. It doesn't affect the flight of the ball at all. It's just so you can grip the ball when it's cold." Many pitchers, perhaps as many as 70 percent, according to Trevor Bauer in 2020, do this, and they defend such usage as a safety measure to protect batters from wayward fastballs. So, pitchers want to know, What exactly is cheating?[33]

Batters have responded to pitchers' persistence to test the boundaries of the rules. Some have resorted to corked bats, believing erroneously that hollowing out the fat end of the bat, filling the hole with light, resistant, cork balls, and then resealing the bat to conceal what they have done would help them hit the ball farther. Norm Cash admitted using a corked bat when he won the American League batting title in 1961. Graig Nettles hit a broken-bat single in 1974 and was chagrined to see six superballs come flying out of it. Amos Otis admitted after he retired in 1984 that "I had enough cork and superballs in there to blow away anything." Albert Belle had his suspicious bat confiscated in 1994. "All Albert's bats were corked," wrote his teammate, Omar Vizquel. And so it goes.[34]

More profoundly, one might debate if players who resort to performance-enhancing drugs, including caffeine, amphetamines, cocaine, and anabolic steroids, are crossing some ethical line as they try to redress the imbalance they believe pitchers have enjoyed for too long. But that is an argument best left to others. Neil Diamond asked where it began. One might also ask where it will end, and perhaps, for wisdom, turn to Martin Quigley, author of *The Crooked Pitch: The Curveball in American Baseball History*. His judgment was simple: "A fair assumption in baseball is that if it can be done, it is being done."[35]

Notes

1. Neil Diamond, "Sweet Caroline," 1969. Lyrics © Universal Music Publishing Group.

2. This essay focuses on players and teams who cheat to gain an advantage, to help them win. The other side of the coin, cheating in order to lose deliberately, usually in exchange for money, is not covered here. Readers interested in this aspect of cheating might begin with Daniel E. Ginsburg, *The Fix Is In: A History of Baseball Gambling and Game Fixing Scandals* (Jefferson, NC: McFarland, 1995), and then wade into the enormous amount written on the 1919 Chicago White Sox, the so-called Black Sox, with Gene Carney, *Burying the Black Sox: How Baseball's Cover-Up of the 1919 World Series Fix Almost Succeeded* (Washington, DC: Potomac Books, 2007), William F. Lamb, *Black Sox in the Courtroom: The Grand Jury, Criminal Trial and Civil Litigation* (Jefferson, NC: McFarland, 2013), and Jacob Pomrenke, ed., *Scandal on the South Side: The 1919 Chicago White Sox* (Phoenix, AZ: Society for American Baseball Research, 2015).

3. On the early history of baseball, see Richard Hershberger, *Strike Four: The Evolution of Baseball* (Lanham, MD: Rowman & Littlefield, 2019), and Thomas W. Gilbert, *How Baseball Happened: Outrageous Lies Exposed! The True Story Revealed* (Boston: David A. Godine, 2020).

4. Hershberger, *Strike Four*, 105–106.

5. Hershberger, *Strike Four*, 71.

6. Hershberger, *Strike Four*, 70–71.

7. Hershberger, *Strike Four*, 72–75.

8. Hershberger, *Strike Four*, 157–166.

9. David H. Nathan, ed., *The McFarland Baseball Quotations Dictionary* (Jefferson, NC: McFarland, 2000), 185.

10. Hershberger, *Strike Four*, 223–224.

11. Hershberger, *Strike Four*, 225–226.

12. Hershberger, *Strike Four*, 229–232.

13. Peter Morris, *A Game of Inches: The Game on the Field: The Stories Behind the Innovations That Shaped Modern Baseball* (Chicago: Ivan R. Dee, 2006), 340–341; Joshua Prager, *The Echoing Green: The Untold Story of Bobby Thomson, Ralph Branca, and the Shot Heard Round the World* (New York: Pantheon Books, 2006), 69–70.

14. Morris, *Game of Inches*, 341.

15. Morris, *Game of Inches*, 47–48.

16. Paul Dickson, *The Hidden Game of Baseball: How Signs and Sign Stealing Have Influenced the Course of America's Pastime* (New York: Walker, 2003), 33; Morris, *Game of Inches*, 48, 341.

17. Dickson, *Hidden Game*, 15, 20, 22.

18. Morris, *Game of Inches*, 343; Prager, *Echoing Green*, 72.

19. Morris, *Game of Inches*, 343.

20. Dickson, *Hidden Game*, 33.

21. Joe Dittmar, "A Shocking Discovery," *Baseball Research Journal* 20 (1991): 52.

22. Dittmar, "Shocking Discovery," 52–53.

23. Dittmar, "Shocking Discovery," 53.

24. Dickson, *Hidden Game*, 55, 91.

25. Morris, *Game of Inches*, 164–167.

26. Morris, *Game of Inches*, 141–142.

27. Rule 27, Section 2, stated: "At no time during the progress of the game shall the pitcher be allowed to (1) apply a foreign substance of any kind to the ball; (2) expectorate either on the ball or his glove; (3) rub the ball on his glove, person or clothing; (4) deface the ball in any manner; or to deliver what is called the 'shine' ball, 'spit' ball, 'mud' ball, or 'emery' ball." *2019 Official Baseball Rules*, MLB.com, https://img.mlbstatic.com/mlb-images/image/upload/mlb/ubo8blsefk8wkkd2oemz.pdf.

28. Morris, *Game of Inches*, 143; John Thorn and John Holway, *The Pitcher* (New York: Prentice Hall, 1988), 167–169.

29. For a detailed examination of the intense competition between the Giants and the Dodgers, see Andrew Goldblatt, *The Giants and the Dodgers: Four Cities, Two Teams, One Rivalry* (Jefferson, NC: McFarland, 2003).

30. Joshua Prager, "Was the '51 Giants Comeback a Miracle, Or Did They Simply Steal the Pennant?," *Wall Street Journal*, January 31, 2001; Prager, *Echoing Green*, 60–65.

31. Dickson, *Hidden Game*, 102–106, 112–117.

32. Thorn and Holway, *Pitcher*, 161–162; "Biggest Cheaters in Baseball," ESPN.com, https://www.espn.com/page2/s/list/cheaters/ballplayers.html.

33. *2019 Official Baseball Rules*; Cliff Corcoran, "Michael Pineda's Pine-tar Fracas Shows Sticky Stuff Not a Real Concern for MLB," *Sports Illustrated*, https://www.si.com/mlb/2014/04/11/michael-pineda-pine-tar-new-york-yankees-boston-red-sox; David Waldstein, "A Yankees Pitcher's Hand Revives Arguments Over Pine Tar," *New York Times*, April 14, 2014; Rob Maaddi, "MLB Reminding Teams about Sticky Substance Rules," USA Today.com, https://www.usatoday.com/story/sports/mlb/2020/03/05/mlb-reminding-teams-about-sticky-substance-rules/111397432/.

34. "Biggest Cheaters in Baseball."

35. Martin Quigley, *The Crooked Pitch: The Curveball in American History* (Chapel Hill, NC: Algonquin Press, 1984), 145.

CHAPTER 2

Cheating versus Gamesmanship: Ethical Relativism in Baseball?

GEORGE GMELCH

As minor league players in the Detroit Tigers organization in the 1960s, my teammates and I engaged in practices that most baseball fans today would regard as cheating. But how much was really *cheating* as opposed to *gamesmanship*? Where do we draw the line? And could it be that fans and players, though from the same culture, have different views about what cheating is in baseball?

One incident from the journal I kept during my playing days speaks to the ambiguity of cheating in baseball. It is July 22, 1968, and I am playing left field in a close game against the Lachine Mets of the Québec Provincial League in their home park. The batter hits a line drive into left field; I dive for it and miss, and the ball rolls past me to the fence. By the time I reach it, I can see the runner heading for third and know that he will score the go-ahead run. Rather than pick the ball up and throw it to my cutoff man, I raise my hand and motion that the ball has gone under the fence. It had not. While the umpire makes his way to the outfield, I turn my back to the infield and push the ball under the fence with my foot. When the umpire arrives, he asks me point blank if I had forced the ball under the fence. I say no. The Mets and their manager, former Dodger Tim Harkness, knew this was practically impossible given the construction of the fence and protested vehemently. But with the ball sitting on the other side, the umpire had little choice but to declare it a ground-rule double.

Was this dishonest? Absolutely. But was it cheating? Hadn't I merely tried to save the run from scoring? Hadn't I done this for the benefit of my team, not for me personally?

When I asked players and coaches if they would call my ball-under-fence episode cheating, nearly all said "No." Some referred to my trying to help my team win the game; some excused it by saying that it had not been premeditated but rather a spontaneous decision. Others noted that it was the act of an individual, not one orchestrated by the team, as was the Houston Astros' now infamous sign-stealing scheme. One person said it was a failure on the part of the umpires to see the play clearly.

Yet when I put the same question to a sample of two dozen baseball fans, most said, yes, it was cheating. And when I asked university colleagues who have no relationship to or interest in baseball, all said that it sure sounded like cheating to them. Among them, women were the most adamant in their belief that my act had been cheating.

My 1968 journal entry suggests that I felt bad about what I had done, but mainly because I had looked foolish in not realizing the near impossibility of the ball rolling of its own accord under the Lachine ballpark fence and because I had lied to the umpire. As outrageous as it may sound, an outfielder trying to shove a ball under the fence in my day was not unknown. Much worse, the 1896 Baltimore Orioles (a National League team unrelated to the current Orioles) were known to have hidden extra balls in the outfield, which they sometimes sneaked into play when a hit got past their outfielders. Did they consider this cheating? We can only wonder. Such actions would be impossible today given the vastly improved field conditions, fencing, and pervasive video coverage in major league parks.

Let me start by making clear how cheating is defined in sports. The definitions offered by most sports scholars boil down to this: cheating is the *intentional* breaking of *rules* in order to obtain an *advantage* over one's opponent.[1]

But what about the many dubious practices ballplayers engage in for which there is no rule? There is nothing in the official rules of baseball, for example, that says a player who traps a ball with his glove cannot pretend that he actually caught it. We've all seen a player proudly thrust his glove in the air, trying to convince the umpire that he caught the ball on the fly. Similarly, there is no rule that says a batter cannot pretend that he was hit by a close pitch. We've all seen players doing so, sometimes leaning into a pitch. Nor is there an actual rule against a hitter peeking out of the corner of his eye to see where the catcher is setting up for the next pitch. Nor is there a rule against the catcher framing a pitch to fool the umpire into thinking it was a strike. All catchers do this, and they are expected to be good at it. Nor is there anything in the rulebook against a player or coach decoding the opposing catcher's signs and relaying them to their hitter. There is a rule, however, against using technology to do it. This was the Astros' cardinal sin.

Most of my sample of two dozen baseball fans of all ages regarded these examples as forms of "cheating." This is consistent with popular belief that baseball is rampant with cheating; as the sports adage has it, "If you ain't cheating, you ain't trying." "Everyone Cheats in Baseball" was the title of the feature article of the March 19, 2010, issue of *The Week*. Thomas Boswell, the former *Washington Post* sports columnist, once wrote, "Cheating *is* baseball's oldest profession. No other game is so rich in skullduggery, so suited to it or so proud of it."[2]

But if there is no rule against a practice, is it really cheating? Are we stigmatizing the sport unfairly? The ballplayers and coaches that I talked to mostly referred to these practices as "gamesmanship," meaning that they are merely players' attempts to get an edge or advantage over their opposition. "If that's cheating," responded former Detroit minor leaguer Bob "Shifty" Gear after listening to my list of actions, "there would be some punishment for them. And there isn't. The umpires don't say anything about it." According to former California Angel Dan Ardell, in baseball, "everyone is always trying to gain an advantage over the competition, and that's not cheating." Andy MacPhail, twice a major league general manager and current head of baseball operations for the Philadelphia Phillies, may have said it best: "There is a culture of deception in this game. . . . It has been in this game for 100 years. I do not look at this in terms of ethics. It's the culture of the game."[3]

Deception in baseball comes in many forms, from phantom double plays to concealment and sleight of hand to an infielder pretending to be receiving a throw in order to get the base runner to slide. After a long rain delay, Norm Cash, the first baseman who played several levels above me in the Tiger organization, would sometimes try to advance to the next base when play resumed—going to third base, for example, when he had been on second.

The more I discussed such practices with players and coaches, the more it became clear that players and other insiders have a different notion of "cheating" from that of its fans. Again, what fans regard as cheating in baseball often fails to meet the definition because there is no rule. In the absence of a rule, the game's insiders, whether it be players, coaches, or umpires, tend to see gamesmanship, not cheating.

This is not to say that real cheating does not occur in baseball, nor that players and fans do not agree in some areas. Ethical relativism tells us that morality is conditioned by the norms of one's culture. While professional baseball—the quintessential American game—mostly reflects the norms of our larger culture, it has its own subculture, with rules and moral standards that sometimes depart from mainstream morality. Let us examine real cheating in baseball and how it is regarded.

Doctoring the Ball

On the playing field, most rule breaking takes place on the pitching mound, rather than elsewhere on the diamond, in the batter's box, in the coach's box, or in the dugout. During a game, the pitcher and catcher have the greatest opportunity to cheat since they handle the ball on every pitch. Official baseball rule 3.01 states, "No player shall intentionally discolor or damage the ball by rubbing it with soil, rosin, paraffin, licorice, sand-paper, emery-paper or other foreign substance." The regulation appears again in section 6.02(c) (4): "The pitcher shall not apply a foreign substance of any kind to the ball." And section 6.02(c) (7) prohibits the pitcher from having in his possession "any foreign substance." Pitchers sometimes enlist the help of their catchers to doctor the ball, as when the catcher scuffs it or applies a substance to it before throwing it back. The penalty for doctoring is unequivocal and stiff: "The umpire shall demand the ball and remove the offender from the game."

Despite the many variables measured by today's analytics, there are none that provide us data on how many pitchers doctor the ball or how often illegal pitches are thrown. However, it is clear from many sources beyond my own interviews that the practice is common. Rob Friedman, an MLB and ESPN baseball analyst, estimates that around 60 percent of big league pitchers use some type of foreign substance on the mound. In a February 2020 HBO *Real Sports* profile, pitcher Trevor Bauer claimed that 70 percent of baseball's pitchers apply some type of sticky substance (most often pine tar) to the surface of the ball. With some hyperbole, Bauer even insisted to reporter Bernard Goldberg that doctoring the baseball "is a bigger advantage than steroids ever were. If you know how to manipulate it, you can make the ball do drastically different things from pitch to pitch at the same velocity."[4] Adding a tacky substance to the ball helps the pitcher get a better grip, which can increase the spin rate, making a fastball fly truer and a breaking ball bite harder.[5] A better grip also gives the pitcher more control over his pitches, especially useful in cold weather when the surface of the ball can be slippery. Some hitters, concerned for their own safety, say they appreciate pitchers having more control. Nevertheless, applying a foreign substance to the ball violates rule 6.02. Although this rule is often not enforced, that may be changing. In 2019, the Los Angeles Angels fired their visiting clubhouse attendant Brian "Bubba" Harkins after learning that he was supplying pitchers with a blend of rosin and pine tar. Harkins sued MLB and the Angels for wrongful dismissal, arguing that he had been singled out for punishment while the many players who illegally used his concoction were being ignored. His attorneys further alleged that MLB began to crack down on pitchers' use of ball-doctoring substances only when it discovered that numerous teams were trying to develop advanced blends to maximize their own pitchers' spin rate.[6]

The other common way some pitchers doctor a baseball is to apply a lubricant, such as saliva, hair oil, or Vaseline. This enables the pitcher to throw a pitch that slides off his fingers without generating too much backspin (it is the opposite effect of making the ball sticky). This technique alters the wind resistance on one side of the ball, causing it to move erratically. Because of its illegality, pitchers must apply the substance without being seen. There are many ways of concealing a glob of the preferred substance somewhere on the body or uniform. Pitchers are rarely caught, though New York Yankee Michael Pineda was ejected from a game and suspended for ten games in 2014 after carelessly placing a large patch of pine tar on an observable place on his neck.

Doc Olms, a teammate of mine in the Class A Florida State League, always kept a dab of Vaseline under the bill of his cap, smearing some of it on the ball, especially when in a jam and needing to get an out. He had much success throwing his "Vaseline ball" until one umpire caught on and word spread around the league. Other umpires then kept an eye out for it. Denied his Vaseline ball, Olms's ERA went from 1.82 in 1966 to 6.19 the next season. Everyone on our team knew that Doc threw a nasty "Vaseline ball," but no one thought any less of him for it. He was just trying to gain an edge.

Many former and current major league pitchers are suspected of throwing doctored pitches, including former stars Don Drysdale, Whitey Ford, Lew Burdette, Rick Honeycutt, Nolan Ryan, Don Sutton, and Gaylord Perry, to name just a few.[7] Whitey Ford would apply saliva to one side of the ball and then rub it into the dirt as he reached for the rosin bag. Rick Honeycutt taped a thumbtack to a finger on his glove hand so he could rough the ball up. He once forgot the tack was there and cut his forehead when he wiped sweat away from his brow. Don Sutton used Super Glue to attach sandpaper to his glove to scuff the ball. Joe Niekro kept an emery board in his back pocket. Gaylord Perry, who had a notorious reputation for throwing a spitter, sometimes put Vaseline on his zipper because umpires would never check a player's groin. Most didn't openly admit to having thrown a spitter, mud ball, shine ball, or Vaseline ball or to having scuffed the surface of the baseball until after their careers ended.[8]

Hardly baseball pariahs for having broken baseball's official Rules 3.01 and 6.02, Perry, Ford, and Ryan went on to be elected to baseball's Hall of Fame. Perry actually flaunted the rule against doctoring the ball during his career when he titled his autobiography *Me and the Spitter* (1974), published while he was still playing. Ford in his book called *Slick* (1988), published after his career ended, revealed several ways he gained an edge over the batter. One was having his catcher Elston Howard scrape the ball on the ground before throwing it back to the mound; another was having a ring for scuffing the baseball custom-made. Scuffing is more difficult today since umpires constantly change the ball, especially after it hits the dirt or is put into play.

Admitting to using pine tar to help his curveball, Ryan told an ESPN interviewer, "Those are things that are done in the game, that are accepted as part of the game." In his autobiography *Throwing Heat* (1990), Ryan wrote, "Cheating is accepted in baseball, so I participated."[9] Ryan also sometimes pitched from in front of the rubber, inching down the mound closer to the hitter. Were Perry, Ford, or Ryan, like many others, ashamed of having bolstered their careers by "cheating"? Their books and interviews suggest otherwise.

Doctoring the Bat

The most egregious violation of baseball rules by hitters also involves altering one of the key tools of the game, in this case, the bat. "Corking" involves drilling a hole in the dense wood of the barrel of the bat and filling it with a less dense substance, such as cork. This makes the bat lighter, which gives a hitter a quicker swing.[10] Corking violates rule 6.03 (a)(5), which states, "A batter is out for illegal action when he uses or attempts to use a bat that, in the umpire's judgment, has been altered or tampered with. . . . This includes bats that are filled, flat-surfaced, nailed, hollowed, grooved or covered with a substance such as paraffin, wax, etc."

Corked bats are rarely discovered unless they break during play. The last time that happened was in 2003, when Chicago Cubs superstar Sammy Sosa's bat shattered; lying on the infield for all to see were the two halves of the barrel and the offending cork interior. Sosa was suspended for eight games. He denied wrongdoing, implausibly claiming that the bat had been made for batting practice and that he had simply grabbed the wrong bat when he went to the plate.

When I played in the 1960s, a few teammates doctored their bats in a very different way. They drove a few nails into the barrel to make the bat heavier in the belief that the greater the bat's mass, the farther the ball would travel. Only in recent decades have players uniformly understood that lightening a bat, as in corking, is far better since it enables greater bat speed. In a 2010 article in *Baseball Research Journal*, Ben Walker notes how slow ballplayers were to recognize that bat speed is more important than bat mass. It was common for players in Babe Ruth's era—the 1920s and '30s—to swing bats weighing 43 to 45 ounces.[11] Babe Ruth is said to have used a 52-ounce hickory bat early in his career. I once had the opportunity to swing one of Ruth's early bats in the basement archives of the Baseball Hall of Fame. Although I am the same height and of similar build to the young Ruth, I found it utterly amazing that he could have gotten such a heavy bat around on a major league fastball. Today's big leaguers favor bats that weigh 33 to 34 ounces.

Cheating with Chemicals

Today, doping is the most widely known form of cheating in baseball. Instead of doctoring the ball or bat, the ballplayer doctors himself by taking an illegal performance-enhancing drug (PED). The most common doping substances are anabolic steroids, which increase muscle size, strengthening the muscles used in hitting and pitching. While we think of doping as being a "modern" phenomenon in baseball, there are accounts of players ingesting substances and elixirs in the nineteenth century with the same goal in mind. In the 1890s, for example, St. Louis Browns pitcher Pud Galvin was a regular user and a vocal proponent of a testosterone supplement made from the testicles of live animals, including dogs and guinea pigs. Galvin was MLB's first three-hundred-game winner and was enshrined in the Baseball Hall of Fame in 1965. In the 1920s, Babe Ruth once experimented with an extract from sheep testicles, but rather than giving him more power at the plate, it made him ill.[12]

When I entered pro ball in 1965, the use of chemicals of any type was unheard of, unless you counted the caffeine in strong cups of coffee. I say this with some certainty, having consulted many teammates and coaches of my era while writing a memoir,[13] and again while doing interviews for this essay. Within a few years, however, amphetamines began to appear in major-league clubhouses, and used, according to Jim Bouton in *Ball Four*, a diary of his 1969 season, not only to enhance performance but also for "relief from a hangover, general fatigue, and whenever a player felt he needed a boost of energy." Bouton claimed that the use of amphetamines, which players then referred to as "greenies" and later "beans," was widespread: "Just about the whole Baltimore (Orioles) team takes them [and] most of the [Detroit] Tigers."[14] Surprisingly, there was no rule against the use of amphetamines in baseball until 2006.

In the 1980s, anabolic steroids replaced amphetamines as the enhancement chemical of choice in what became known as the "Steroid Era" of baseball (the late 1980s to the early 2000s). What is still unclear is the percentage of ballplayers at any one time who were using steroids or other PEDs. Some players have made wild claims to the media and in tell-all books about the frequency of steroid use, giving figures as high as 80 percent (José Canseco), 50 percent (Ken Caminiti), or 25 to 40 percent (David Wells).[15] Probably more reliable was the finding of an anonymous poll of 143 players done for ESPN in 2014. It found that about 9 percent of then-current players were taking some type of PED.[16]

While MLB did not ban the use of steroids until 2005, more than a decade earlier, in 1991, Commissioner Fay Vincent sent a memo to all teams telling them that steroid use was against the rules. He said the memo was intended as a moral statement to the players rather than a legal one. League-wide testing of players for PEDs did not begin until 2007. In what MLB now considers its poststeroid era, the league conducts more than ten thousand drug tests a year. The latest test results to be released in 2018 showed a marked decline in PED use, with only 1.2 percent of players in the majors and 1.6 percent of players in the minors in violation. Some of these violations were for recreational drugs and masking agents.[17]

Baseball's steroid problem received major media coverage in March 2007, contributing to the sport's image as being a haven for cheating. Ten star players and MLB executives were summoned to appear before the House Committee on Oversight and Government Reform. The committee was hoping to pressure baseball to toughen its policy against steroids. Under oath in an eleven-hour hearing, the ballplayers—including some of its biggest stars, among them Mark McGwire and Sammy Sosa—denied using steroids or evaded the questioning. Baltimore Orioles star Rafael Palmeiro lied when he pointed his index finger at the panel and expressed indignation over the accusation against him made by former slugger José Canseco in his tell-all book. The images of McGwire, Sosa, and Palmeiro as baseball heroes would never be the same. In a Gallup poll taken five months after the congressional hearing, eight in ten fans said performance-enhancing drugs were a serious problem for the game.[18] Unfortunately, we do not have enough testimony from players and coaches to know to what extent they shared the public's concern about steroid use in the game. There has been a clear consensus among both insiders and outsiders, however, in condemnation of the most recent example of cheating.

The Houston Astros' Cheating with Technology

While the problem of PEDs in baseball never fully went away, there had not been a major team cheating scandal in baseball for over a century. That is, until the Astros' sign-stealing story broke in 2020. Unlike the use of PEDs, which was always done by individual players, the Astros' cheating was orchestrated by the team and its coaches. As teamwide dishonesty, it crossed the line: the Astros' use of technology permitting a catcher's signals to be digitally recorded and deciphered superseded all previous known attempts to spy on a catcher's signs. The only known scheme close to what the Astros did was the New York Giants use of a telescope to steal the opposing catcher's signs in the last month of their 1951 pennant-winning season. Its use was not widely known until *Wall Street Journal* reporter Joshua Prager revealed it in an article in 2001 and then in his book *The Echoing Green* (2006).

Before the Astros, only the infamous Black Sox scandal, in which eight members of the Chicago White Sox colluded to throw the 1919 World Series against the Cincinnati Reds in exchange for money from a gambling syndicate, had been a bigger cheat. But there is a significant difference: the White Sox were trying to lose a World Series; the Astros were trying to win one, and in doing so, they would deprive the opposing Los Angeles Dodgers of a World Championship and all the accolades and monetary benefits that go to the winning team.

There can be little doubt that the Astros knew the seriousness of their cheating scheme, as suggested by their electronic spying operation's being referred to as "Dark Arts" within the Astros front office. The use of technology to steal signs had long been taboo in professional baseball. In 1961, the National League had banned the use of any "mechanical device" to steal signs, and in 2001 MLB issued a memorandum stating that teams could not use electronic equipment to communicate with each other during games, especially for stealing signs. In September 2017, after the Boston Red Sox were fined for using an Apple Watch to steal signs, MLB Commissioner Rob Manfred sent a memo to all thirty teams warning that future incidents of electronic sign stealing "will be subject to more serious sanctions, including the possible loss of draft picks."[19]

Among major league ballplayers the reaction to the Astros' cheating scheme has been unforgiving, perhaps more so than any other scandal in baseball history. Dodgers closer Kenley Jansen characterized it as "worse than gambling, worse than steroids." Pitcher Trevor Bauer told reporters at spring training in 2020, "I'm not going to let them forget the fact that they are hypocrites, they are cheaters, and they've stolen from a lot of other people and the game itself." Some players said they expected opposing teams to retaliate against Houston hitters by throwing at them. When asked about throwing at Houston hitters, Dodgers pitcher Alex Wood said, "You'd be hard-pressed to say no. I mean, they messed with a lot of guys' lives." Astros manager Dusty Baker, who replaced the fired A. J. Hinch, asked MLB to try to prevent opposing pitchers from throwing beanballs at the Astros hitters after some had been targeted during spring training games. Former Tigers minor leaguer Dennis Grossini wrote to me, "It's so, so disappointing. In our time [1960s], stealing signs was an art, a skill mastered by observant players and base-coaches on the field. This is a crime."[20]

Former MLB pitcher Mike Bolsinger filed a lawsuit against the Astros, alleging that the banging scheme used against him while he was pitching for the Toronto Blue Jays in 2017 had affected his career. After giving up four runs and getting only one out against the Astros on August 4, 2017, he was demoted to the minor leagues. He never made it back to the majors. In the words of ESPN columnist Buster Olney, "Front-office staffers around baseball cannot remember a circumstance of such widespread and loud player-to-player condemnation."[21] Regarding punishment, New York Yankees star Aaron Judge said that the Astros should be forced to give up their title and that the players should have been punished. Hall of Famer Hank Aaron may have taken the hardest line in saying, "I think whoever did that should be out of baseball for the rest of their lives." Most of my sample of players and coaches thought that the Astros should have forfeited their World Series title but stopped well short of a lifetime ban. Mike Young, who became a scout for the Cubs and the Giants after his minor-league career, said, "If you break the rules to win in the Olympics they take away your medal. Should be the same in baseball. End of story." Matt Thomas, a catcher on the Harvard baseball team who believes the Astros' sign stealing cost his hometown LA Dodgers the World Series title, offered a novel suggestion: "The Astros should be 'relegated' [demoted] to AAA for the next season, like they do in English soccer for the bottom finishing teams."[22]

Fans have been no less forgiving. Some taunted the Astros with banners and signs at spring training games. More elaborate protests were planned for when the season opened, but then the coronavirus pandemic hit and shut down the season in March. When an abbreviated season began months later, the games were played in empty ballparks. Denied the chance to boo the Houston players in person, some fans turned to social media to shame the team for their cheating.[23] Three lawsuits against the Astros were filed by former Astros season ticket holders, each alleging that the ticket holder had been defrauded by the sign-stealing scandal because the play on the field was not what it was billed to be.

My sample of fans was especially critical of commissioner Manfred's granting immunity from punishment to the Astros players. (Manfred did so in exchange for their cooperation with Major League Baseball's investigation.) In an ESPN survey of 1,010 adults, 58 percent said that the players should have been penalized. Adding to the ire of both fans and players was the feeling that the Astros were not sufficiently apologetic, that some of their apologies were lame or seemed insincere. One fan said he was infuriated when an Astros player smirked, minimizing his guilt. Houston owner Jim Crane was widely criticized in the media for an apology that rang hollow to many.

It probably did not help that the Astros had a checkered reputation before the scandal broke. According to Jeremy Venook of *The Atlantic*, the culture of the Astros organization under Crane and Luhnow had "developed a reputation for a cutthroat, win-at-all-costs mentality that sacrificed the human element of the game for marginal gains on the playing field."[24] Some teams had long suspected the Astros of cheating. On a Houston radio station in 2010, Phil Garner, who had once managed the Astros, admitted that during his reign the team had used corked bats in the 2005 season and World Series.

Is There a Generational Difference?

As a longtime college professor, I wondered if young baseball fans of college age who have grown up with electronic technology might view the Astros' cheating differently from my generation. In teaching a course on the anthropology of sport, I had encountered a huge difference in how my students viewed Pete Rose's exclusion from the Baseball Hall of Fame as compared to my generation. While most older adults oppose Rose's ever being inducted, my students think just the opposite, arguing that he deserves induction based solely on the numbers he put up, having more hits than any player in the history of the game. Well, could these same young people also be more accepting of what the Astros did? To my surprise, the students were no more forgiving of the Astros' cheating than were the older adults.

Conclusions

A lot of what baseball fans regard as "cheating" really is not, since it does not violate any of the sport's official rules. Rather, it is better regarded as "gamesmanship." We have seen that what is most often regarded as cheating involves the use of technology, whether it be applying a dab of Vaseline or pine tar to the surface of the baseball, lightening a bat with cork, injecting or ingesting performance-enhancing chemicals, or employing video and electronics to spy on a catcher's signs. Stealing signs using human guile alone is considered acceptable, but once technology is employed the line between gamesmanship and cheating has been crossed.

The strong reaction by players and fans to the Houston Astros' sign-stealing scheme suggests that cheating is deemed worse when it involves whole teams and not just individual athletes. It is worse still when it involves operatives who are positioned outside the playing field (e.g., the Astros stationed one person above centerfield and others in the team's video room).

It is unlikely that the ethically borderline activity in baseball, whether cheating or gamesmanship, will ever be rooted out. The competitiveness of athletes will always encourage them to seize any possible advantage. The excessive emphasis on winning inclines players to engage in borderline activities, if not actual rule breaking, as long as there is a good chance they can get away with it. In the words of George Bamberger, former manager of the New York Mets, "You often don't decide whether to cheat based on if it's right or wrong. You base it on whether or not you can get away with it and what the penalty might be."[25] As former White Sox manager Ozzie Guillen put it, "If you don't get caught, you're a smart player. If you get caught, you're cheating."

"Cheating in sport," asserts sport sociologist Stanley Eitzen, "stems from participation in a morally distorted sports world in which winning supersedes all other considerations and where moral values have become confused with the bottom line."[26] While talking to former teammates and reflecting on my own baseball life, I began to wonder if the questionable behavior we had engaged in had resulted in a laissez-faire attitude toward cheating generally. Had we become more willing to fudge on our income taxes, cheat at cards or on an exam, improve our lie on the golf course? I can't answer this question, but research on the outcome of sports participation shows little evidence that involvement in sports results in moral development and good citizenship.[27] Clearly, there are enormous benefits to participating in sports—exercise and health, discipline and perseverance, teamwork and social skills, to name just a few. But doesn't baseball, as just one example from the world of sport, also teach us that it's okay to cheat—if you don't get caught? Put differently, baseball's ethical relativism too often implies the pernicious attitude that "anything goes."

Notes

1. Jay Coakley, *Sport in Society: Issues and Controversies*, 8th ed. (New York: McGraw-Hill 2004); D. Stanley Eitzen, *Fair and Foul: Beyond the Myths and Paradoxes of Sport* (Lanham, MD: Rowman & Littlefield, 2016).

2. Thomas Boswell, "The Miracle of Coogan's Bluff Tarnished," *Washington Post*, February 1, 2001.

3. Quoted in Jason Turbow, *The Baseball Codes: Beanballs, Sign Stealing, and Bench-Clearing Brawls* (New York: Anchor Books, 2010), 182.

4. Jacob Bogage, "MLB Pitchers Cheat, Too. They Use Pine Tar Instead of Trash Cans," *Washington Post*, January 17, 2020, https://www.washingtonpost.com/sports /2020/01/17/mlb-pitchers-cheat-too-they-use-pine-tar-instead-trash-cans.

5. At the time of this writing in August 2020, there are social media conversations speculating that the dominating performance of New York Yankees pitcher Gerrit Cole this season has been due to his illicit use of pine tar, which is increasing the spin rate on his four-seam fastball. Manny Gomez, "New York Yankee Gerrit Cole in a Sticky Situation," Call to the Bullpen, August 8, 2020, https://calltothepen .com/2020/08/09/new-york-yankees-gerrit-cole-sticky-situation/.

6. Alden Gonzalez, "Fired Los Angeles Angels Clubhouse Attendant Names Pitchers in Ball-Doctoring Case," ESPN.com, December 8, 2021, https://www.espn .com/mlb/story/_/id/30671790.

7. See for example, J. Francis Wolfe, "Top 15 Pitchers Who Dominated Baseball by Cheating," The Sportster, April 14, 2015, https://www.thesportster.com/baseball/top-15-pitchers-who-dominated-baseball-by-cheating/, and Jay Jaffe, "11 Tales of Pitchers Using Spitters, Sandpaper and Scuffing," SI.com, May 3, 2013, https://www .si.com/mlb/2013/05/03/a-gripping-saga-11-tales-of-pitchers-using-spitters-sand paper-and-scuffing.

8. See Wolfe, "Top 15 Pitchers," and Jaffe, "A Gripping Saga."

9. Bogage, "MLB Pitchers Cheat."

10. Some hitters prefer lighter bats because they can swing them faster, allowing the batter more time to react to an incoming pitch and adjust his swing. However, research by physicist Alan Nathan and his colleagues at the University of Illinois have found that the distance gained by using a corked bat may be negligible. They conclude that "there is no advantage to corking a bat if the goal is for the batted ball speed to be as large as possible, as is the case for a home run hitter." Emerging Technology from the ArXiv, "The Misleading Myth of the Corked Bat," *Technology Review*, September 16, 2010, https://www.technologyreview.com/2010/09/16/200387. See also David Waldstein, "Even in a Pandemic, Everyone Still Hates the Astros," *New York Times*, August 18, 2020, https://www.nytimes.com/2020/08/18/sports/base ball/houston-astros-joe-kelly-cheating.html.

11. Ben Walker, "Properties of Baseball Bats," *Baseball Research Journal*, Summer 2010, https://sabr.org/journal/article/properties-of-baseball-bats/.

12. Robert Smith, "A Different Kind of Performance Enhancer," npr.org, March 31, 2006, https://www.npr.org/templates/story/story.php?storyId=5314753; Allen Wood, "Baseball & P.E.Ds: A 120-Year History," The Joy of Sox, February 15, 2009, http://joy ofsox.blogspot.com/2009/02/baseball-peds-120-year-history.html.

13. George Gmelch, *Playing with Tigers: A Minor Chronicle of the Sixties* (Lincoln: University of Nebraska Press, 2018).

14. I have never been convinced that their use at that time—the late 1960s—was as widespread as Bouton claimed, nor have any of my former teammates whom I have questioned. By the time my playing days ended in 1970, I hardly knew a teammate who used amphetamines. It isn't that I would not have recognized the pills for

what they were, for I, like some of my classmates at Stanford University, were using them to stay awake when preparing for a big exam. To be fair, I was in the minor leagues, and Bouton was describing their use in the major leagues.

15. In "Totally Juiced," in the June 3, 2002, issue of *Sports Illustrated*, Ken Caminiti spoke to Tom Verducci about the steroids problem in baseball. Verducci believed that steroid use is much more pervasive than these figures suggest. The two books were David Wells, *Perfect I'm Not: Boomer on Beer, Brawls, Backaches, and Baseball* (New York: It Books, 2004), and José Canseco, *Juiced: Wild Times, Rampant 'Roids, Smash Hits & How Baseball Got Big* (New York: ReganBooks, 2005).

16. Alex Skillin, "MLB Players Talk PED Usage in Anonymous Poll," SBNation .com, March 24, 2014, https://www.sbnation.com/mlb/2014/3/24/5543452.

17. Anthony Fisher, "Does Major League Baseball Still Have a Drug Problem?," *Inside Hook*, February 17, 2018, https://www.insidehook.com/article/sports/baseball -mlb-ped-steroid-problem.

18. Mark Gillespie, "Steroids a Strike Against Baseball," Gallup, August 12, 2005, https://news.gallup.com/poll/17788/steroids-strike-against-baseball.aspx.

19. The *New York Times* reported that the Red Sox used an Apple Watch to steal signals from the Yankees. A Red Sox trainer was caught looking at his watch and then relaying a message to players. Anita Balakrishnan, "MLB Fines Red Sox and Yankees for Improper Use of Technology in Games," CNBC.com, September 15, 2017, https://www.cnbc.com/2017/09/15/mlb-fines-red-sox-and-yankees-for-use-of-apple -watch-and-phones.html.

20. Norm Frauenheim, "Bellinger: Altuve Stole MVP from Yankees' Judge," Associated Press, ABC News, February 14, 2020, https://abcnews.go.com/Sports/wire Story/bellinger-altuve-stole-mvp-yankees-judge-68995910; Justin Sayles, "The Anti-Astros Sign-Stealing Big Mad Player Rankings," The Ringer, February 19, 2020, https://www.theringer.com/mlb/2020/2/19/21143952.

21. "Olney: MLB Players Angry Over Sign Stealing While Astros Wait to Say They're Sorry," ESPN.com, February 2, 2020, https://www.espn.com/mlb/insider /story/_/id/28614624.

22. Des Bieler, "Hank Aaron Thinks Sign-Stealing Astros Players Should Be Banned from Baseball," *Washington Post*, February 7, 2020, https.//www.washing tonpost.com/sports/2020/02/07/hank-aaron-thinks-sign-stealing-astros-players -should-be-banned-baseball/.

23. Waldstein, "Even in a Pandemic, Everyone Still Hates the Astros."

24. "The Astros' Cheating Scandal Rewrites a Decade of Baseball History," *The Atlantic*, January 19, 2020, https://www.theatlantic.com/culture/archive/2020/01/the -astros-scandal-rewrites-a-decade-of-mlb-history/605185/.

25. Quoted in Turbow, *Baseball Codes*, 182.

26. Eitzen, *Fair and Foul*, 69.

27. Eitzen, *Fair and Foul*, 84. A large study of athletes by the sport psychologists Bruce Ogilvy and Tomas Tutko also found no empirical support for the widespread notion that sport builds character.

CHAPTER 3

"This Is Not a Cultural Issue": The Astros' (and Baseball's) Willingness to Overlook Domestic Violence

KATHERINE MURRAY

On the blue level, where our most expensive boxes are, we experimented for a week to determine what light looked best on ladies' makeup and clothes. Listen, every day here will be ladies' day.
JUDGE ROY HOFHEINZ, OWNER OF THE COLT .45S FRANCHISE, ON THE ASTRODOME[1]

I just beat the hell out of [my wife] Sylvia and kick the dog and whatever else I've got to do to get it out.
METS MANAGER DALLAS GREEN ON HOW HE DEALS WITH LOSING[2]

In the top of the ninth of game 6 of the 2019 ALCS, pitcher Roberto Osuna gave up a two-run homer that nearly cost the Astros a shot at the World Series.

Despite this blunder, assistant GM Brandon Taubman chose to yell "I'm so fucking glad we got Osuna!" at a group of female reporters during the postgame celebration. It certainly seemed an odd moment to praise Osuna, given that his performance that night made him the least valuable player in the clubhouse. It certainly seemed an odd moment to direct these remarks to a reporter who was wearing a domestic violence awareness bracelet and had covered Osuna's domestic violence charges.

Two days later, Stephanie Apstein of *Sports Illustrated*, one of the female reporters in the clubhouse, published "Astros Staffer's Outburst at Female Reporters Illustrates MLB's Forgive-and-Forget Attitude toward Domestic Violence." The fact that the later cheating scandal received considerably more media attention than Taubman's behavior only reinforced Apstein's thesis. While Major League Baseball may prefer to pretend that such malfeasance is a one-off rather than an indication of institutionalized maltreatment, Taubman's tirade reflects the repercussions of long-embedded misogyny on the analytics-based thinking of recent years. It is a form of cheating to sign players who have been devalued through their own actions: if you prioritize numbers over people, you sign domestic abusers and justify this choice as something clinical and calculated. Yet the bloodlessness of this decision stands at odds with the image of a red-faced Taubman taunting a woman in a fetid postgame clubhouse and the Astros' attempt to excuse his behavior as justifiably "getting caught up in the moment." Cornell-educated, Ernst & Young–pedigreed Taubman was of the *Moneyball* generation that prefers to reduce people to numbers, but to do so only further compromised the team's humanity. GM Jeff Luhnow's insistence that Taubman's tirade did not reflect "a cultural issue" confirmed that his tirade absolutely reflected a cultural issue.

In May 2018, Osuna, then of the Blue Jays, was reported to have assaulted Alejandra Román Cota. Major League Baseball found that he violated the league's Joint Domestic Violence, Sexual Assault, and Child Abuse Policy and suspended him for seventy-five games. Prosecutors dropped the charges against Osuna after Cota declined to testify and chose to stay in Mexico rather than return to Toronto. While the details of Osuna's assault are still unknown to the public, the length of the suspension invited dark speculation from curious fans. If Aroldis Chapman received a thirty-game suspension for choking his girlfriend in front of their daughter and firing a gun into their garage, what crime would merit a suspension twice that long? To what extent must Osuna have brutalized the mother of his child?

Domestic Violence in Sports

Our current understanding of domestic violence was born around the same time as the Astros' rainbow uniforms (but thankfully, the former had more staying power).[3] In 1977, Francine Hughes poured gasoline over her husband, who had passed out in a drunken stupor after he raped her for the last time. She loaded her children into the car and set fire to her home.

During the trial, her lawyer was the first to invoke the term "battered woman syndrome" in court. Hughes was acquitted by reason of temporary insanity caused by thirteen years of abuse, marking a watershed moment for victims of domestic violence who have all been told some variation of Hughes's husband's favorite refrain: "There is nowhere you can go, bitch, that I won't find you."[4]

Since Hughes's trial, the term "battered woman syndrome" has entered common parlance, allowing greater visibility and understanding of victims of domestic abuse. Despite the potential for empathy enabled by the vocabulary of violence, the available rhetoric has yet to be perfected: "Battered Women's Syndrome, the chief narrative available to women who fight back, forces women to plead for mercy and subjects their behavior to extensive scrutiny and evaluation. Stand Your Ground, the chief narrative men can now use to justify provoking deadly fights, often allows men to escape evaluation altogether by granting immunity from prosecution and even from arrest."[5] Despite the progress of the forty-three years since Hughes's trial, victims of domestic violence are plagued by the same taboos and shamed limitations as they were in the era of Head and Master laws, which held that only husbands were allowed to administer community property, until that law was finally removed from the books in 1979. In the age of social media, domestic violence victims are held to greater scrutiny than ever. While idealists maintain that the internet offers survivors a platform from which to access resources and condemn their abuser, the sober reality is that the internet also makes it easier for abusers (and their supporters) to track and intimidate their victims. Like many of the resources of the digital age, the ease of access to information initiates a one-step-forward, two-steps-back dance. Any victim of domestic violence fears unwanted visibility, and victims of the seemingly untouchable caste of professional male athletes are held to the scrutiny of keyboard warriors' kangaroo courts.

As Apstein explained in her article, malfeasance by male celebrities—particularly athletes—often goes uncondemned by fans who are eager to forget. Fans are notoriously willing to grant clemency in exchange for the entertainment provided by athletic talent, but claiming that celebrity creates a sphere of invincibility is nothing new. Younger generations are better acquainted with Mike Tyson's appearance in *The Hangover* than they are with his 1991 rape conviction. Kobe Bryant's 2003 sexual assault case left his career relatively untarnished. The 2009 beating of Rihanna by Chris Brown could have represented a landmark moment for survivors of domestic abuse, but instead we watched fans rally around Brown as he continued performing around the world. In 2014 we finally witnessed public condemnation of an abuser after TMZ published the video of Ray Rice dragging his beaten, unconscious fiancée out of an elevator. Yet even with the indisputable video evidence of Rice's violence, some fans still protested his initial two-game suspension. In December 2020, fans applauded Johnny Manziel's return to professional football in the new Fan Controlled Football League, happy to forget the photos of his heavily bruised girlfriend.[6]

Women are still facing the same violence at home that they were fifty years ago, but now we have a better vocabulary to understand the primordial ooze of toxic masculinity and rape culture. The talent of the athlete is indirectly proportional to the sympathy for his victim and directly proportional to fans' usual misogynistic ad hominem claims: she's a tease, she's crying for attention, she's a falsely accusing gold digger. As detailed in the 2015 Sundance Film Festival documentary *The Hunting Ground*, Erica Kinsman was doxxed, threatened, and harassed by Florida State fans and students after she accused quarterback Jameis Winston of rape. In a 2007 interview with Nancy Grace about Michael Vick's dog fighting operation, CNN sports anchor Larry Smith claimed that "while Kobe Bryant is a situation we can sort of compare this to, this really is much worse. Not only can you argue that the crimes are much worse in terms of, you know, killing dogs and that kind of thing, but as an NFL starting quarterback, you are the most visible face in that city."[7] Smith's appraisal of dog fighting as worse than rape highlights the ugly flip side of the camaraderie of sports fandoms: while professional athletes indisputably possess the potential to unify a city, they also possess the power to set the perceived standard of masculinity. As Mike Bates points out, allowing baseball players convicted of domestic violence to still be set on a pedestal "runs counter to what a sport predicated on fair play is about."[8]

In 2015, MLB and the Major League Baseball Players Association announced an agreement to address domestic violence committed by or against players through four action points: (1) treatment and interventions; (2) investigations; (3) discipline; and (4) training, education, and resources.[9] Before this policy was put in place, the league did not punish players for domestic violence.[10] The immediacy and number of suspensions suggests that this should have been implemented sooner.[11]

- In March 2016, Aroldis Chapman was the first player penalized under this policy after he was suspended for thirty games for choking his girlfriend and then firing eight shots into their garage. The investigation report lists the weapon as "hands/feet/fist/teeth."[12]
- In February 2016, José Reyes was placed on leave and then suspended for the first fifty-one games of the season after grabbing his wife by the throat and shoving her into a sliding glass door.
- In April 2016, Braves outfielder Héctor Olivera was charged with one misdemeanor account of assault and battery after assaulting a female acquaintance.
- In March 2017, Mets pitcher Jeurys Familia was suspended fifteen games for violence against his wife.

- In September 2017, Tampa Bay catcher Derek Norris was suspended for choking his fiancée.
- In December 2017, Red Sox pitcher Steven Wright was arrested at home and charged with domestic violence against his wife. He was suspended fifteen games.
- In March 2018, a video surfaced of Tigers minor leaguer Danry Vásquez dragging his girlfriend by her hair and beating her in the stadium stairwell. He shoves her head so forcefully that her glasses fall off. After he drags her down the stairs, he shoves her glasses back onto her face, fracturing her nose. The Tigers organization released him in 2018 when the video surfaced and went viral. Video proof made Vásquez's guilt undeniable, and the swift responses decrying his actions demonstrated the ease of condemning visible violence. Then-Tiger Justin Verlander tweeted "[middle finger emoji] you man. I hope the rest of your life without baseball is horrible. You deserve all that is coming your way!," a "stance" that would come back to haunt him.
- In September 2018, Cubs outfielder Addison Russell was suspended for abusing his wife.[13]
- In October 2018, the Padres released relief pitcher José Torres after he pled guilty to an aggravated assault of his wife.
- In May 2019, Phillies outfielder Odúbel Herrera was arrested after assaulting his girlfriend.
- In September 2019, Pirates pitcher Felipe Vázquez was charged with twenty-one felonies, including statutory assault and indecent assault of a person less than sixteen in at least three states.
- In January 2020, Yankees pitcher Domingo Germán was suspended for eighty-one games after hitting his girlfriend.
- In January 2022, former Yankees pitcher Sergio Mitre was convicted of raping and murdering his girlfriend's two-year-old daughter.[14]

There will undoubtedly be more.

The Acquisition of Osuna

Despite Osuna's impressive stats (he is the youngest player in MLB history to reach one hundred saves), Toronto fans praised the Blue Jays' swift release of their reliever. The Blue Jays had previously demonstrated their commitment to maintaining an ethical atmosphere (as evidenced by the 2012 suspension of Yunel Escobar after he wrote a homophobic slur on his eye black and the 2017 suspension of Kevin Pillar after he directed a homophobic slur at Jason Motte), but the unbothered Astros apparently viewed Osuna's actions as an opportunity for a discount.[15]

The baseball world was divided by the hasty enthusiasm of the acquisition and the willingness of the Astros to look the other way. As Jeff Passan notes in his refreshingly blunt article "In Trading for Roberto Osuna, the Houston Astros Show They Have No Conscience":

> The pattern is reprehensible, and yet it's of no surprise, because for all of the lip service the game pays about wanting to snuff out mistreatment of women, it's at the mercy of teams that don't pretend to have some kind of zero-tolerance policy. The Astros are far from alone, though this is no time for whataboutism, because this is fresh, and it felt positively gross: the visceral details, the clumsy deceit, the haphazard explanations. The entire production is just a reminder that the sports we watch, the teams we love, are ready to feed a steady diet of nonsense in hopes that allegiance might obfuscate something so obviously wrong.[16]

Yet some fans willingly gobbled this diet of nonsense despite the moral indigestion it caused in countless cases.

The Astros clubhouse attempted to present a united front. The *Houston Chronicle*, which portrayed Osuna as a polarizing figure for the Astros," reported, "Luhnow, the general manager, also announced that the team had a zero-tolerance policy toward abuse. When it was pointed out to him that dealing for a player who had served a seventy-five-game suspension for abuse was in violation of a zero-tolerance policy, Luhnow hemmed and hawed. 'What I meant and the way that was interpreted and what it really means are two different things. . . . So that's one I'd like to have back.'"[17]

Though he had tweeted his disgust with the Danry Vásquez video, now-Astro Verlander took a less firm stance on the acquisition of Osuna: "It's a tough situation. . . . I think the thing for us to remember here is that the details have not come to light. We don't know the whole story. Obviously, I've said some pretty inflammatory things about stuff like this in the past. I stand by those words."[18] Verlander's suggestion that "stuff like this" can be "inflammatory" implies that the deplorability of domestic violence is debatable. Verlander's refusal to condemn a new teammate echoed David Ortiz's insistence that the anticipated punishment of Aroldis Chapman and José Reyes was unjustified: "These are good guys, I feel so bad for them. . . . I know José well. José is not a trouble maker. He's a good guy."[19] Verlander's public flip-flopping only further perpetuated the notion that the victimizer is also the victimized.

Facing backlash from fans, Luhnow tried to justify the acquisition of Osuna: "The due diligence by our front office was unprecedented. We are confident that Osuna is remorseful, has willfully complied with all consequences related to his past behavior, has proactively engaged in counseling, and will fully comply with our zero tolerance policy related to abuse of any kind."[20] As Passan rightly countered, "[Luhnow] traded the goodwill built up by a clubhouse full of likable players who soon will be sharing a uniform, field and dugout with one currently standing trial for beating a woman."[21] Many Astros fans advocated the separation of the artist from the art, among them *The Athletic* editor Jenny Dial Creech, who tweeted: "Athletes are role models. Men who abuse women should not be. Sports fans, two things can be true at the same time: 1—you can unconditionally love your team and cheer for them. 2—you can also be disappointed and demand better when it acquires a player with a history of assault." On September 1, Astros fan Kevin Jukkola was ejected from Minute Maid Park for holding a sign that read "Houston Domestic Violence Hot Line 713.528.2121." His ejection was allegedly justified by the Astros' claim that anyone holding a sign unrelated to baseball can be ejected. Other fans chimed in their approval and offered suggestions: "I think the sign should be irrelevant in the ballpark because the Astros should already have one instead of us needing to bring one."[22]

Apparently surprised by public condemnation, the Astros took further steps to appease fans. In October, owner Jim Crane donated $214,000 to Family Services of Southeast Texas. According to MLB.com, he also donated $10,000 to the Montgomery County Women's Shelter.[23] While thousands of dollars might signify a generous contribution, the sum of the donations constitutes "less than five per cent of the base salary that the Astros paid Osuna in 2019."[24] Perhaps Crane's intentions were actually good, but the timing of the gesture reduces it to little more than a slimy PR tactic to placate ticket buyers.

Meanwhile, Osuna was met with boos when he took the mound against his former Blue Jays. His Instagram account was set to private; as of this writing, his official Instagram account features only two posts, and the comments are disabled. His sound bites reflect remorse for the possibility of punishment, not his actions, and he appears either unapologetically oblivious or inexcusably smug.

In an interview given in anticipation of his September 2018 hearing, Osuna stated, "Hey, if I'm guilty, you can say whatever you want."[25]

Responses to Clubhouse Incident

The candor of Osuna and Taubman stood in stark contrast to the female reporters' responses and reflected a consistent trend in sporting spheres: men's emotion is valorized as authentic, while women's emotion undermines their credibility. To deflect both allegations of distracting emotion and the feeling of crushing institutionalized impostor syndrome, female reporters must use the same kind of analytics-based thinking that front office peers use for major acquisitions. The freedom to speak and write off the cuff is a luxury achievable only when your listeners are not dissecting your words with toxic confirmation bias.

In her article, Apstein carefully delineated the systemic failures of organizations whose success depends on the public conviction in their players' infallibility: "This is the miscalculation that teams make over and over again. They acquire players with reprehensible pasts for less than market rate and concede that they will have to pay a price in public trust. But when the bill comes due, teams act like they, not the people their actions wounded, are the aggrieved party. How dare you keep reminding us of the past? Don't you understand we have baseball games to play?"[26] The sobering truth of her article was only further validated by the outrage it catalyzed.

After Apstein's story was published, the Astros released the following statement: "The story posted by *Sports Illustrated* is misleading and completely irresponsible. . . . An Astros player was being asked about a difficult outing. Our executive was supporting the player during a difficult time. His comments had everything to do about the game situation that just occurred and nothing else—they were also not directed toward any specific reporters. We are extremely disappointed in *Sports Illustrated*'s attempt to fabricate a story where one does not exist."[27] As the story developed, it became glaringly obvious that Apstein was in the right.

Hannah Keyser, a baseball writer for Yahoo! Sports who was one of the three female reporters in the clubhouse, corroborated Apstein's story: "Much of what Luhnow said on Thursday attempts to perpetuate the convenient delusion that what happened at the ALCS was a standalone incident and not a sobering tip of the iceberg."[28] While the third reporter asked to remain anonymous, [mostly female] reporters offered sympathetic takes. *New Yorker* staff writer Louisa Thomas agreed that "the long catalogue of unforced errors" includes the Astros' "resisting the suggestion that the rot ran deeper."[29] Just as Verlander had previously demonstrated, it is far too easy to claim to have always been on the "right side," and those who had stayed silent now hurried to position themselves in a more flattering light. *Houston*

Chronicle sports reporter Hunter Atkins confirmed the *Sports Illustrated* report after it was published, tweeting, "The Astros called this @stephapstein report misleading. It is not. I was there. Saw it. And I should've said something sooner." (Atkins's Twitter account was deleted after his arrest, but fans took screenshots of his tweet. It is possibly relevant to note that a few weeks later Atkins was arrested for soliciting and assaulting a fifteen-year-old.)[30]

As these events unfolded in the simpler, pre-COVID fall of 2019, I closely followed Apstein's story, and just before I opened Twitter to skim posts and read articles about the incident, I remember foolishly hoping that the two years since #MeToo had at least somewhat enlightened the internet. I eagerly imagined the barrage of tweets by both male and female fans, the thrill of camaraderie I would feel with fellow sports fans who understand that "feminist" is not a bad word.

As always, Twitter did not fail to destroy my faith in humanity.

- On October 22, 2019, at 1:56 p.m., @mariokracst tweeted, "Was that the proper environment for someone who was allegedly wearing a DV bracelet to be in? There's a time and place to make a statement. I'm not condoning a stupid action but I'm also not going into shark infested waters with a bleeding cut."
- On October 22, 2019, at 6:18 p.m., @jkeebz07 tweeted, "Presently, we have a sissy ass PC culture that protects media at all cost. This story should be filed in the folder that says Who Gives a F."
- On October 21, 2019, at 8:07 p.m., @DavidMorant48 tweeted, "Since Stephanie is a die-hard Yankees fan and Altuve just broke her heart. . . . I HIGHLY doubt her version of this. Just bitter obviously. As another tweeter said . . . why would he yell that right after Osuna just blew the save? Something sounds fishy here."
- On October 22, 2019, at 6:24 a.m., @SevenM3 tweeted, "Sounds like a bunch of he said she said to me with the overwhelming stinch [*sic*] of Yankeeism. If it's true disciplinary action should be taken but as of rt now it should be a non-story. Let's talk WS & Stros."

Much of the Twitter conversation demanded that Apstein "stick to sports," a commonly used phrase that commentators employ when they do not like the "political" commentary rather than discuss topics perceived to be sports-adjacent. However, demanding that sports reporters stick to sports instead of considering athletes' off-field lives merely mitigates malfeasance, rendering athletes even more untouchable and unrelatable. To place athletes on a different plane entirely is to dehumanize them to mere sources of entertainment and compartmentalize them as objects that fulfill a need, much as misogynists compartmentalize the women around them. Denying athletes the right to be tried as human sets them on a crumbling pedestal that will inevitably collapse. As MacAree astutely noted, "'Stick to sports' misses the fundamental point: putting misogyny and baseball (or racism and soccer, or etc.) on the same moral plane is absurd. There is no cost-benefit analysis for teams to fiddle with here; the evil of domestic violence isn't mitigated by how tightly the perpetrator can spin a slider."[31]

I can only imagine how difficult it must have been for Apstein and Keyser to craft those articles after the clubhouse incident. A female journalist decrying the actions of a powerful man must tread lightly, removing all traces of emotion from her writing lest she be declared too unreliably sensitive (or, in the terms of Victorian quasi-doctors that unfortunately still linger in the dialogue about women, "hysterical"). A female writer of sports is held to much higher scrutiny than her male peers; she must fight for her right to write and her right to belong in the pages and spaces she occupies. The authenticity of her fandom is doubted; her knowledge of and love for the game is questioned; her credibility is jeopardized by the ease of labeling her just another angry feminist.[32]

The Baseball Wives of Instagram

The shift from print to digital has altered not only our consumption of sports journalism but of sports themselves. We still haven't quite figured out how to handle social media as it shortens the distance between athlete and fan, offering a tantalizing glimpse into our idols' personal lives. Often, these glimpses of reckless glamour stand in stark contrast to carefully curated statements by front offices that, once upon a time, were our main source of insight into players' lives.[33] The game that looks so good on TV is not done the same justice on a phone, and as the jungle of cable television becomes increasingly maddening to navigate, more fans are crafting their own narratives of the game through multiple platforms. Within our media milieu, doggedly conservative baseball struggles to maintain its foothold: the way we engage with baseball is changing, and baseball must take the leap to adapt or risk erasure. According to a 2017 Gallup poll, only 9 percent of Americans claim baseball is their favorite sport to watch.[34]

Baseball has always maintained a curiously selective relationship with female fans. Judge Hofheinz's claim that "every day here will be ladies' day" because carefully designed lights supposedly flattered women's makeup reflects an unfortunately embedded tradition of misogyny: female fans are welcome as long as they look good.[35] As sociologist Kim Toffoletti delineates, female fandom "validates heterosexuality as the norm within sports that are heavily invested in hegemonic versions of masculinity": the masculine ideal of male players is confirmed by the presence of female spectators who invest time and money to watch them perform, and the players' perceived athletic ability is bolstered by their desirability to beautiful female fans.[36] The early entrepreneurs of Ladies Day promotions hoped that the presence of women would mitigate the unruliness of drunk male fans. The ideal female fan apparently has not evolved much as she remains halfway between a cheerleader and a scarecrow, a passive enforcer without agency who validates male players' belief that they deserve to be watched.

Social media—particularly Instagram—amplifies the ugliness of baseball's attitude towards beautiful women. Baseball players' wives occupy a puzzling position, since they are encouraged to appear relatively conservative and take part in wholesome team-led philanthropic projects, while NBA and NFL wives are allowed to occupy a bolder spotlight (a perception perhaps amplified by shows like VH1's *Football Wives* and *Basketball Wives* and the Kardashians' collective attempt to seemingly date the entire NBA). With rare exception (two-time gold medalist soccer player Mia Hamm [Nomar Garciaparra], three-time gold medalist beach volleyball player Misty May-Treanor [Matt Treanor], and model-actress Kate Upton [Justin Verlander]), baseball wives are often depicted as content to be cheerleaders rather than cheered.

Just as social media narrows the gap between fans and male athletes, so too does Instagram allow for greater surveillance of and speculation about players' wives, enabling access to women who are further objectified. They appear to have it all: travel, financial security, access to luxury, time to enjoy vocational charity work, a sorority of supportive fellow team wives in adorable matching denim jackets bejeweled with their husbands' numbers. The new generation of media continues to sell fantasies we wish we could be part of: John Hughes movies told us we should wish to date Jake Ryan, and now Kourtney Turner [Josh Turner]'s Instagram tells us we should wish to swim in an infinity pool overlooking the ocean (and we do).[37]

In the process of writing this article, it felt incredibly grubby to comb through the Instagram accounts of players' wives to monitor the onslaught of comments from male fans, but it felt even more offensive—but somehow necessary—to speculate about the Instagram accounts of MLB wives who have been abused. As social media perpetuates the illusion of connectivity while also making victims more isolated, it places undue pressure on them to appear "fine," but how is this phenomenon amplified when the victim is in the public eye? How is it amplified when she occupies a far less secure position than the abuser on whom she financially depends? What public image is expected of her, and what lengths must she go to in order to project an image of a healthy relationship? To what extent is her husband monitoring her posts, and to what extent does he control them?

Considerable scholarship has been conducted to determine the lasting effects of social media's perpetual location-tagging and relationship-displaying on modern relationships. An abused wife in 2021 who is plotting an escape has a much wider vocabulary to discuss her situation than Francine Hughes did in 1977, though her potential accidental divulging of location information on social media adds another layer of worry to the usual concerns of money, children, and perceived shame that so often prevent women from leaving. Stephanie Kohlman and her colleagues demonstrate that image-based social networking is becoming another tool by which abusers "establish an imbalance of power and control in relationships."[38] Law professor Andrew King-Ries demonstrates that "efforts to match their expectations about intimate relationships to their peers'" encourages young adults to place an unhealthy emphasis on visibility of relationships on social media, and "there is a significant similarity between the dynamic in adult-battering relationships and the use of technology by teenagers in their intimate relationships."[39] As Kelly Carlyle and her colleagues show, this dynamic is further muddled by conflicted impressions of intimate partner violence as something to be "viewed in a public health context, or simply as an interpersonal, private issue with implications for the criminal justice system."[40] The ambiguity of domestic violence as a public health versus private health issue further complicates its perception and categorization; its connotation of taboo and shame makes it difficult to incorporate into necessary dialogues in settings that do not proactively work to destigmatize this conversation.

I continue to return to the case of Aroldis Chapman because his thirty-game suspension seemed to set the precedent for offering a proportional number of suspensions to the level of violence committed. On October 30, Chapman choked his girlfriend and fired eight shots into his garage. Cristina was allowed to take some belongings from the house and take her children to stay with a family member. On November 4, she posted a selfie to Instagram with the caption "En la vida no pierde el que es traicionado, si no el que no valoró un gran amor que tenía a su lado!!!" (In life, the one who is betrayed does not lose, but rather the one who does not value a great love that he had by his side). On November 8, she posted a photo of herself and her baby daughter on a boat with Chapman with the caption "#blessed."

I invoke Cristina's posts as an example of the complexity of the dynamic of domestic violence. Considerable scholarship demonstrates that strangulation is an important risk factor for homicide of women, and the homepage of the Training Institute on Strangulation Prevention features an anecdote by author Stephanie Land that reflects a common experience: "I was embarrassed. I wanted to keep living out this fantasy perfect relationship thing I had created on social media. . . . Even though there were red flags, I wasn't sure. I was like, 'he seems committed and he really wants to do this.' And so I was like: 'this is fine.'"[41] I cannot judge Cristina for her response, because leaving an abuser—particularly the enabler of financial security and the father of your children—is tremendously difficult to accomplish.[42] However, I do worry about how describing the return to a partner who strangles you as a #blessed life appears on social media and the ramifications it has for impressionable followers who normalize this behavior. Domestic violence rates are skyrocketing during COVID, and they will continue to skyrocket while men who demonstrate no remorse for their treatment of women remain on unapologetic pedestals.[43]

Creating Our Own Narratives, Assembling Our Own Archives

While many of these pedestals still stand, we do not have to worship at their feet. As Apstein rightly pointed out, "No matter what Taubman thinks about it, the rest of us can choose to remember for as long as we want."[44] This oddly echoes Osuna's comment that if he's guilty, we can say whatever we want. Just as easily as deleting an Instagram post, we can pretend to selectively curate our private archives. Our submissions to public archives, however, cannot be revoked.

As fans, we try to make ourselves believe in the myth of meritocracy, that the talented players we admire are inherently good and deserving of our deference. We want to believe that the front office executives pulling our team's puppet strings are well-intentioned. We want to believe that the players whose jerseys we buy and whose motions we imitate deserve such hero worship. As fans, our greatest fear is not that our heroes will disappoint us on the field, but that they will reveal themselves to be unworthy of the time we have invested in the relationship. Like a wife in denial of her husband's true nature, a fan who has pledged fealty to a player feels more compelled to defend them.

On November 12, 2019, Ken Rosenthal and Evan Drellich's article unveiled the cheating scandal, and the Osuna affair receded into the shadows of an energized news cycle. But we can always choose to remember.

Notes

1. Liz Smith, "Giltfinger's Golden Dome," *Sports Illustrated*, April 12, 1965, https://vaulti.si.com/vault/1965/04/12/giltfingers-golden-dome.

2. "Baseball: Green Quip Angers Women, *New York Times*, August 5, 1983, https://www.nytimes.com/1993/08/05/sports/baseball-green-quip-angers-women.html?searchResultPosition=1.

3. In this chapter, I focus on intimate partner violence committed against women by men. But to ignore the fact that men can be abused by women only perpetuates the cycle of toxic masculinity. According to the National Coalition Against Domestic Violence (https://ncadv.org/), one in three women and one in four men have experienced some form of physical violence by an intimate partner.

4. Anna Boots, "'The Burning Bed' Recalls the Case That Changed How Law Enforcement Treats Domestic Violence," *New Yorker*, July 9, 2020, https://www.newyorker.com/culture/video-dept/the-burning-bed-recalls-the-case that-changed-how-law-enforcement-treats-domestic-violence.

5. Mary Ann Franks, "Real Men Advance, Real Women Retreat: Stand Your Ground, Battered Women's Syndrome, and Violence as Male Privilege," *Miami Law Review* 68 (2014): 1009, https://lawreview.law.miami.edu/wp-content/uploads/2014/09/Real-Men-Advance-Real-Women-Retreat.pdf.

6. The "Athletes and Domestic Violence" Wikipedia page does not even have a section for baseball (featured headings include "American Football," "NCAA," "NBA," and "Boxing/Floyd Mayweather"). While some may interpret this as evidence of the relative scarcity of domestic violence in the baseball world as compared to other sports, I am more inclined to view this as evidence of an issue of publicity and visibility.

7. "Nancy Grace: Vick, Three Others, Plead Not Guilty on Federal Dog Charges," CNN Online, July 26, 2007, http://transcripts.cnn.com/TRANSCRIPTS/0707/26/ng.01.html.

8. Mike Bates, "MLB's Record on Domestic Violence Worse Than NFL's," SBNation.com, July 28, 2014, https://www.sbnation.com/mlb/2014/7/28/5936835/ray-rice-chuck-knoblauch-minnesota-twins-mlb-domestic-abuse-violence.

9. Paul Hagen, "MLB, MLBPA Reveal Domestic Violence Policy," MLB.com, August 21, 2015, https://www.mlb.com/news/mlb-mlbpa-agree-on-domestic-violence-policy/c-144508842.

10. In January 2017, the NBA followed MLB's example and issued a new collective bargaining agreement with a new "joint NBA/NBPA policy on domestic violence, sexual assault, and child abuse." A 1996 *Harvard Law Review* article postulated that leagues would be resistant to implementing such policies because they "might be construed as an attempt to usurp the role of the government . . . when the league seeks to enact rules in a realm in which it has no specialized knowledge and in

which public government intervention is desirable—such as domestic violence—the legitimacy of such private action must be questioned." "Out of Bounds: Professional Sports Leagues and Domestic Violence," *Harvard Law Review* 109, no. 5 (1996): 1053–1054, https://doi.org/10.2307/1342260.

11. In 1997, the Red Sox did nothing after outfielder Wil Cordero was arrested for hitting his wife. Pedro Astacio still started on opening day for the Rockies after he was arrested for hitting his pregnant wife. The Phillies did nothing after Brett Myers was arrested for punching his wife while arguing on the streets of Boston. The Dodgers gave Milton Bradley the Roberto Clemente award in 2005, the year that police made three separate domestic violence calls to Bradley's home. The Mariners' "Refuse to Abuse" partnership with the Washington State Coalition Against Domestic Violence had garnered positive PR until their 2010 acquisition of Josh Lueke after his rape conviction. However, it is worth noting that despite the lack of formal policy, the Astros did release Julio Lugo in 2003 after he hit his wife; in 2007, the Mariners sent Julio Mateo back to Triple-A after he turned himself in for assaulting his wife; in 2014 the Twins canceled the induction of Chuck Knoblauch to their team hall of fame after he was arrested for assaulting his wife.

12. Tim Brown and Jeff Passan, "Police Report: Aroldis Chapman Allegedly Fired Gunshots, 'Choked' Girlfriend in Domestic Incident," Yahoo! Sports, December 7, 2015, https://sports.yahoo.com/news/aroldis-chapman-s-girlfriend-alleged-he-choked-her-according-to-police-report-023629095.html.

13. Addison Russell's ex-wife posted on her blog, "The first time I was physically mistreated by my spouse, I was in shock. I couldn't wrap my head around what just happened. . . . Why did he get so angry? What did I do for him to want to put his hands on me? Of course I forgave him & assumed it would never happen again." Emily Caron, "Addison Russell's Ex-Wife Shares Blog Post Detailing Disturbing Story of Emotional, Physical Abuse," *Sports Illustrated*, September 21, 2018, https://www.si.com/mlb/2018/09/21/chicago-cubs-addison-russell-melisa-reidy-abuse-relationship-violence-divorce.

14. Dan Lyons, "Former MLB Pitcher Sentenced to 40 to 60 Years for Rape, Murder of Toddler,"*Sports Illustrated*, January 21, 2022, https://www.si.com/mlb/2022/01/21/sergio-mitre-guilty-rape-murder-toddler-prison-mexico.

15. In her analysis of Blue Jays manager John Gibbons's statement, lawyer Sheryl Rings notes its lack of qualifications and other language-padders often used by teams when issuing similar statements about their players' "alleged" misconduct:

> It's troubling because the Blue Jays evidently believe these allegations to be sufficiently credible that they are willing to ignore possible damage to Osuna's reputation if they're wrong. After all, the language "conduct associated with this incident" pretty much takes for granted that the incident happened. And that means that the allegations against Osuna are likely pretty serious. Whatever Osuna is alleged to have done—and, as I write this, we don't know exactly what it is—it's pretty serious. Canada, like the U.S., follows the British common law, so their assault laws are fairly similar to what you might expect in the States. And that covers such a broad range of behaviors that it's impossible at this point to know what type of conduct we're talking about (Sheryl Rings, "Roberto Osuna, the Blue Jays, and the Limits of Presuming

Innocence," last modified May 10, 2018, https://blogs.fangraphs.com/roberto-osuna
-the-blue-jays-and-the-limits-of-presuming-innocence/).

16. Jeff Passan, "In Trading for Roberto Osuna, the Houston Astros Show They
Have No Conscience," Yahoo! Sports, July 31, 2018, https://sports.yahoo.com/trading
-roberto-osuna-houston-astros-show-no-conscience-134758777.html.

17. Louisa Thomas, "The Stories That the Houston Astros Have Told," *New Yorker*,
October 25, 2019, https://www.newyorker.com/sports/sporting-scene/the-stories-that
the-houston-astros-have-told.

18. In a February 2020 interview, Trevor Bauer criticized Verlander's hypocrisy:
"I mean, I don't know anything about the whole [Roberto] Osuna situation, right?
But if you're Justin Verlander and you decide to take a stance against domestic violence and speak out 100% against it and then you flip-flop your opinion when someone is now on your team and it's affecting you, that's not having character. That's not
taking a moral stand. That's just pandering to the public. It's the same thing as cheating." Bobby Nightengale, "Trevor Bauer Takes Aim at Houston Astros' José Altuve,
Alex Bregman, Justin Verlander," *Cincinnati Enquirer*, February 15, 2020, https://
www.cincinnati.com/story/sports/mlb/reds/2020/02/15/trevor-bauer-fires-houston
-astros-players-jose-altuve alex-bregman/4768418002/.

19. Michael Rosen, "David Ortiz on Alleged Domestic Abusers," Fusion TV,
February 24, 2016, https://fusion.tv/story/272479/david-ortiz-on-alleged-domestic
-abusers-those-are-good-guys-i-feel-so bad-for-them.

20. Khadrice Rollins, "Astros Convinced Roberto Osuna Is 'Remorseful' for Domestic Violence Incident," *Sports Illustrated*, July 30, 2018, https://www.si.com/mlb
/2018/07/30/astros-roberto-osuna-trade-statement-domestic-violence-allegation.

21. Passan, "In Trading for Roberto Osuna, the Houston Astros Show They Have
No Conscience."

22. Steve Campion, "Astros fan curious why he was kicked out of game over domestic violence sign," ABC13.com, September 4, 2018, https://abc13.com/houston
-astros-fan-domestic-violence-sign-abuse/4137979/.

23. Alyson Footer, "Astros Commit to Anti-domestic Violence Cause," MLB
.com, October 15, 2018, https://www.mlb.com/astros/news/astros-join-cause-to-pre
vent-domestic-violence-c297882304.

24. Thomas, "The Stories That the Houston Astros Have Told."

25. Charlotte Carroll, "Roberto Osuna Breaks Silence On Domestic Violence
Charge: 'Everybody is Quick to Judge Me,'" *Sports Illustrated*, August 29, 2018,
https://www.si.com/mlb/2018/08/29/roberto-osuna-domestic-violence-charge
criticism-statement.

26. Stephanie Apstein, "Astros Staffer's Outburst at Female Reporters Illustrates
MLB's Forgive-and-Forget Attitude toward Domestic Violence," *Sports Illustrated*,
October 21, 2019, https://www.si.com/mlb/2019/10/22/houston-astros-roberto-osuna
-suspension.

27. Arthur Weinstein, "Astros Dispute Story That Team Executive Taunted Female Reporters about Roberto Osuna," *The Sporting News*, October 21, 2019, https://
www.sportingnews.com/us/mlb/news/astros-dispute-story-that-staffer-taunted
-female-reporters-about-roberto-osuna-after-alcs/gkg17mragu161rvubrqsnwzm8.

28. Hannah Keyser, "The Astros Don't Think They Have a 'Cultural' Problem. Here's Why They're Wrong," Yahoo! Sports, October 25, 2019, https://www.yahoo.com/lifestyle/the-pen-the-astros-dont-think-they-have-a-cultural-problem-heres-why-theyre-wrong-183116740.html.

29. Thomas, "The Stories."

30. Far more tactful allyship was performed by *Seattle Times* columnist Larry Stone, who admitted his own compromising of journalistic integrity. In response to *Sports Illustrated*'s exposé of the abuse Milton Bradley committed against his wife, Stone acknowledged:

> Finally, I felt regret for whatever minuscule role I might have played as a media enabler. It's not that I swept Bradley's long history of legal scraps and on- and off-field battles under the rug. I dutifully reported them. But I also had at least one 'Bradley's not as bad as portrayed' story, quoting former teammates, managers and executives about Bradley's sensitive side. It was written with a desire for balance and fairness, but in retrospect it's the kind of thing that lets people like Bradley skate through. It also shows how difficult it can be to ascertain, from the outside looking in, just how volatile and dangerous a person really is (Larry Stone, "Domestic Abuse by Milton Bradley Is a Cautionary Tale We Must All Learn From," *Seattle Times*, April 11, 2015, https://www.seattletimes.com/sports/mariners/domestic-abuse-by-milton-bradley-is-a-cautionary-tale-we-all-must-learn-from/).

31. Graham MacAree, "The Astros Have a Misogyny Problem Because Sports Have a Misogyny Problem," SB Nation, October 22, 2019, https://www.sbnation.com/2019/10/22/20926423/astros-houston-world-series-brandon-taubman-roberto-osuna.

32. As *The Atlantic* journalist Jemele Hill noted, "The immediate reaction from a still-too-large segment of the public is going to be, 'That's why women shouldn't talk sports.' Even though most guys that are in [my] position probably would make a similar mistake, but it's never going to be about their competence. It's never going to be about their gender, where it will be for me." Michael Serazio, *The Power of Sports: Media and Spectacle in American Culture* (New York: New York University Press, 2019), 189.

33. As of February 2021, the most popular current/former MLB players' Instagram accounts belong to: 1. David Ortiz (2.2 million followers); 2. Mike Trout (1.8 million followers); 3. Bryce Harper (1.7 million followers). In other professional sports, Odell Beckham Jr. has 14.3 million followers, LeBron James has 80 million followers, and Cristiano Ronaldo has 265 million followers.

34. "Sports," Gallup Organization, https://news.gallup.com/poll/4735/sports.aspx. Seventy percent of viewers of MLB and NBA games are male, and baseball fans are perceived as not only too male but also too old and too white. See also Derek Thompson, "Which Sports Have the Whitest/Richest/Oldest Fans?," *The Atlantic*, February 10, 2014, https://www.theatlantic.com/business/archive/2014/02/which-sports-have-the-whitest-richest-oldest-fans/283626/.

35. Susan Cahn, "Sport Remains a Key Cultural Location for Male Dominance, a Site Where Traditional Patriarchal Values Are Upheld and Transformed in Re-

sponse to Changes in the Broader Society," *Coming On Strong: Gender and Sexuality in Women's Sport* (Urbana: University of Illinois Press, 2015), 278.

36. Kim Toffoletti, *Sport and Its Female Fans* (London: Routledge, 2012), 105.

37. I would like to add that Kourtney and I were classmates at UCLA, and she is a lovely person who works to feed thousands of families in Los Angeles through the Justin Turner Foundation.

38. Stephanie Kohlman, Amber Baig, Guy Balice, et al., "Contribution of Media to the Normalization and Perpetuation of Domestic Violence," *Austin Journal of Psychiatry and Behavioral Sciences* 1, no. 4 (2014): 1018, https://austinpublishing group.com/psychiatry-behavioral-sciences/fulltext/ajpbs-v1-id1018.php.

39. Andrew King-Ries, "Teens, Technology, and Cyberstalking: The Domestic Violence Wave of the Future?," *Texas Journal of Women and the Law* 20, no. 2 (2011): 154, http://scholarship.law.umt.edu/faculty_lawreviews/118.

40. Kellie E. Carlyle, Jeanine P. D. Guidry, Sharyn A. Dougherty, and Candace W. Burton, "Intimate Partner Violence on Instagram: Visualizing a Public Health Approach to Prevention," *Health Education & Behavior* 46, no. 2 (2019): 90S–96S, https://doi.org/10.1177/1090198119873917.

41. Sa'iyda Shabazz, "Strangulation: The Red Flag of Domestic Violence That We Never Discuss," Strangulation Training Institute, December 27, 2019, https://www.strangulationtraininginstitute.com/strangulation-the-red-flag-of-domestic -violence-that-we-never-discuss/.

42. The website of the National Domestic Violence Hotline cites the common reasons people stay in an abusive relationship: fear, normalized abuse, shame, intimidation, low self-esteem, lack of resources, disability, immigration status, cultural context, children, and love. "Why People Stay," https://www.thehotline.org/support -others/why-people-stay/.

43. Megan L. Evans, Margo Lindauer, and Maureen E. Farrell, "A Pandemic within a Pandemic—Intimate Partner Violence during Covid-19," *New England Journal of Medicine* 383, no. 24 (December 10, 2020): 2302–2304, https://doi.org/10.1056 /NEJMp2024046.

44. Apstein, "Astros Staffer's Outburst."

CHAPTER 4

Round Up the Usual Suspects: Cheating in Baseball

RICHARD C. CREPEAU

American culture is deeply immersed in competition. The entrepreneurial economy is highly competitive and at times cutthroat in character. Middle-class lifestyles are competitive in terms of status. Sports are competitive and are often obsessed with winning. At times the pressures to succeed or win are overwhelming, and when that level is reached, there is a tendency to go beyond the rules and regulations to achieve victory regardless of the sphere. Lying and cheating are easy to slip into, and anything offering a winning edge can seem legitimate, if not entirely ethical or legal. When the rewards increase in sport, the willingness to take risks increases proportionally.

Forms of cheating to increase the odds of winning are many and varied, and they are found all across American society and American sport. There is a remarkable range of words and descriptions for the forms of cheating, and they are used for a range of reasons. Alternatives include lying, dissembling, fudging, withholding information, lacking full disclosure, misinformation, spying, discerning, analyzing, copying, plagiarism, and stealing. This obfuscating vocabulary allows the participants or practitioners to deny that what they are doing is cheating.

This sort of practice, call it hypocrisy or something else, can be found across many societies and throughout history. American culture is riddled with it. Cheating is embedded in many compartments of our lives, although it goes by many names. Cheating per se is unacceptable, but when it goes by other names it is condoned and even admired. It is within this context that the Houston Astros' sign-stealing scandal should be understood and judged: "It's not that cheating is socially acceptable in baseball; the shock and indignation over the steroids era are proof that is very much not. It's that *certain kinds* of cheating are socially acceptable in baseball, and being competitive means engaging in the ambiguous negotiation of the acceptable vs. the unacceptable."[1]

I contend that the scandal involving sign stealing by the Houston Astros is no more serious than many other cases of sign stealing in the history of the game. It is also no more serious than various other forms of stealing or cheating. What distinguishes it is the use of a combination of technology and crude communication, as well as the perceived success of their methods that some see as propelling them to a World Series victory. In point of fact, what was done by the Astros has a long history in the game, and much of that history is regarded with a wink and a nod or simply seen as charming nostalgia.

We grow up in a world of advertising and consumption, at the heart of which is lying about the attributes of the product. The essence of advertising is to stretch the truth, often beyond the breaking point. Furthermore, advertising is at the center of our daily lives. At the center of American capitalism is competition, and the point of competition is to win, as it is in our sports culture. At the extremes are cutthroat competition and forms of business espionage. Politics, too, is steeped in dissembling, half-truths, innuendo, and outright lies. Truth from politicians is unexpected and rare, especially in the competitive arena of elections.

All of these examples could be classified as cheating, but clearly they are not. To a certain degree, those who are the beneficiaries and those who are the victims differ on their view of what is and what is not cheating. What is acceptable or not depends on context and on what is regarded as the "seriousness" of any particular act or actions. The nature and extent of the Astros' operations in the "trash can scandal" should be judged within this broad cultural context.

To some, the Astros simply made clever and effective use of a combination of technology and baseball knowledge to gain a competitive edge. In essence, the scheme made it possible for hitters to know what pitch was coming from the pitcher they were facing. There is no doubt that this would offer at least some hitters an advantage over the pitcher and should have been reflected in performance. That was not always the case.

The reaction to these revelations across the world of baseball and beyond was, for the most part, condemnation. The Astros had cheated to win. It was despicable. It violated a sacred trust and a basic tenant of fairness in sport. It seemed as if everyone in and outside of baseball reacted strongly to the Astros' transgression, but how sincere was the condemnation?

This reaction reminded me of the scene in the 1942 film *Casablanca* when Captain Renault leads a raid on Rick's nightclub and casino, saying, "I'm shocked, shocked to find out that gambling is going on in here!" No sooner were the words out of his mouth than the croupier handed Captain Renault his winnings. Captain Renault's hypocrisy was blatant, but it was also necessary. As a personification of the law, Renault was required to maintain the fiction that he was enforcing the law.

There is in sport a delicate balance surrounding rules and the adherence to them. In one sense, rules are designed to keep the playing field fair, but in another, rules cannot be allowed to inhibit the pursuit of winning. Then again, break the rules and you are a cheat, but only if you get caught. The opposite of winning is losing. No one likes to lose, and seldom is anyone satisfied to lose. The whole point of competition is to win, in sport and elsewhere. "Winning isn't everything; it's the only thing," goes the popular phrase.

Basically, people cheat because they want to win.[2] If you watch children play at games, all sorts of games, athletic, card, or board games in which there is a winner, it is common for them to try to bend the rules or ignore the rules. Children start cheating at an early age. Is it natural or just something they learn very early in their life? Is there a culture of cheating? And, of course, if you don't get caught, then good for you. There are aphorisms on cheating that are culturally instructive: "It is only cheating if you get caught." If you are not caught, it is because you are "smart" and "clever."

"If you're not cheating, you're not trying," a phrase central to the culture of the Oakland Raiders under Al Davis, has come into widespread use in sports. In point of fact, we tend to "applaud cheating" when someone gets away with it. The examples from baseball alone are legion.

Cheating in baseball goes back to its beginnings. In the nineteenth century, as soon as baseball changed from being a social and recreational activity to one in which winning was important, teams began bending rules and ethics in order to increase wins. "Ringers" were brought in to play. Those who were not members of the club were recruited for their abilities to play baseball. Social class or occupational category, initially a membership requirement, gave way to winning.

The next step down this road was logical: pay someone to come and play in the games while continuing to insist that this was an all amateur affair. The key here is the need or desire to win. Everyone seemed content to live with this fiction, until they were not. Nineteenth-century baseball organizations collapsed under the strain of this hypocrisy, the result being the demise of the National Association of Base Ball Players, then succeeded by the National Association of Professional Baseball Players. Professionalism was preferred to amateurism, and winning turned out to be the most important thing.[3]

There were any number of cheating scandals that attest to the prevalence of shady practices in the game. The first major sign-stealing scandal in 1899–1900 involved the Philadelphia Phillies, who used a set of binoculars, a buzzer system, and a backup catcher to detect the signs given by opposing catchers and then passing them on to the batter via the third-base coach. From 1910 to 1914, the Philadelphia A's used binoculars and a weather vane to signal batters. Binoculars seemed to be the essential piece of equipment in all these schemes involving the Cleveland Indians, the Cubs, and the White Sox.

One of the most notorious of the sign-stealing incidents involved the New York Giants, who used a powerful telescope looking out from its centerfield clubhouse in towards home plate. This led to the now legendary, and literary, home run by Bobby Thomson off Ralph Branca to defeat the Brooklyn Dodgers in the 1951 National League pennant playoff final. Had it been exposed at the time, the reaction would have been comparable to the reaction to the Astros' sign stealing.[4]

Sign stealing was an important skill for Rickey Henderson, the all-time base stealing leader. Henderson handled the stealing of signs on his own. He was able to get a long enough lead when at first base, where he could see the catcher's signs. Henderson soon deciphered the code to know when a breaking pitch was coming, adding one more edge to his already blinding speed and acceleration. Was he cheating, or just a smart player?[5]

For hitters, another of the ways of cheating is using a corked bat. In this iteration, the barrel of a bat is hollowed out and cork, or in some cases superballs, is loaded into the barrel. Then the end of the bat is refilled with wood and smoothed and sealed to hide any marks of corking. Among the better-known corkers was Sammy Sosa of the Cubs, whose bat broke open during play revealing the cork. Sosa claimed it was all a mistake. He only used corked bats for batting practice, he said, and somehow he had mistakenly picked up a corked bat when he came to bat that one time. Few found Sosa's explanation convincing.

Some players are caught when an umpire or opponents, suspecting some foul play, ask that the bat be removed from play and sent to the league office for X-rays. All corkers, of course, were not caught. Norm Cash, the four-time All-Star first baseman and 1961 American League batting champion of the Detroit Tigers, admitted long after he retired that he had played his entire career with a corked bat.[6] Not much outrage—as in none—followed that admission.

Out on the mound, cheating through doctoring of the baseball has been widespread and again is as old as the game itself. In 1920, the spitball was outlawed, but somehow it never disappeared. The best known of the spitball pitchers is Hall of Fame member Gaylord Perry. He was long suspected of using the spitball, but no one seemed able to catch him. After his excellent 1974 season, Perry wrote *Me & the Spitter*, in which he admitted that the spitball was a key part of his pitching repertoire, adding that he wasn't throwing it anymore. Gene Mauch observed that Perry wasn't throwing it any less, either. Perry's spitball became a running joke in the game.

There were any number of other foreign substances used by pitchers through the years, from the simple K-Y Jelly and Vaseline to more elaborate concoctions such as Whitey Ford's mix of turpentine, rosin, and baby oil. These substances were put on locations on the pitcher's body, on the uniform, on the cap, or wherever the pitcher found it most convenient to access the illegal substance.[7]

The other major means of doctoring the ball was scuffing its surface. The number of ways of doing this seem to be infinite: a tack in the pitcher's glove, a sharp fingernail, sandpaper, or an emery board. My favorite case, because I was a witness to it, occurred when Joe Niekro was caught using an emery board to scuff the baseball. A few days after he was caught, the Minnesota Twins had a special giveaway night. "The Joe Niekro Emery Board" was given to fans on the night that his cheating was honored at the ballpark.

Over a period of a quarter-century, Bobby Valentine managed three major league teams and one team in Japan. As new players arrived, one of the first things Valentine asked each of them to do was to provide him with the signs being used by their previous team. When asked for his views on the Astros scandal, Valentine said that if he had been managing the Astros, he would not have tried to stop the sign stealing because "every at bat is a life-or-death situation."

While managing, Valentine estimates that he was witness to at least twenty major attempts to steal signs. Also, there were surveillance cameras and bugged rooms used across baseball to steal signs and spy on opponents. Valentine thinks that one point that is being missed in all the noise about the Astros is that sign stealing is relatively easy to counter by frequent sign changes during the course of a game.[8] It is also part of the game, a game within the game.

In and around baseball, those who condemned the Astros were not unlike Captain Renault. The practice of sign stealing in baseball is as old as the game itself, and it is a given that teams will nearly always try to steal the signs of their opponents. Indeed, within the culture of baseball, it is expected that teams and individual players will push at the edges of rules and ethics to gain a competitive edge. The question is: Where is the line and who decides when it is crossed? To be clear, this is not a case of everyone cheats, and so will I. Rather, it is a case of the general acceptance of sign stealing and long list of other practices that may or may not violate rules but that push the boundaries of honesty and fair play.

The outrage over the Astros' sign stealing was clearly an overreaction. No one was using drugs, and no one was injured. Other teams lost when the Astros won, just as would be expected. There are winners and losers in sporting contests. The object of baseball, and of sport generally, is to win. That is why the score is recorded. The difference in this situation is that the transgressions occurred at the World Series and the playoffs.

For all of the shock expressed after the commissioner issued his report on the Astros, it seems likely that there was little that came as a surprise to players across the major leagues. The *Washington Post* reported on numerous instances in which charges were made against the Astros, and suspicions of the Astros were discussed within opposing teams well before the investigation. One of the more interesting of these came from the Washington Nationals as they prepared for the 2019 World Series. Nationals players and coaches were given numerous tips and warnings from major league players about the Astros' activities. As Valentine suggested, the Nationals took counteractions and developed multiple sets of signs for use during the Series.[9]

In an interview with Jim Rome, Hunter Pence, who once played with the Astros, but not in 2017, said that no team was above suspicion at that time. The Astros had mastered the techniques, but "a lot of teams were doing suspicious things during those times."[10] Among suspected teams were the Red Sox, Yankees, and Dodgers.

The new analytics has led to an increased interest in spin rate, which in turn has led to an increased interest in the use of foreign substances by pitchers. The website *The Athletic* reported the results of a survey of players and coaches on the use of foreign substances. The conclusion was that anywhere from 75 to 100 percent of pitchers were enhancing their spin rate. Trevor Bauer wrote that he had spent eight years trying to find the most effective way to increase spin rate.[11] Many of these were illegal under the rules.

In 2020, the Los Angeles Angels clubhouse attendant, Brian Harkins, sued the team for unlawful dismissal. The attendant was fired when MLB informed the Angels that Harkins was supplying pitchers with an illegal substance of rosin and pine tar. Harkins's attorney introduced a text from Gerrit Cole to Harkins asking Harkins to help him out of a "sticky situation" by getting him some of the stuff he had from the previous year. In an interview, Harkins also named a litany of future Hall of Famers who were using the substance.

Perhaps the most notorious cheating scandal before the Astros' activities was the use of performance enhancing drugs that helped produce the home run explosion of the 1990s. As in the Astros' case, there was public outrage and condemnation of the activity when it became "official" public knowledge.[12] Of course, it had been "unofficial common knowledge" for over a decade. The names Barry Bonds, Mark McGwire, Alex Rodriguez, and Roger Clemens are perhaps the best known in this category of cheaters. There were many more suspected and proven PED users.

One of the more interesting aspects of the PED scandal has been the variation in the treatment and reputation of the users. McGwire has returned to baseball as a batting coach. Rodriguez has carved out a broadcasting career on the national stage with ESPN. Clemens and Bonds are now garnering votes for the Baseball Hall of Fame. Those seen as enablers of the drug culture, at least in its home-run aspect, such as former Commissioner Bud Selig and Tony LaRussa, have made their way into the Baseball Hall of Fame with very little objection. Others have not escaped public condemnation and are banned from baseball or life.

It is clear, then, that cheating in baseball is not unusual, but reactions to it seem puzzling at times. There is an air of ambivalence surrounding cheating as well as the reactions to it. A certain amount of cheating is expected and tolerated. Some forms of cheating are acceptable while others are not. Reactions to cheating run the gamut from condemnation to passive acceptance to amusement. The lines between these three are blurry.

Sometimes cheating is admired, especially if it is revealed well after the fact. Occasionally, it is praised or applauded, especially if it is known but never caught. No one would now suggest that the Giants victory in the National League playoff of 1951 be stricken from the records or that the Giants be stripped of their pennant. The sign stealing by the Giants has even taken on a whimsical charm in some quarters.

On the other hand, cheating seems to be most roundly condemned when the cheaters are exposed during or shortly after the cheating has taken place. The scale or degree of cheating also seems to play a role in the intensity of public reaction. Baseball's claim as the national pastime no doubt plays a role in the public reaction. A violation of the honesty and integrity of the national game may be seen as a violation of national ideals as well as sporting ideals. Not all cheating carries that sort of gravitas, but some does, if it is on a large scale or on a large stage. The seeming inconsistencies of public reaction or institutional reaction may seem hypocritical, but it is important to understand that hypocrisy has its uses, one of which is protecting institutions, values, and the maintenance of common sense.

It is here that some understanding of the reaction to the Astros scandal may be found. First and foremost is the fact that what was done by the Houston Astros may have taken place on the biggest stage in baseball, the World Series. The perception also is that cheating was what got them to the World Series. If, as the commissioner's report concludes, the Astros' sign stealing went on throughout the 2017 regular season and playoffs, the scale of the cheating was outsized. The fact that the Astros were held up as a possible dynasty that had risen from the depths of the National League in a remarkable rebuilding effort to become a model for all of baseball added to the backlash when it came.

Then there are the aggrieved parties in the scandal. Several teams assumed the role of victim. Foremost among them was the Los Angeles Dodgers, which had assumed that having spent so much money and accumulating so much talent, the World Series trophy was by right theirs. The self-righteousness of a number of Dodgers in the face of the revelations from the commissioner's investigation was a bit over the top, even if understandable. Complaints from both the Red Sox and Yankees seemed ludicrous, given their own track records.[13]

Adding to the outcry were the Astros themselves, as both players and executives exhibited a level of hubris that was hard to digest. Claims of ignorance, innocence, and, perhaps worst of all, that none of this factored into winning were particularly inflammatory. The Astros' defiance and lack of contrition did not endear them to the public. And, given that no apologies were forthcoming, the Astros did not endear themselves to baseball fans.[14]

The Astros had developed a reputation of being at the cutting edge of analytics. They made extensive use of algorithms, making computers and software developers required equipment. The Astros organization was profoundly changing the grand old game of baseball. Topping that commitment to technology with a crude system of banging on a trash can as part of their success may have been too much of an extreme juxtaposition for their critics to bear.

So why did the Astros cheat other than to win? The Civil War historian Bruce Catton once observed that a fundamental rule of modern technology and the machine age requires that what you *can* do you *must* do, and in our technological age this often unleashes forces that mere humans cannot control. One wonders in what ways this might apply to the Astros.

Notes

1. Ben Lindbergh and Sam Miller, *The Only Rule Is That It Has to Work* (New York: Henry Holt, 2016), 48.

2. "The Psychology of Cheating in Sports," Exercise Science, AU Online, Au-

rora University, August 16, 2019, https://online.aurora.edu/psychology-of-cheating -in-sports/.

3. David Voigt, *American Baseball* (University Park: Pennsylvania State University Press, 1983), 1:14–22.

4. Tom Verducci, "How MLB Handled Sign Stealing before Punishing Astros," *Sports Illustrated*, January 23, 2020, https://www.si.com/mlb/2020/01/23/sign -stealing-history-astros-red-sox.

5. Peter Gammons, "Gammons: Catfish Hunter, the Beatles, New Year's Eve, and How the World Turned," *The Athletic*, December 21, 2020, https://theathletic.com /2286987/2020/12/31/gammons-catfish-hunter-new-years-eve/?source=weeklyemail.

6. David Wade, "Inside the Rules: Bat Corking," *Hardball Times*, December 13, 2010, https://tht.fangraphs.com/inside-the-rules-bat-corking/.

7. "Everyone Cheats in Baseball," *The Week*, March 19, 2010, excerpt taken from Jason Turbow and Michael Duca, *The Baseball Codes* (New York: Pantheon Books, 2010), https://theweek.com/articles/495902/everyone-cheats-baseball.

8. Zach Helfand, "Is Stealing Signs in Baseball Really So Bad? Bobby Valentine Has Some Thoughts," *New Yorker*, February 13, 2020, https://www.newyorker.com /sports/sporting-scene/is-stealing-signs-in-baseball-really-so-bad-bobby-valentine -has-some-thoughts.

9. Barry Syrluga and Dave Sheinin, "The World Just Learned of the Astros Cheating. Inside Baseball, it was an Open Secret," *Washington Post*, February 11, 2020, https://www.washingtonpost.com/sports/mlb/astros-cheating-open-secret/2020/02 /11/1830154c-4c41-11ea-9b5c-eac5b16dafaa_story.html.

10. Jim Rome, Rome Podcast, October 7, 2020.

11. Eno Sarris, "'Almost everyone is using something': Getting a Grip on How MLB Pitchers Are Cheating," *The Athletic*, November 9, 2020, https://theathletic .com/2183861/2020/11/09/pitchers-pine-tar-grip-mlb-time-to-legalize/.

12. Tom Verducci, "How MLB Handled Sign Stealing Before Punishing the Astros," *Sports Illustrated*, January 23, 2020, https://www.si.com/mlb/2020/01/23/sign -stealing-history-astros-red-sox.

13. Wade, "Inside the Rules: Bat Corking."

14. Jeff Passan, "What to Make of Houston Astros Owner Jim Crane's Non-apology," ESPN.com, February 14. 2020, https://www.espn.com/mlb/story/_/id/286 93762/what-make-houston-astros-owner-jim-crane-public-non-apology.

PART II

THE SCANDAL UNFOLDS

A Seattle Mariners fan holds a sign that reads "Banging on a Trash Can" during the first inning of a baseball game between the Mariners and the Houston Astros on Saturday, April 17, 2021, in Seattle. The sign referred to the sign-stealing scandal involving Astros teams from the 2017 season. (AP Photo/Ted S. Warren)

CHAPTER 5

Finally, a Fun Baseball Scandal

WILL LEITCH

One of the most exhausting things about being a baseball fan is the constant debate over whether the game has Lost Its Way. Baseball always seems to be fighting for its own soul. PEDs. Pace of play. Juiced baseballs. Labor vs. management. Too many strikeouts. The shift. The demographic breakdown of the player pool. The unwritten rules. Every conversation about baseball, it seems, is so weighted down with grave concern about what has happened to America's pastime that it honestly can be exhausting to talk about the sport at all. Any disagreement, however slight, inevitably comes down to some sort of cultural chasm in which what's really at issue is the basic human value of your opponent—almost as if you're talking politics.

Which is why the current controversy that's rocking the sport, I have to say, feels so . . . glorious and freeing?

Last week [November 12, 2019], reporters for *The Athletic*, Ken Rosenthal and Evan Drellich, dropped a bombshell on the baseball world with a report that in 2017, the year they won the World Series, the Astros had been using live video feeds to steal opposing signs and signal to their hitters what pitches were coming. Their scheme, as detailed by former Astros pitcher Mike Fiers, basically the Baseball Whistleblower, was so straightforward that it's almost embarrassing. The Astros would watch the signs the catcher was giving from a centerfield camera, and if the pitch was an off-speed pitch, they would bang a trash can in the dugout for the hitter to hear. If the pitch was a fastball, no garbage can bang. That's it. That's the mechanism. They would hit a trash can with a bat.

But the thing about baseball is that there are literally thousands of hours of footage of baseball games going back decades, footage that is publicly available for fans to sift through at their leisure. So a cottage industry, led by an enterprising and incredibly entertaining baseball YouTuber named Jimmy O'Brien and his growing Jomboy Media empire, has sprung up, attempting to find every example of the Astros' cheating in 2017 (a year the team won the World Series) by listening for those bangs. And you can hear them. Baseball Prospectus' Rob Arthur actually ran audio data through a, uh, well, whatever you run audio data through, and discovered that not only could you capture the garbage-can bangs in an audio chart, the bangs actively tracked, on a near-perfect basis, to off-speed pitches thrown. And a Jomboy Media video detailing precisely how the scheme worked has more than 1.6 million views on YouTube and, to this writer's eyes, appears to definitely damn the Astros.

(I really can't overstate how much fun Jomboy Media's videos are, by the way. Before the Astros scandal, O'Brien was most famous for hilarious breakdowns of cartoonishly profane baseball brawls. His description of a Reds brawl back in July made me understand the way baseball is actually played better than anything Red Smith or George Will ever wrote.)

Basically: Baseball now has its Deflategate. And baseball really needed a Deflategate. The Tom Brady deflated-balls scandal was patently ridiculous in every way—it might be the dumbest ongoing sports story of my lifetime—but it was also completely harmless. It felt like an antidote for our current sober age: a cipher in Brady, whom people, in equal measure, could line up in lockstep defense behind or attack with blind, self-righteous fury. Stephen A. Smith could scream about it, we could all fight online about it, Brady could use it as further fuel for his competitive fire, and none of it really mattered or made any sort of lasting impact at all. It was just fun for everybody to yell at each other about. The perfect, weightless sports scandal. It didn't have a human toll, like concussions or domestic violence. It didn't echo the real world, like labor strife. It didn't even pose a threat to the game itself, like juicing. It was just a silly story about how much air is in a football.

Baseball teams have been stealing signs and clawing for every competitive advantage as long as they have been adjusting their cups and spitting. The Astros introduced new technology into it, and they make for convenient villains with their data-driven, win-at-all-costs, hedge-fund-bro-asshole mentality witnessed last month with former executive Brandon Taubman's rant at female baseball reporters about Astros pitcher Roberto Osuna, who had been suspended for domestic violence. (And the team's ham-fisted initial response to the incident.) But to think that they are the only team in baseball trying everything they can to steal signals from the other team is absurd. The Pittsburgh Pirates were using telescopes and bells to steal signs in the '70s; this is what teams do. The live feed adds a tech-era feel to it, but this is fundamentally what baseball has always been about: deception and trickery. You can argue, if you want, that the Astros were doing something fundamentally against the spirit of baseball . . . but man, you are really not having enough fun with this.

Because this is the sort of controversy that generates endless amounts of "evidence" to sift through, the story is already elevating itself into myth. Conspiracies are everywhere. Fans of teams with former Astros executives are nervous that their teams will get drawn into this; the Mets, in perfect Mets fashion, just hired a new manager in Carlos Beltrán, who played for the 2017 Astros and is already a target of the ongoing investigation. Cubs pitcher Yu Darvish, who was famously knocked around by the Astros in the 2017 World Series, in a fashion that had many observers speculating that he was tipping his pitches, became a trending topic in the wake of the scandal, which led to former MVP Christian Yelich going after him on Twitter, saying, "Nobody needs help facing you." Twitter fights in baseball! How delicious! What is this, the NBA?

This is the advantage of the NFL having surpassed MLB (and all North American sports) as the national pastime. An NFL scandal, like when Cleveland Browns defensive end Myles Garrett hit Steelers quarterback Mason Rudolph with his helmet, gets elevated to national disgrace, with desperately serious op-eds about Why Myles Garrett Is Like Donald Trump in national newspapers and references on *Saturday Night Live.* But baseball doesn't have to be constantly fighting for its soul as much when it's just another game rather than a stand-in for something in the national character. The Astros' cheating scandal is very much in the spirit of the game itself, and nobody's falling to the fainting couches and wailing "what about the children?!" They're instead deep-diving into game video, updating endless Reddit threads, and watching players fight about it on Twitter. Yes, yes, cheating is bad. Yes, yes, the Astros must be punished. Yes, yes, the commissioner's office must act. But c'mon. After years of people screaming at each other about PEDs and moral rot, a good old-fashioned sign-stealing scandal is just what the doctor ordered. If you'll excuse me, I'm going to go dial up a random Astros-Orioles game from three years ago, listen for trash-can bangs, and breathlessly write up my findings. And then we can have a good clean fight about it. Isn't it great? Isn't this what it's supposed to be all about?

The article originally appeared in *New York Magazine*, November 19, 2019.

CHAPTER 6

What Is the Sound of One Bat Slapping?
Reading the Houston Astros' Trash Can

ROBERTA J. NEWMAN

On January 14, 2020, at 6:51 a.m., one day after Major League Baseball Commissioner Rob Manfred issued his official statement regarding the Houston Astros' sign-stealing scheme, the intrepid anchors at FOX 29's *Good Day Philadelphia* scooped every other news outlet in the United States and beyond with its hard-hitting interview with T. C. (short for Trash Can), purported to be the very rubbish receptacle implicated in the scandal. Calling its employment the "worst job in sports," T. C. defended itself against anchor Mike Jerrick's accusations of complicity, responding, "All I did was sit there. I thought I was going to be part of the team. I thought I was going to help them keep their area clean, and what did they do? They took a stick to me, Mike, they took a stick to me!"[1] Shockingly, no other news outlet picked up the interview, much less commented on it, except to mock it. Such is the case with the ever-reliable *New York Post*, which called it the "trashy tell-all no one asked for."[2]

Despite T. C.'s claim that it is in the "trash can protection program,"[3] the veracity of its identity is in question. After all, T. C. is dirty beige, while the trash can in question is forest green, as is characteristic of the bins placed in Minute Maid Field by its owner, Waste Management (WM), a national carting company. T. C.'s dubious assertions notwithstanding, it is certain that a trash can was involved. It is well documented that the 2017 Houston Astros concocted a sophisticated sign-relaying system, which is widely suspected to have aided in the team's successful quest to win the World Series. The system, though it employed advanced video technology, ultimately depended upon that humblest of items, a large, molded plastic garbage receptacle, upon which an assigned player banged with a bat, or on occasion, a massage gun—once for a breaking ball, twice for a changeup, and not at all for a fastball. Much space has been devoted to the system and the scandal it created. But with the exception of the *Good Day Philadelphia* interview, little, if any, attention has been paid to the trash can. Many questions regarding the trash can remain unasked and, therefore, unanswered. What is it about this trash can that made it an exemplary vehicle for transmitting signs? Historically speaking, is there something about this trash can, of all trash cans, and of sanitation, in general, that explicitly connects them to the sport of baseball? And what might be the trash can's uses and meanings, both literal and figurative, beyond the dugout? I will attempt to answer these and other trash can–related questions by examining topics as diverse as the early history of drumming, the acoustical properties of large, plastic garbage receptacles, the birth of the sanitation movement in Great Britain and the United States, the introduction of statistical analysis to baseball, and the commercial uses of trash can imagery. In addition, it will attempt to make historical connections between sanitation, in general, and trash cans, in particular, and baseball, in ways that are both direct and oblique. Finally, it will consider the functions of codes and code breakings, all in an attempt to read the Houston Astros' trash can.

As a vehicle for communication, the green WM trash can was, for all intents and purposes, a drum, and as such, one with deep roots.

According to the *Yamaha Musical Instrument Guide*,

Beating on things to produce a sound, and through that sound express various emotions, is said to have begun in the early stages of human development, where people stomped on the ground or beat their own bodies. Producing sounds by beating things served not just as an accompaniment to dancing but also as a means of communicating with other people over long distances. It has also been used effectively to win over the hearts and minds of people, such as in religious ceremonies.[4]

"As the 'keeper of rhythm,'" continues the *Yamaha Guide*, "the drum provides the foundation for the overall sound of music. Because a drum only has to be hit to make a sound, it is one of the simplest of the instruments."

The archaeological record tells us that some of the earliest drums were little more than holes dug into the earth, covered with animal skins, planks, or the palms of the drummer's hands. All worked on the same principle. Exploiting the resonant properties of the hole, the drummer created sounds that carried.[5] Technically speaking, as the *Yamaha Guide* says, "striking the head of the drum changes its shape and compresses the air inside the shell. The compressed air presses on the bottom head and changes itself. Then, these changes are transmitted to the drum shell and reflected back, and this action is repeated, creating a vibration." The Astros' WM trash can, constructed of two interlocking pieces of molded plastic, had neither top nor bottom head. Still, the trash can functioned in precisely the same way as a proper drum: striking it produced vibrations and hence sound. Given the trash can's large size, it became, in essence, the bass drum of trash cans. Like those made by playing a bass drum, the loud, deep sounds made by the signaling player from just outside the Astros dugout would have easily been heard by the batter, his teammates, and his coaches, not to mention the opposing team's catcher, nearby security guards, and fans sitting behind the dugout.

But the trash can's baseball story extends well beyond its effective use as a drum. The connection between this trash receptacle and, by extension, all trash receptacles and baseball is a very old one, reaching back to the origins of both the nineteenth-century sanitation movement and the formalization of the game. As is widely regarded as true of baseball, the sanitation movement first developed in England before migrating to the United States. Prior to the mass urbanization that marked the development of Europe from the seventeenth century onward, trash, which, for the most part, consisted of organic materials, was reclaimed for use as fertilizer, pig slop, and for the manufacture of soap, candles, bricks, and other useful items. In this regard, it was not refuse at all. Rather, it was a resource.[6]

Urbanization brought with it a new set of issues when it came to trash disposal. At the outset, scavengers did the job, collecting manure and human and animal waste for fertilizer, ash for soap and bricks, and rags for repurposing. But the Industrial Revolution changed everything. While slow urbanization was a constant in early modern Europe, the population of cities, most particularly capital cities such as Paris and London, grew at a faster rate beginning in the early seventeenth century.[7] But from 1750 until the 1840s, urban industrialization grew exponentially, the result of new employment opportunities coupled with economic hardship in rural areas. In the United States, industrialization along with waves of immigration also led to the growth of cities. With increased industrialization came the increased availability of consumer goods to an ever-expanding consumer base. And the by-product of all this new stuff was trash. The first response of both producers and consumers was to find a place to bury what couldn't be scavenged, preferably right outside city centers. If burial wasn't possible, trash was often dumped into what amounted to large hills like the one overseen by Charles Dickens's Golden Dustman, Nicodemus Boffin, in *Our Mutual Friend*. Failing that, trash could be thrown into the nearest body of water or simply tossed out windows. But as cities grew—London and others in England's industrial north, in particular—trash burial and dumping sites were at a premium. With no place and, for the working class, no means to cart trash to external sites, garbage hills became a regular feature of the urban landscape, as did streets strewn with often noxious refuse. To compound issues, sewage disposal was crude, at best. As such, working class, urban Britons were forced to live in crowded, unsanitary conditions in slums plagued by refuse-related, water-borne diseases like cholera, typhus, and indirectly, by the mosquito-borne yellow fever, surrounded by trash.[8]

Half a century before the introduction of the germ theory of disease, such epidemic sicknesses were thought to originate from the miasma—an unseen fog of smells arising from rotting garbage and sewer gases.[9] In response to the crisis, in stepped a man dedicated to the eradication of the miasma, the self-taught statistician and onetime contributor to the notorious poor laws turned reformer, Sir Edwin Chadwick, generally acknowledged to be the father of public health. In an 1838 study leading up to his landmark *Report on the Sanitary Condition of the Labouring Population of Great Britain* (1842), Chadwick described the living conditions of slum dwellers in this way:

> They were surrounded by filth, accumulated in cesspools and privies and stagnant surface drains; they breathed the exhalations of undrained marsh land, graveyards, and slaughter-houses; They had no choice but to live in narrow alleys and close courts. [The conditions] were removable, however, by intelligent arrangements of public authorities: by a system of sewers, a plentiful water supply, an effective service of scavengers, by control of building, and regulations against overcrowding and noxious trades.[10]

Though Chadwick's proposal didn't solve all of nineteenth-century England's garbage problems, his observations led to generally improved conditions and a reduction of disease for England's working class. Relying first and foremost upon the new scientific method of statistical analysis to prove his point, Chadwick was behind the passage by Parliament of the Public Health Act of 1848, followed by the more robust Public Health Act of 1875.[11]

The sanitation movement pioneered by Sir Edwin Chadwick found a foothold in the United States approximately a decade and a half after the passage of England's first public health act. In 1866, New York City's Metropolitan Board of Health—the first municipal board of health in the United States—cracked down on errant garbage disposal, outlawing the "throwing of dead animals, garbage, or ashes into the streets."[12] A cleaner city was no doubt appreciated by those middle-class men playing the still nascent game of baseball.

Like effective sanitation, the efficacy of which Chadwick proved by statistical analysis, baseball was, almost from the outset, also governed by statistics. And like the sanitation movement, baseball, too, had its "father." According to his *New York Times* obituary, Henry Chadwick "invented the approved system of scoring" and was "an acknowledged authority on all (the game's) technicalities."[13] In the 1860s, he began the process of introducing the scientific method of statistical analysis to the game, collecting and systematizing information on batters.[14] As their common surname suggests, Henry and Edwin Chadwick were, in fact, connected by a closer bond than a mutual admiration of statistics. They were half-brothers. And like Sir Edwin before him, Henry was a social reformer. Baseball, he asserted, built character. "He believed in the efficacy and good moral influence of hearty outdoor sports," noted the *Times*. "His influence has been measurable in eliminating rowdyism and gambling from the game."[15] In essence, Henry Chadwick fought against the game's figurative garbage, just as his half-brother fought against England's literal garbage.

What would the brothers Chadwick have made of the Astros' sign-stealing scandal? While it is only speculation, it may be safe to say that Sir Edwin Chadwick, the sanitarian, may have appreciated the ubiquity of receptacles meant to aid in the systematic removal of refuse. In his 1838 study, Sir Edwin noted that living in a filthy environment also had a negative effect upon the mental health—though he did not use the term—of poor city dwellers and could lead to criminal behavior. Henry, by contrast, would no doubt have been deeply distressed by the whole affair. Henry Chadwick had no sympathy for those who would sully baseball, no matter what social class the offenders belonged to. As an 1886 profile of baseball's father makes clear, he had no "mercy for base ball 'crooks,'"[16] be they slum dwellers, middle-class players, or wealthy gamblers.

By the time the aforementioned profile appeared in print, trash cans, as we know them, were in fairly common use. Made of wood or metal, they held ash from recently burned garbage, which was generally collected weekly, depending upon location, or garbage itself. In New York City, Henry Chadwick's home, their contents were hauled off to incinerators, the first of which was located in the harbor on Governors Island.[17] In fact, wood, or more commonly, metal trash cans would be the norm until the mid-twentieth century.

The Astros' can, however, was made of neither wood nor metal but of molded plastic. Although plastic in one form or another had been around since the turn of the century, it was not used for garbage disposal until much later. By the 1940s, sturdy injection-molded polymers were made into a vast variety of consumer goods like radios, telephones, jewelry, and toys.[18] But hard plastics such as Bakelite, which was nonconductive and could be used in place of glass and ceramics, were not used for the manufacture of garbage bins. Metal, most particularly galvanized steel, remained in use. Plastic trash cans were first introduced in the mid-1960s by industrial designer Charles Harrison, the first African American executive at Sears. Made of polypropylene, Harrison's molded plastic receptacles served as an excellent substitute for the heavy steel cans, especially in the retail market. Trash cans were not the only item Harrison designed for Sears. In fact, he was behind the form and function of as many as 250 Sears products, the majority of which were constructed of molded plastic. Most notable among them were the View-Master and the first portable Lady Kenmore sewing machines. As the designer of the Lady Kenmore, Harrison's connection to baseball extends beyond plastic trash cans into pop-culture history, however tangentially. After all, were it not for Harrison's designs, Coach Larry Hockett of the fictional Durham Bulls would not have been able to advise minor league slugger Crash Davis not to quit his day job, saying, "Sears sucks, Crash. Boy, I once worked there. Sold Lady Kenmores. Nasty. Nasty work," in Ron Shelton's classic baseball film *Bull Durham*.[19]

The trash can at the center of the Astros' cheating scandal belonged to private waste hauler Waste Management (WM), "North America's largest environmental solutions provider," as its website would have it. WM, too, has a connection to baseball. The garbage giant traces its origins back to 1893, when Harm Huizenga, a Dutch immigrant to Chicago, began charging to collect trash in his horse-drawn cart. For-profit trash collection became the family business. And unlike much of the private trash collection and waste hauling industry, which would become mob controlled in the new century, the Huizenga family business remained unusually clean. Flash forward to 1968, as Waste Management's corporate website tells us, "Harm's grandson Wayne Huizenga and two other investors, Dean Buntrock and Larry Beck, had a vision. They wanted to serve their community by properly managing the waste produced by a rapidly growing population consuming more and more products built for convenience."[20] Wayne Huizenga sold his controlling interest in WM in 1984, twelve years after having taken the company public, also founding AutoNation and corporatizing Blockbuster Video in the process. Huizenga's success as a titan of industry may have cemented his reputation among a certain percentage of the population, but for others, the trash mogul will be forever associated with the Florida Marlins—the 1997 Marlins, in particular. Having built a World Series–winning team as owner, Huizenga quickly sold-off his star players, thereby disillusioning fans, making his name a dirty word in baseball circles. Profit was everything for Huizenga, and the Marlins, despite their success, were not profitable. Shedding large contracts allowed him to sell the team at an attractive price. Given Huizenga's role in the story of WM and in the story of the Marlins, it's possible to draw a fairly straight line in between Huizenga, a clean operator in the traditionally corrupt business of trash carting, baseball, and the green bin upon which Houston's ballplayers beat their dishonest tattoo.

Despite its fraudulent claims, T. C., the *Good Morning Philadelphia* trash can, made one important point. Addressing the hosts, T. C. asked, "Have you ever seen a baseball dugout? They never use me. There's stuff all over the floor."[21] T. C. is correct. According to pitcher Dillon Gee, "Nobody throws anything in the trash can in the dugout. Some dugouts don't even have trash cans."[22] *Wall Street Journal* sports reporter Joshua Robinson concurs, writing:

> Since no one seems able—or willing—to locate the trash can, the dugout floor can be as foul as any part of the stadium. By the end of nine innings, it is usually covered by an unholy mixture of water, spit, Gatorade, bubble gum wrappers, sunflower seed shells, clumps of dirt, all slowly inching toward the built-in drains. The flotsam on that evil liquid is made up of dozens of crushed paper cups.[23]

In fact, a dugout in use more closely resembles the London streets prior to Chadwick's intervention than an integral part of a twenty-first century, state-of-the-art baseball stadium. Given the trash can's almost total irrelevance in the dugout, it is more than a little ironic that one served as the drum on which were beaten signals to Astros batters, signals that would soil the game.

No matter what its use in the sign-stealing scheme, the trash can was not culpable. There is no indication that WM disciplined the garbage receptacle in any way. It is, after all, an inanimate object with no agency, despite T. C.'s objections. Some of the human perpetrators, however, were punished. Managers and coaches were dismissed and suspended; the Astros general manager was suspended and fired; and the assistant general manager was suspended. Draft picks were forfeited, and the team was fined. Yet the players faced no repercussions. According to Commissioner Manfred, punishing players was simply too complex. Although he acknowledged that the entire team was likely in on or at least aware of the scheme, Manfred stated, "I am not in a position based on the investigative record to determine with any degree of certainty every player who should be held accountable, or their relative degree of culpability."[24] But some of the players suffered their own form of punishment at the hands of fans of opposing teams. On the first day of Spring Training 2020, a Yankees fan made a ruckus at Astros camp in West Palm Beach, thumping on a trash can behind home plate as Houston's star players took batting practice.[25] It is highly likely that trash can wielding fans would have made appearances at any number of ballparks during the 2020 season, had the 2020 season been anything like normal. But with no fans in the stands, there were no trash cans in ballparks—at least none that were expressly meant for a purpose other than trash disposal. Two dedicated fans did manage to bang a few cans outside Target Field before a postseason matchup between the Twins and Astros.[26] And pitcher Trevor Bauer fired off his own salvo, wearing custom cleats decorated with little trash cans, though not while facing the Astros.[27] Such heckling paled in comparison to what might have been.

COVID-19 did nothing to stop Astros haters from circulating trash can–related memes or manufacturers of unlicensed merchandise from producing and selling items depicting those and other memes on T-shirts, stickers, and posters. On REDBUBBLE.com, for example, shoppers could purchase the ubiquitous shirts as well as baseball cards, banners, and face masks featuring trash receptacles, all made by small companies and marketed through the site.[28] Departed Soles, a small brewery in New Jersey, introduced Trash Can Banger beer, a session IPA, priced at seventeen dollars for a four-pack of cans emblazoned with neon orange stripes clearly evocative of Astros uniforms of old.[29] Applying the principle of meaning transfer, by which purchasers consume the meanings of products along with the products themselves, Trash Can Banger drinkers imbibed the ugly 1970s uniforms as well as the team's perceived shame along with their beer.[30]

Licensed trash can distribution in Houston actually reaches back more than a decade. Perhaps presciently, WM sponsored a 2007 mini-trash-can giveaway, the item imprinted with the slogan, "Return of the Good Guys" and WM's green and yellow logo.[31] On July 7 of that year, Astros fans were treated to a seventeen-inning loss at the hands of the New York Mets, but at least the first lucky ten thousand fans in attendance received brightly printed wastebaskets.[32] In a sense, the WM giveaway may be seen as representative of the Astros' 2007 season. With a 73–89 record, the team discarded Manager Phil Garner and General Manager Tim Purpura just twenty days after the WM event.[33] Though it may have provided a glimpse into the Astros' future behavior, whatever connection there may be between this WM trash can and the 2017 model is purely incidental.

As information about the scandal came to light and promotional planning for the 2020 season got underway, at least two minor league teams announced trash can–related giveaways. The Staten Island Yankees, then the Yankees' short season New York Penn League affiliate, planned a "Mini Trash Can Giveaway" for September 3, 2020, when the team was set to take on the Valley Cats, the Houston affiliate. This was to be the SI Yankees' final giveaway of the season, which was canceled as a result of the COVID-19 pandemic. Sadly, it was also the final giveaway of the SI Yankees' existence, their league having been disbanded in 2021.

On a lighter note, the ever-creative and ever-popular St. Paul Saints, now a Twins affiliate, planned an "Astro the Grouch" bobble-lid talking trash can for the 2020 season. The promotional receptacle featured Orbit, the Astros mascot, furtively peeking out. On its best days, Orbit, ostensibly a space alien, appears to be a human child/Muppet hybrid, wearing a baseball cap and sporting antennae. Ensconced in the promotional trash can, the mascot bears an uncanny resemblance to Oscar the Grouch, the trash can dweller of *Sesame Street* fame. In addition to being distributed to all fans in attendance in July 2020, the item was available for $35 on the Saints website. With 10 percent of the proceeds benefiting Athletes Committed to Educating Students (ACES), dedicated to reducing the "academic achievement gap," Astro the Grouch was meant to have a positive impact on childhood education, much like his namesake and role model.[34] Fortunately for Saints fans, talking collectible lovers, and Astros haters, not to mention the team's bottom line, the Saints played a shortened 2020 season, and the giveaway trash cans were distributed at the ballpark as planned.

What, then, does the trash can mean? Its literal meaning, at least outside of a dugout, is fairly clear. The trash can is exactly that—a can, though plastic rather than metal—in which to throw trash. As such, it is a signifier of cleanliness, of sanitation, and, by extension, of public health. Presumably, trash thrown in it will be properly disposed of so as not to create a miasma or the twenty-first century germ-theory version thereof. Taken in the context of the scandal, however, its uses and meanings are more obscure. Empty of litter, it is liberated from its original purpose. It is, in essence, an empty vessel waiting to be filled. But if not by litter, then by what? In this particular case, it was transformed into a drum, waiting to be struck, and thereby filled with vibrations that were translated into sound. The sound, in turn, was used for the communication of encoded message.

The code—one thump for a breaking ball, two for a changeup, and none for a fastball—taken at face value, is actually quite simple. But it is the result of a complex process. It is an interpretation of a far more layered code, the generation of which required the thumper to function as a codebreaker as well. To generate the code, the player monitoring the video was charged with deciphering the opposing team's signs. At first glance, this also seems to be simple. The catcher conventionally puts down one finger for a fastball, two for a curve, three for a slider, and either four fingers, or wiggled fingers, for a changeup. But as baseball aficionados and even casual fans know, reading signs requires more than just an understanding of a single set of hand signals. With a runner on second base, the signs change, according to a coach's indicator—yet another sign that informs the fielding team of the meanings of the new signs. In this regard, the sign stealer must also be an ace decoder. In turn, he becomes a writer as well as a reader, creating the new code, which he transmits to the batter. Empty of trash and filled with encoded vibrations, the image of cleanliness, of sanitation, and of health becomes a sign for pollution, sickness, and corruption.

From a commercial and promotional standpoint, the trash can has yet another meaning. Moved one step further away from its original purpose and placed on a T-shirt or transformed into a bobble lid collectable, the actual trash can is translated into the image of a trash can. While not quite a simulacrum of a trash can—an image that has become a reality (i.e., a picture of a trash can that supersedes the existence of actual trash cans)[35]—it is a parody of a trash can. It is both a sign of dirtiness and an indication that the collector, purchaser, waver, or wearer is an in-the-know Astros hater and, perhaps, a fan of one of the aforementioned minor league teams.

Ultimately, one good thing may have come out of COVID-19's role in vastly altering the 2020 baseball season. The pandemic had a direct effect on dugout sanitation and possibly on trash can use, or the lack thereof. Before the shortened season began, CNN reporter A. J. Willingham noted that the professional sport would be cleaned up. Writes Willingham, "It will look a lot different than the hallowed summer pastiche we're used to. Gone will be the roaring crowds, the call of the hot dog seller, and the grunting of thirty or so grown men hocking loogies and slapping each other on the butt in the dugout."[36] The move toward dugout sanitation seems to have gone even further than just outlawing spitting. Images show not just an absence of seed shells and other less pleasant expectorants but also a dearth of gum wrappers, Gatorade cups, and the other detritus that accumulates during baseball games. This suggests that trash cans were, in fact, in use where they weren't before. With the exposure of the Astros' cheating scandal and its repercussions, baseball's trash cans may have been restored to their original meaning. Freed from secondary and tertiary significations, freed from substituting for drums, baseball's trash cans are free to be just that: places to throw trash.

Notes

1. "Trash Can Accused in Astros Scandal Goes on the Record with Good Day," FOX 29, January 14, 2020, https://www.fox29.com/video/644181.

2. Michael Blinn, "Fox 29 Airs Weird Interview with Astros Trash Can: 'Worst job in sports,'" *New York Post*, January 14, 2020, https://nypost.com/2020/01/14/fox-29-airs-weird-interview-with-astros-trash-can-worst-job-in-sports/.

3. "Trash Can Accused."

4. "Drums," *Yamaha Musical Instrument Guide*, https://www.yamaha.com/en/musical_instrument_guide/drums.

5. Matt Dean, *The Drum: A History* (Toronto: Scarecrow Press, 2012), 12.

6. Richard D. Oram, "Waste Management and Peri-urban Agriculture in the Early Modern Scottish Burgh," *Agricultural History Review* 59, no. 1 (June 2011): 3.

7. David R. Ringrose, "Capital Cities, Urbanization, and Modernization in Early Modern Europe," *Journal of Urban History* 24, no. 2 (January 1998): 164.

8. "Report on the Sanitary Conditions of the Labouring Population of Great Britain: Historical Context," The Health Foundation, 1842, https://navigator.health.org.uk/theme/report-sanitary-conditions-labouring-population-great-britain#.

9. Martin V. Melosi, *The Sanitary City: Environmental Services in Urban America from Colonial Times to the Present* (Pittsburgh, PA: University of Pittsburgh Press, 2008), 31.

10. R. A. Lewis, *Edwin Chadwick and the Public Health Movement, 1832–1854* (New York: Augustus M. Kelley, 1970), 36.

11. Melosi, *The Sanitary City*, 35–36.

12. Trash Cans Unlimited, "The History of the Trash Can (and All Its Dirty Secrets)," September 23, 2016, https://medium.com/@sunlimitedoutreach/the-history-of-the-trash-can-and-all-its-dirty-secrets-b12c6853e81b#.

13. "Father of Baseball," *New York Times*, April 21, 1908.

14. Andrew Schiff, "Henry Chadwick," SABR Bio Project, https://sabr.org/bioproj/person/henry-chadwick/.

15. "Father of Baseball."

16. "Henry Chadwick," *Rochester Democrat and Chronicle*, June 30, 1886, 8.

17. Trash Cans Unlimited, "History."

18. Susan Freinkel, "A Brief History of Plastic's Conquest of the World," *Scientific American*, May 29, 2011, https://www.scientificamerican.com/article/a-brief-history-of-plastic-world-conquest/.

19. Ryan Fagan, "*Bull Durham*: Ranking the 37 Best Quotes from the Classic Movie," *Sporting News*, December 27, 2020, https://www.sportingnews.com/us/mlb/news/bull-durham-ranking-the-37-best-quotes-from-the-classic-baseball-movie/nb6vi55npoh71fs7yx6dzwh70.

20. "Going from Waste Collection to Waste Management," Inside WM: Our Story, https://www.wm.com/us/en/inside-wm/our-story.

21. "Trash Can Accused."

22. Dillon Gee, quoted in Joshua Robinson, "An Insider's Guide to the Dugout," *Wall Street Journal*, July 21, 2011.

23. Robinson, "Insider's Guide."

24. "Statement of the Commissioner," January 13, 2020, https://img.mlbstatic.com/mlb-images/image/upload/mlb/cglrhmlrwwbkacty27l7.pdf.

25. Dan Gartland, "Yankees Fan Bangs on Trash Can During Astros Stars' Batting Practice," *Sports Illustrated*, February 18, 2020, https://www.si.com/extra-mustard/2020/02/18/astros-spring-training-fan-batting-practice-trash-can.

26. Gabriel Fernandez, "Twins Taunt Astros with Trash Cans Outside Target Field Ahead of MLB Playoff Series," CBS Sports, September 29, 2020, https://www.cbssports.com/mlb/news/twins-fans-taunt-astros-with-trash-cans-outside-target-field-ahead-of-mlb-playoff-series/.

27. Matt Leode, "Trevor Bauer Gets Savage on the Astros, Then Gets Owned by Chicago's Tim Anderson," *Sports Illustrated*, September 20, 2020, https://www.si.com/mlb/indians/news/trevor-bauer-goes-savage-on-the-astros-then-gets-owned-by-chicagos-tim-anderson.

28. Redbubble, https://www.redbubble.com/shop/houston+astros+trash+can.

29. Katie Sobko, "Jersey City Brewery's 'Trashcan Banger' IPA Pokes Fun at Houston Astros," northjersey.com, May 28, 2020, https://www.northjersey.com/story/food/beer/2020/05/28/jersey-city-brewery-departed-soles-trash-can-banger-ipa-astros/5279124002/.

30. Grant McCracken, "Who Is a Celebrity Endorser? The Cultural Foundations of the Endorsement Process," *Journal of Consumer Research* 16, no. 3 (December 1989): L311.

31. "2007 MLB Stadium Giveaways," *Tuff Stuff's Sports Collectors Monthly*, July 17, 2008, https://www.tuffstuff.com/news/baseball/2007_mlb_stadium_giveaways.

32. "Beltran Lifts Mets to Win in Their Longest Game Since '93," ESPN.com, July 8, 2007, https://www.espn.com/mlb/recap?gameId=270707118.

33. "Astros Fire Manager Garner, GM Purpura," Associated Press, August 27, 2007, https://www.espn.com/mlb/news/story?id=2993335.

34. "Astro the Grouch Talking Collectible Now on Sale," Saint Paul Saints, https://www.saintsbaseball.com/news/detail/astro-the-grouch-talking-collectible-now-on-sale.

35. Jean Baudrillard, "Simulacra and Simulations," in *Jean Baudrillard, Selected Writings*, ed. Mark Poster (Stanford, CA: Stanford University Press, 1988), 167.

36. A. J. Willingham, "There's No Crying, Er, Spitting in Baseball Anymore. But Why Was It a Thing in the First Place?," CNN.com, July 1, 2020, https://www.cnn.com/2020/07/01/us/baseball-spitting-mlb-season-changes-history-trnd/index.html.

CHAPTER 7

Blame Is a Tangled Mess in Astros Sign-Stealing Scandal

EVAN DRELLICH

The blame game that has sprung from the Astros sign-stealing scandal cannot be won, because the culpability is everywhere.

Naturally, the Astros—that broad collective—are the guiltiest party. But any quest to understand who, what, when, and why involves different people and topics at different times.

What happened in Houston is the result of a collision of subcultures, with outside forces at play as well, be it league policy or the historically insular nature of locker rooms.

The origin of the Astros' cheating is not singular. Such a determination depends on how far back you want to trace the system, and which set of circumstances you view as most important. The environment, the conditions, and the choices that helped foster one of the worst cheating scandals in baseball history are complicated.

There were even two threads of electronic sign stealing to follow: what happened with the trash can and the television monitor in the dugout tunnel, and what happened with the video-replay room. They're intertwined, but not identical.

Here is an exercise. Go ahead and try to rank these factors that powered the sign-stealing scandal, and consider how they feed into one another.

Across MLB

- Major League Baseball instituted instant-replay challenges in 2014 and sanctioned the development of video-replay rooms. In addition, the league allowed teams to position those rooms close to dugouts, if the teams wanted. MLB also permitted the use of live video and technology by teams in other capacities, including the in-game review of at bats.

- MLB punished the Red Sox and Yankees in September 2017 for sign stealing via the replay room, but did not put any on-site enforcement into replay rooms until 2018. In fact, a full regular season of play passed in 2018 before MLB instituted full-time, in-person monitoring in the replay rooms.

- In MLB's eyes, there was a gray area in the 2017 season regarding sign stealing and replay rooms. While electronic sign stealing was broadly prohibited—and something like the trash can scheme with a video monitor clearly prohibited—the rules did not include specific wording about those replay rooms. MLB's own interpretation of the rules in September 2017 gave credence to the idea of a gray area. The punishment issued then to the Red Sox and Yankees was not centered on the act of using the video-replay room to decode signs but on how the teams relayed the information from the replay room to the field—via an electronic device. Was that interpretation correct, or merely practical, as the problem had already begun to spread under MLB's nose? MLB changed its rules for the next season to expressly prohibit the use of the replay rooms during games to figure out signs.

- Throughout the history of this sport as well as others, the culture among players and inside locker rooms is generally secretive and protective, a brotherhood. Such a culture, while widely accepted, can nonetheless help facilitate and cover up wrongdoing. Functionally, locker-room culture makes it difficult for anyone on the outside—league officials, media, fans—to learn exactly what goes on with a team. Particularly in real time.

- The highest-ranking body involved here is the commissioner's office. MLB was certainly well aware of the secretive nature of clubhouses following the scandals of the performance-enhancing drug era. As technology spread throughout the sport, could MLB have forgotten some of the lessons from PEDs—specifically, how necessary it is to be diligent and proactive in policing the different ways players and teams seek an edge? Did the league invest the necessary resources and dedicate enough personnel to heading off major problems with its on-field product, such as this one?

- The MLB Players Association has a seat at the table as well. At union meetings in recent years, players have discussed the drag on the pace of game created by electronic sign stealing. Union officials did not make sign stealing a top priority at that point.

- Not every rule in the sport is strictly enforced or policed, perhaps adding incentive for teams and players to push the envelope. Pitchers are rarely stopped for using substances to aid their grip on the ball, for example.

- Players and teams are highly competitive and want to gain every edge. If they believe one team is getting away with something, they may be inclined to do it themselves.

In Houston

- The Astros front office showed support for the act of electronic sign stealing via the development of "Codebreaker," an Excel algorithm that could have been used legally as an advance scouting tool but was also deployed illegally.
- The Astros front office showed further support for sign stealing via email communications about the team's sign-stealing schemes, including the progress reports sent from staffer Tom Koch-Weser to general manager Jeff Luhnow, as reported by the *Wall Street Journal.*
- Luhnow did not forward necessary league-issued bulletins related to electronic sign stealing to dugout personnel.
- In general, MLB and the teams alike may not have done as much as they could have to make sure such bulletins were front and center for players, that notice of the rules was given.
- Players should be expected to have an innate sense of right and wrong, just as any person should, regardless of the prominent posting of those rules.
- The same expected sense of right and wrong goes for anyone else who knew of the Astros' schemes. By the end of the season, that was virtually everyone in proximity to the dugout and the team, including manager A. J. Hinch and the coaching staff.
- The culture Luhnow built in Houston under owner Jim Crane was a win-first, bottom-line-oriented culture, without enough concern for other factors—a leadership philosophy that can and likely did have a trickle-down effect, even if that was not always directly evident.
- Carlos Beltrán and Alex Cora spearheaded the specific development of the trash can-banging system that used a video monitor and a center-field camera feed, the most egregious example of rule breaking committed by the Astros.
- What blame falls on those who initiate something compared to those who benefit from something and/or do not stop it? Other players went along with the trash can banging and did not stop it—and even enjoyed its fruits. As *The Athletic* reported, some in the Astros clubhouse said they indeed felt they could not effectively stop the trash can-banging system. Should they

have felt that way? The explanation for inaction is not inherently an excuse for inaction.

- The setup of that video monitor with the center-field feed required help from other Astros staff.
- Other teams, including the A's, complained to MLB about the Astros. Published reports also cast doubt on the Astros' actions. But MLB did not get to the bottom of the matter until it launched an investigation following *The Athletic*'s report on November 12. Full-fledged investigations are hard for a league to commence without hard proof, and schemes can take place both behind the scenes and with some air of plausible deniability—a fact a team could leverage.
- The buck is supposed to stop with the manager, Hinch. Hinch twice destroyed the screen but never put his foot down, a task his role demanded.
- The buck is supposed to stop with Luhnow, who was in charge of the entirety of baseball operations, including Hinch and the players.
- The buck is supposed to stop with the owner, Crane.
- The buck is supposed to stop with the highest-ranking authority in the sport, commissioner Rob Manfred.
- The players and lower-level staffers should know better, even if they're not ultimately responsible in a standard management hierarchy.

Seems like we're running in circles now. The Astros' sign-stealing scandal is a mess, all the way around, rife with failure at so many turns.

This article originally appeared in The Athletic, *February 13, 2020.*

PART III

FANS AND THE SCANDAL

Houston Astros World Series shortstop Carlos Correa holds the trophy as he and George Springer join Mayor Sylvester Turner and Astros owner Jim Crane in Houston Police Department tower truck 69 during the Houston Astros World Series victory parade downtown on Friday, November 3, 2017, in Houston. (Karen Warren/Houston Chronicle via AP)

CHAPTER 8

Interview with a Bang Counter:
A Q&A with Tony Adams

Editor's note: Tony Adams is a lifelong Astros fan who took it upon himself to document all the times the Houston Astros banged the trash can during the 2017 season as a way of understanding the length and depth of the sign-stealing efforts. For his work, he was given a Society of American Baseball Research Award in 2021.[1]

Jonathan Silverman: How did you become an Astros fan?
Tony Adams: One of the things that journalists picked up on with me is that my story was very much a symbolic story of Astros fans and Houston in general. I started out as an Astros fan when I was thirteen. They had the rainbow jerseys at the time, which was very unusual and intriguing and a lot of fun. And they had some exciting players like J. R. Richard and José Cruz. My mom picked up on my fandom, and she would watch the games with me. So that was time that we could spend together.

I started going to games at the Astrodome, an amazing spectacle sensory overload type of experience, particularly for a young kid. They had a huge scoreboard, which would do the animations of the cowboy and the bulls whenever they hit a home run. I'm re-creating the scoreboard with a little LED matrix right now. It will follow the game feed, and whenever the Astros hit a home run, it will play the animations. I posted a quick link to it, and people have already asked me if I'm selling them.

I bought my own season tickets in high school and went with a friend of mine for most of the games. When I was younger, I would listen to every game and keep score. I followed everything I could about them. I started to get into analytics in high school. I bought my first Bill James book in 1984, which was very early for analytics. And so I was really into the numbers and the stats and all that stuff.

In 1986, we went to the NLCS against the Mets, and it was an exciting series, but we lost in six. The Mets that year were just one of those teams with destiny on their side. Every time we came back or thought we had had them beat, they would come back. As a baseball fan, as a kid, you have all this optimism, and with the Astros, you would get so close, and that hope gets so big that all the disappointments kind of push you down a little bit.

JS: What was the low point of your fandom?
TA: We went through most of the '90s and never really accomplished much. In the late '90s and early 2000s, we started winning again. We finally made it to the World Series in 2005 but were swept by the White Sox. But even that series was exciting. It had to be the closest sweep in MLB history.

In the early 2010s, the Astros weren't on TV for most Houstonians, so it was hard to follow the team. The previous owner kept the payroll low to make the team more sellable, so the talent wasn't there, and they lost more. But the stadium was still relatively new, and it was really fun to go to. It was an old-school stadium that harkens back to the playground days. They had the hill in centerfield with the flagpole in the middle. Many people went to see the stadium, but the team was not great.

JS: What happened when Jim Crane bought the team?
TA: When they were sold to Jim Crane, the Astros moved to the American League West, and the issues with the local TV coverage got resolved, so they were back on TV. At the time, I was anti-DH [designated hitter]. It didn't feel like the same kind of experience. They decided not to put a lot of resources and money into current players and focused on developing their younger players. They were losing a lot, and it was tough to get excited. Obviously, by losing a lot, they were getting draft picks, so there was still hope that these young kids would eventually come up and turn it around.

JS: What happened when the Astros hired Jeff Luhnow?
TA: Jim Crane brought in Jeff Luhnow to be general manager. Jeff is a very rational and analytical person. Rather than go by feel, he wanted to use data analytics in their decision making more than any other team had previously.

For example, Houston was one of the first teams to bring in high-speed cameras to look at pitchers' spin rates. They could see if a player's fundamental ability was there for them to work with. They were looking at every metric available to evaluate players. It removed a lot of the human element from the process. The Astros started firing scouts, which angered some people in the organization.

JS: How quickly did Luhnow get results?

TA: It was a very quick turnaround. It's one thing to have a plan to say we're going to use our analytics and the data to pick the right guys, and it's another thing to execute it. It's still a skill to figure out what the right metrics are and adjust your metrics as you go along. So, even though they brought into this analytical attitude, the Astros were willing to say that they didn't know everything and needed to be able to adjust and learn and change.

One of the things that Jeff Luhnow doesn't get a lot of credit for is that he did take in a lot of other input, and he did adjust. It wasn't just throwing numbers into a computer and having something spit out and just following it blindly.

As we know now, they drafted very well, and the team started playing much better. There was a lot of excitement for the high draft picks coming up. We had a lot of young stars, including José Altuve, who, because of his size, became a fan favorite. George Springer was a great player and a very nice guy. The excitement level started to really increase, and I began to think that we could become a great team.

JS: When did you really think the Astros had a chance to win a World Series?

TA: For the 2017 season, they signed Carlos Beltrán and brought in some other veteran players. Before the season started, I told my wife that I would not be surprised if they won the World Series that year.

That was the first time since I was a kid that I had that level of optimism. In Houston, we don't have that level of optimism for sports teams. We've been disappointed too many times. But that year, with the young talent getting better and adding the veterans, I thought it could happen.

There were so many different personalities on the team. It was easy to find a favorite player to root for. It was a really great year, and we obviously made the playoffs.

We beat Boston pretty handily in the division series. Then we won the ALCS against the Yankees in seven exciting games. And we were off to the World Series!

JS: Tell me about Hurricane Harvey and how it impacted you.

TA: Hurricane Harvey hit the Texas coast in August. The hurricane itself didn't hit Houston—it hit further south—but it stalled and dumped an extraordinary amount of rain on us. My family didn't evacuate at first. The rising water kind of snuck up on us. My wife, my daughter, and I were in our home, and the water came in the house and started to rise.

At first, it was a couple of inches, but then it was one foot, and then two feet. The weather forecast said it was going to continue to rain. There was an alert that people in our area needed to go to a shelter. The shelter in our neighborhood was a couple of blocks away. We were wading through chest-high water trying to get to the shelter, but we saw that a street we had to cross was basically a river and didn't know what to do, so we turned back. As we turned back, we met a neighbor that we'd never met before, who said that another neighbor down the street had a house that was built up out of the floodplain and was taking in people. She took in five or six families that night.

There were army helicopters picking people off roofs in our neighborhood. We were fortunate that we found someone to take us in. We lost our house; the house was not repairable. We had a lot of help from many Houstonians and a lot of people from out of state. The city really came together and helped each other. If you could see my block after the waters went down, there were people everywhere helping others clean up. People were driving down the street with pizzas and sandwiches. Complete strangers were handing out food to those in need. It was really a moment that, while tragic, showed the spirit of Houston and how the community could come together when necessary. No one asked my religion, or where I was from, or who I loved; they just helped. It reinforced my admiration for the human spirit and that we are all in this together.

JS: What was the relationship between hurricane recovery and the Astros' World Series win?
TA: The hurricane took a long time to get over, both the practical aspects of fixing the city and the emotional aspects of what happened. We were in the middle of the baseball season. The Astros had to play in Florida one series because the stadium was unavailable. As the city moved forward from Harvey those next few weeks, we were looking for something to give us joy and take our minds off what we were going through. A family friend took us in and watched the games as much as I could. Watching a game gave a lot of Houstonians a moment to forget about all the issues they were dealing with due to the flood. The Astros were going to help as much as they could. The city really got behind the team even more after Harvey.

JS: What was it like being an Astros fan and finally winning a World Series title?
TA: Going to the World Series was exciting, and it was what the city needed to help us through the tough times. The series against the Dodgers was thrilling—seven amazing games. The team played very well, but the Dodgers were a great team, so it was very competitive.

When the Astros won, I was kind of stunned. All those years of frustration were over. It was hard to believe. I talked to my brother, who is a huge Astros fan, and we were like, "Can you believe it, man? It just happened." Even if there was no Harvey, just being an Astros fan, all that disappointment over the decades and now having that finally pay off in a championship was terrific.

It was also a justification for the process for analytics. For me, as a scientific-minded person, the fact that data science can show how things actually are instead of how we perceive them is fascinating. But the moment of winning, that wasn't in my head. It was just the excitement of it all. The feeling of somebody who's just won the lottery. There were so many emotions—it's hard to put into words.

Astros fans had followed most of the players from when they were young. All these storylines came together in a World Series championship. It was a fantastic ending to the drama we followed for years.

The town was just crazy excited. A million people came out for the parade. I bought the shirts and all the championship paraphernalia.

For a few months after the World Series, it was hard to believe it happened. I texted my brother a few times, saying, "They won the World Series, didn't they?"

I was also excited that the Astros had a manager and general manager who seemed like they could sustain this success. They had a proven process to continue reloading the team's talent. I thought we had a manager for life. I thought we had a potential dynasty, that we could be a contender every year. The following year, the Astros again played very well and went to the ALCS but lost to Boston. The next year, 2019, was amazing to watch. In my opinion, it was one of the greatest teams ever. We barreled through the playoffs, but we came up against a hot team in the Nationals and lost in the World Series. That one hurt but winning two years before helped ease the pain.

JS: How did the revelations in *The Athletic*'s article about sign stealing impact you?

TA: The article in *The Athletic* came out early in the morning [on November 12, 2019]. There had been rumors about the Astros and cheating previously, but these were specific allegations from a former Astro. It didn't take long until some videos online showed the banging and then correlated that with breaking balls. It was clear from the videos that the allegations were true: it happened. One of the things that people really responded to was that it was so obvious they were cheating: you could hear it. And so there was really no way that you couldn't accept it. I texted my brother and my nephew: "It looks like they cheated."

It was disappointing. For a while, I was trying to process its scope. Obviously, it became a huge story, and it caught on like a wildfire, with fans of other teams weighing in and Astros fans defending their team. Initially, I wasn't sure how to feel about it and what it really meant about the championship.

Then more material started coming out. Jomboy put out a video that became extremely popular in which he breaks down the banging.[2] Another YouTuber released a video highlighting charge whistles before breaking balls in game 5 of the 2017 World Series. Some news websites picked up that video, and people started saying they were using whistles to cheat.

But that video only looked at a few pitches out of the almost two hundred the Astros threw that game. It's easy to cherry-pick a subset of data to make it look like something happened.

I sat down and listened to the entire game. I logged every charge whistle that I could hear and put out a video showing all the whistles throughout the game. It turned out that there were forty-six whistles instead of just five. Only a few of them were before breaking balls, and many of them were during the Dodgers at bats. The video that tried to show that the Astros were cheating using the charge whistle had about a million views. My video that looked at the entire game and every charge whistle got twelve thousand to fifteen thousand views, so it was really kind of an example for me how these narratives get established.

So even if charges are false, it's hard to correct that narrative once it's established: "A lie travels halfway around the world, while the truth is still putting on shoes." That is particularly true these days with the way social media gets information out there. It also points to confirmation bias. People want the "truth" they're looking for. I don't think many people wanted to understand the actual truth of what happened, so they were willing to believe anything that confirmed the Astros as the villains.

It was still a huge story in the next few weeks, and people were trying to understand what it meant. Many analytical people were looking at things like their performance at home versus away versus the strikeout rates, how they performed against breaking balls, and so on, trying to analyze the Astros' performances. Still, they didn't really have any hard data to work with. They were in the dark and trying to figure out what had happened.

JS: What was the process of logging the bangs?
TA: I expected somebody to come out with details about when and how often the Astros were banging on the trash can, but it didn't happen. I started looking at the data using my experience with the previous video and my knowledge as a web developer and an application developer.

Major League Baseball puts previous years' games on YouTube, and there were a lot of the Astros games from 2017 available. I was looking at the data from it. I noticed there was a time stamp for each pitch, so I had the kind of "aha" moment. I could pull that data into a database and, with the application, match up the time stamp for each pitch with this video from YouTube.

I thought that if I could do that, I could listen for bangs before each pitch and write an application to log this. Looking at it as a problem to solve from an application aspect allowed me to do it. If you were just to try to listen to the entire game, it's three hours, and trying to write down each pitch wouldn't work. But the application that I wrote allowed me to jump to a few seconds before a pitch, listen for the bang, log it, and then jump to the next pitch. I didn't have to listen to all the time in between, so it would take about twelve seconds per pitch instead of listening to a complete game. A game would take me thirty minutes to process instead of three hours.

I wrote a quick app to process a few videos, take the data, and match them together. It was pretty exciting at the time. I was having some difficulties with my job and programming in general because I still had some PTSD from Harvey. So for me, this application reignited my joy for writing applications and programming. That and I really wanted to know what happened. That was my biggest thing. I texted my brother and my nephew when I wrote this app and said, "I can do this. I'm going to log all the bangs."

The original *The Athletic* article quoted Fiers saying that not everybody used the banging. I wanted to know who did it and for how long. At that point, the data showed that a few players, including José Altuve, hadn't participated, so I was curious about which players did participate.

My brother asked me, "Are you trying to exonerate somebody here on the Astros?"

I said, "No, I just want to know the truth."

It was very important for me that if this was going to come out, I wanted it to be an Astros fan. I didn't want it to be sensationalized. I wanted it to be just the information, instead of trying to make a big deal out of it or using it to try to be the next Jomboy.

My brother said, "Be careful—you may not like what you find." That's a quote from the *Planet of the Apes* when Charlton Heston goes down the beach and finds the Statue of Liberty. As a joke, I took that image from the *Planet of the Apes* and replaced the Statue of Liberty with the Astros bobble-head and sent it back.

But I wanted to know the scope of what happened. I figured it would come out eventually and that it would be best to have an Astros fan do it. I wanted to do it without sensationalism and push back on all the conspiracy theories, myths, and rumors. I was attempting to get empirical data and get this story back to the facts.

So, I started developing the app. You need to be able to get the videos and be able to log the bang, and you need to create spectrograms for every pitch. I had a couple of weeks off for Christmas that year, so I was able to concentrate on it. I wrote the app, and then I started going back and listening to all the games.

Fifty-eight Astros home games had videos. I went through the long process of listening to pitches. I don't know why I didn't think about how long it would take to do that, but it was over at 8,200 pitches that I listened to, and some I had to go back and listen to again. But the application allowed me to do that very efficiently.

I could go back and listen to a particular pitch or listen to all the breaking balls in the game and jump around and listen for when they were banging on the trash can. So for the next few weeks, I would wake up early and do a few games or come home and do a few games in the evening. On weekends, I would try to do a few games. I was trying to get it done as quickly as I could. I knew that the commissioner was coming out with his report, and I was hoping to beat him to the punch. In some ways, I was hoping that I could help inform what MLB was doing, but it was taking longer than I expected.

During this time, the rumors and the sensationalism of the story continued. The Astros did not respond to the accusations. So there really were no answers. In that void, people were filling it up with all the speculation.

When I was listening to the games, I believed that I should not make a judgment call on whether something was a bang. I marked it as a bang if it could possibly be a bang. I didn't want somebody to come back and say, "oh, you missed that one," because that would then make people question the data that I was gathering. I wanted to err on the side of overreporting versus underreporting. I knew people would question this report coming from an Astros fan—they would assume I had a bias.

JS: What conclusions could you draw from the logging you did?
TA: I thought I heard very few bangs in the early season, but looking back, those were probably other noises. But the banging started to pick up in midsummer, and then it was pretty constant. They were banging every game.

It didn't matter if they were up ten runs—they would still be banging on the trash can. I was thinking about it at the time: "Why are you doing it now? You're up ten runs in the eighth inning, and you are banging that stupid trash can? This doesn't make sense."

I wouldn't really look at which player was up when I went through the pitches. I was focused on listening and watching the spectrogram for bangs. As I was jumping from pitch to pitch during a game, there would be several pitches where there were some bangs, and then there would be a series of pitches where there were no bangs. It wasn't until I stopped and looked back at the data by players that I noticed that those gaps were usually when [José] Altuve and Josh Reddick were at bat. They were usually back-to-back in the lineup, so the gap was even more apparent.

If there were bangs during Altuve's and Reddick's at bats, it seemed like a mistake by whoever was banging the trash can. The pattern was different from the other players. It appeared for their at bats where there were bangs, the first breaking ball would have a bang, and the rest of the breaking balls wouldn't. This doesn't make sense because the system doesn't work if you're not receiving the signal for all breaking balls. The batter would think that a breaking ball is a fastball without the bang.

The banging continued throughout the season until a game against the White Sox late in September [21], which was detailed in the commissioner's report.

JS: Why did it stop in September?

TA: Danny Farquhar was a relief pitcher for the White Sox, and when he came in that day, he noticed that whenever he threw a breaking ball, there was a sound. And he told himself that if I hear the sound the next time I call for a breaking ball, the Astros are stealing signs. He called the catcher to the mound and said, "they got the signs." That's what stopped it. There were no bangs for the rest of that game and nothing for the rest of the season.

After that game, Farquhar said he waited around in the locker room for any reporter to come up and ask him what happened because he was ready to tell it all. That would have all broken the story right then, but nobody came up and asked.

The commissioner's report stated that the Astros panicked when Farquhar stepped off the mound. They were afraid that they were caught, and they were caught! They took the TV down and put it in an office at that exact moment.

JS: What did you think of the commissioner's report?

TA: When the commissioner's report came out, I hadn't released the data. The report talked about how the Astros messed around with some methods early in the season but decided to go with the banging. It spoke of the Farquhar incident and how the Astros panicked, matching my data. It was very interesting to read the report and see how it reaffirmed that the data I collected was accurate.

The commissioner's report said it continued into the playoffs. I tried to log the playoffs, but there are problems with the audio. I could hear pretty well in the Boston series, and I couldn't detect any bangs. The audio quality is horrible in the New York series and the ALCS. I don't know if it was because of the crowd noise or something else. I can't say for sure. It sounds like the base level is clipped. It could be that they had to mike the stadium differently because of the crowd noise. I spent hours trying to process the audio and clean it up, but I was not able to do that. But, if you think about it, if you have a system based on the audible signal coming from the dugout, one of the things that could make that system break down is crowd noise. The excitement level grows as the Astros get further into the postseason. The stadium is full; obviously, fans want to make noise. It's a domed stadium, and it was closed every game. It can be a loud stadium. It could have been that they tried to use the banging system, and I can't detect it, or they could have tried to use it, but it wasn't effective because they couldn't hear it when they were at the plate.

Carlos Correa talked about how the trash can was there in the playoffs. They tried using it, but they didn't use it very often. But I can't say yes or no to the playoffs.

But one of the things that Correa talked about is that people on other teams were suspicious. There are reports that the Dodgers were suspicious and changed their signals frequently even without a man on second. This was something that the announcers talked about several times during the series. It's one of the things that we still don't have the answers for.

It was wrong and would have tilted the playing field if they cheated during the World Series. Was it enough to affect the outcome? Nobody can say for sure. I don't think anyone can say they stole a World Series.

I suspect they tried to use it in the playoffs, but if they did use it, they didn't use it nearly as much as [in] the regular season because it was hard to hear the bangs. You're not going to trust that signal anymore, and so you might say, "screw it," I'll just hit. Many players don't like to get the signs from a man on second because they want to respond to the pitch. They don't want to think about it. Some studies on my data suggest that knowing the pitch reduced the batter's power. They were just trying to make contact, but it wasn't good contact. This means the pitcher will throw more and wear down quicker than usual.[3]

JS: What do you think happened in the World Series?
TA: I initially felt stronger than I do now about it, partly because I don't know what happened in the World Series. Correa came out and talked about some of the details, saying that we used it, but it wasn't very effective, which kind of matches up with what I was hearing or not hearing.

So, I feel better about it. I'm not 100 percent confident that nothing happened or that the outcome would have been the same. I don't think anybody can really say for sure. The Dodgers can say the Astros stole the World Series from them, but if the Astros were bringing on a trash can and someone hits a home run, there is no way to know if they would have hit a home run otherwise.

If you look at Yu Darvish, he pitched in two games in the series. He gave up eight runs in two-and-a-third innings. He was the only Dodgers pitcher that gave up earned runs in those two games. If they were cheating, you would think it would be effective against all the Dodgers' pitchers.

I'm not necessarily pointing to that as an indicator of innocence. Maybe Darvish wasn't changing the signs because he wasn't familiar with the catcher. He hadn't been with the team very long. So there were a lot of aspects to it. Their batting stats show that the Astros didn't perform very well offensively during the World Series.

Some think that if you know every pitch that is coming, you will hit a home run every time. It didn't work that way. Going back to the data I collected, it shows us that the Astros were frequently wrong about what the pitch was. Often, they thought a breaking ball was coming, but it was a fastball or vice-versa. They were wrong about 12 to 14 percent of the time.

Baseball Prospectus showed a significant advantage for most players when the signal was right, but it was a considerable disadvantage when it was wrong. In the end, the advantages and disadvantages are balanced out for the most part. The benefit was not nearly as great as people think.

JS: Did the punishment of the players and GM fit the crime?
TA: Luhnow says he didn't know about the banging scheme. Looking at the story, I believe him. The Astros were decoding signs between games, but that is legal, and every team does it at this point. The Astros crossed a line at some point, but other teams have definitely crossed the same line. So, with Luhnow, I'm not sure if his punishment was justified. It was only a one-year suspension, but he lost his $30 million contract with the Astros. It was a substantial financial hit for him. It also spoiled his reputation.

Some are upset that none of the players were suspended, but the MLB labor agreement didn't allow it. But it's not like they got away with it. Their reputations and even the World Series championship—some say it should be taken away. It's not the same as other people's championships. Most Houstonians still have great pride in the championship. They think it's legitimate, but how many other fans believe that?

And that's one of my frustrations with the scandal. I thought they could win the World Series before the season started; they were projected to be one of the top teams. I don't think they needed it. I don't know if Carlos Beltrán, with his declining performance, felt he needed it just as a personal thing. But when they started the banging, they were up nine games in the division. It wasn't like they needed to start performing better; they were already performing well. They performed well from the start of the season; they performed well on the road. They were even better on the road and had a better record and better offensive statistics. It was a really, really good team, and that's one of the things that I don't quite understand—why they felt that this was something they had to do.

JS: What are some other contexts for this incident?
TA: That initial video by Jomboy was obviously a milestone in social media as far as sports reporting goes. I'm actually surprised that *The Athletic* didn't try to do something like that. I've talked to him a few times, and he did what he did well. Then he did the buzzer stuff.[4] He was instrumental in spreading that rumor, and he should have known better. He retweeted Beltrán's niece's tweet.[5] Within minutes another reporter actually said that that's not Beltrán's niece, and instead of saying, "my bad; I'm sorry. Let me take this down," he kept it up and said, "well, I've heard this from other people." But if he's heard from other people, why did he go with the Beltrán's niece who said she was in the dugout?

I hadn't released my data at that point, so people didn't know that he [Altuve] didn't participate in the banging scheme. People can say, "well, he didn't stop it," but nobody stopped it, including the manager. When things like this happen, everyone thinks, "I would have stopped it," but the reality is most people wouldn't have. Every player interviewed on another team said he was outraged. Still, the reality is if they were in the same situation, the vast majority of them would have gone along with it.

People have a visceral response when they hear the trash can bangs. I think the reaction to the scandal would have been like the Red Sox Apple Watch thing if the Astros had used a different method to communicate the signs.[6] It's the fact that they went with such a stupid method and the fact that it's so easily detectable and somebody like me can go back and log every time they cheated that made it worse. People think it was a high-tech scheme when actually it was as if a caveman did it. It's not like *Mission Impossible*. They watched a TV and banged on a trash can with the bat. It's more like *The Flintstones*.

JS: Are you going to do more work along these lines?
TA: I don't know if you heard that I won the SABR research award this week. It's obviously a great honor, but the situation that led to it is not positive.

It's kind of odd. I wasn't doing baseball analytics at all two years ago, so I couldn't have imagined it.

So now I'm doing some other things as far as pitch analysis. I want to use video to determine if people are tipping pitches. It opened up my mind to using applications to analyze video and the data. Other people are doing this with much more advanced techniques, but for me, it's still kind of a hobby. At this point in my life, I'm doing things that I enjoy more than the things that are advancing my career.

As the Astros were attacked more and more for things that I didn't feel were based on the evidence, I felt myself defending the Astros because I was trying to keep things based on the truth. It pushed me back into my fandom.

It's weird. The Commissioner didn't really put out a lot of evidence. He said he had a lot, but he didn't put it out. In general, MLB has the attitude that it's okay to cheat until you get caught. They've always kind of accepted a certain level of cheating.

It was a tough year for the Astros fans, particularly on social media. If you're an Astros fan, and you get on social media, or the Astros post something, there's always someone replying with "cheater."

For example, the Astros tweeted when Jimmy Wynn died. He was an Astros player in the late '60s and early '70s. And the first comment was somebody saying "cheater." I responded to the guy and said Jimmy Wynn hadn't played for the Astros in decades. He had nothing to do with the cheating. He said, "you're right," and deleted that post. The response was over the top, and I don't think it fits the crime. It seems like hating the Astros became the national pastime for many people.

All these different rumors about buzzers and stuff—I wish people would try and stick to what we know and what is provable. It's frustrating, and it's really made me more of a defender of the Astros.

This story is going to be written about for a long time. I feel confident that the data I logged is accurate and will help those telling the story know what really happened. I'm proud that I got us a little closer to that truth.

Notes

1. The interview has been edited for length and content and approved by Adams.
2. James Vincent Michael O'Brien, known by his nickname Jomboy, is a prominent YouTuber who often analyzes baseball games.
3. Andy Martino, *Cheated: The Inside Story of the Astros Scandal and a Colorful History of Sign Stealing* (New York: Doubleday, 2021). Martino asserts in his fine book that the Astros did use the system in the World Series but were instead more circumspect. Adams contributed his work to the book.

4. This refers to the mostly disproven allegation that José Altuve wore a buzzer to receive signals.

5. A Twitter user, claiming she was Carlos Beltrán's niece, asserted that she had information about the scandal, including proof that Altuve used a buzzer.

6. The Red Sox were punished for using an Apple Watch to communicate signals in 2017.

CHAPTER 9

Reckoning with Tainted Love: What the Astros Scandal Reveals of Sports Fandom

MATTHEW KLUGMAN

"The Astros have pushed the envelope in so many ways, but I never thought my love of the team would be one of them." So mused "CKuno," one of the longtime writers of the Houston Astros (SB Nation) fan website, the Crawfish Boxes, on January 15, 2020.[1] The surprise of CKuno mirrored that of many people in the baseball world as they sought to understand the ramifications that the scandal would have for baseball fans.

Much of the way that baseball fans reacted to the Astros' sign-stealing scandal was relatively straightforward. The followers of opposing teams were frequently outraged and condemned the behavior of the Astros players and team management. As spring training for the 2020 season began, the Astros players were showered with boos and insults.[2] Some opposing fans called for Houston's World Series title to be vacated and bemoaned the way their teams had been cheated out of a chance for glory.[3] Others indulged in the common sporting emotion of schadenfreude, delighting in the misery that was now being heaped upon the Astros. A popular @AsteriskTour twitter account was developed to chronicle the way opposing fans in different cities reacted to the "Astros 2020 Tour of Shame." The promise of "One year to shame them all, one year to jeer them, one year to boo them all and from your seat deride them," was yet another thing that was ultimately undone by the Covid-19 pandemic, which not only delayed the baseball season but also led to most games being played in stadiums empty of supporters.[4] Still, a substantial number of people made or purchased products that proclaimed the misdeeds of the Houston team to the world. Among other items, "Houston Asterisks" T-shirts are still available for sale.[5]

The responses of Astros fans like CKuno, however, revealed more of the complexities of sports fandom. What was at stake for many were matters not only of personal and communal identity but also of the heart. This chapter explores what the experience of Astros rooters reveals of sporting fandom. At issue are questions of love, heartbreak, guilt by association, idealism, strength, and notions of honor.

Sports fandom has been approached in many ways. Contemporary scholars frequently think of sports fans as consumers or as individuals who identify closely with a team or athlete for relatively rational reasons, such as the sense of belonging that this can engender.[6] But the history of the terms that have been used to designate baseball followers points to something more excessive.

The behavior of many of the early baseball followers in the 1880s was so extreme that they were deemed *cranks*, a term first popularized to denote the insanity of President Garfield's assassin. Not only were the baseball cranks obsessed over a mere game, but they also tended to become highly emotional while watching their teams play. Indeed, viewing the pastime of baseball was an act that engaged body, mind, and soul. During the course of a single inning, the crank might whoop and holler with delight, shriek and stamp, rave and curse, tear at his or her hair, abuse players on both teams as well as the umpire, sigh, and even begin to pray when things became particularly intense.[7]

By the early 1900s, as the designation of the baseball *fan* replaced that of the *crank*, the powerful emotions of baseball followers were becoming seen as an antidote to the ills of the modern world. Watching the game was an act of catharsis. Baseball was a safety valve that allowed people to go momentarily wild and let loose the steam that might otherwise threaten productive work, law and order, and even democracy itself.[8] In 1914, the prominent essayist Simeon Strunsky even argued that baseball was akin to the religion of democracy. The game was "a great democratic rite, a ceremonial which is solemnized on six days in the week during six months in the year by large masses of men with such unfailing regularity and such unquestioning good faith that I cannot help thinking of it as essentially a religious performance."[9]

Yet while the emotional behavior of (generally white) baseball fans was now often celebrated as legitimate, the allusions to madness remained. Sports cartoonists, in particular, frequently drew attention to the way baseball seemed to drive supporters crazy. "Jim Nasium" (Edgar Forrest Wolfe) of the *Pittsburgh Press*, for example, coined the illness "Dementia Americana" to describe the pathology evident at ballparks.[10] Clare Briggs of the *Chicago Tribune* meanwhile detailed the way "The Conservation of Lunacy Is the Life of the Baseball Business," astutely observing that the owners of baseball teams profited from the frequently irrational hopes and dreams of fans.[11]

So what leads baseball fans to indulge in such powerful emotions over the playing of mere games? The word that most frequently came up when Houston Astros followers sought to explain themselves to each other, as well as to a hostile baseball world, was "love." This matches my research of other sports fans who also explained that their fandom is based on love.[12]

Not only is love the emotion most frequently associated with intense human passions and behavior, *but* it can also lead people to identify with the object of their affection—be that another person, a nation, or even a sports team.[13] Indeed, the beloved team comes to feel like it is part of the self. What happens to the team is experienced as happening to the individual who loves that team as well. "We won," proclaim triumphant fans, or "we got crushed," mourn devastated supporters. It's an absurd form of belonging that is grounded in passionate attachment.

For some of those who had supported the Houston Astros, the clear cheating of the team ended their passionate affection for the team. "After the Astros cheated, I ended my love affair with the franchise" wrote "Texas Oiler" in response to a column on the complications of being an Astros fan in 2020:

> I don't see how anyone with any moral values can still be a fan of this team. I have small children that are just getting into the game, how can I, in good conscience, allow them to become Astros fans only so they can be ridiculed endlessly?[14]

For Texas Oiler, sports like baseball were supposed to uphold values such as fair play, and it was immoral to love a team that blatantly went against these values. Yet such decisions to break off the relationship with the Astros seem to have been rare, as "1BIGFandyPackler" found out in February 2020. Aware that a number of Astros fans frequented the LSU fan site TigerDroppings, 1BIGFandyPackler created a thread entitled "Ditching the Astros."[15] "I cannot root for this team until the franchise has different ownership," explained 1BIGFandyPackler. "How many other (former) Astros fans are with me?"

If the question was intended as a rallying cry, it succeeded only in bringing out those fans who were sticking with the team. 1BIGFandyPackler was derided as weak and abused as a "bitch" and a "pussy."[16] The more substantive posts were sometimes politer but nevertheless resolute in defending the decision to stick with the team:

> "Been an Astros fan since 1970. Not giving up on them."

> "I will never surrender my Astros fan hood."

> "Once a Stros fan always a Stros fan."

"I'm disappointed but been an Astro fan since my dad started bringing me to games when Mike Scott was throwing heat in the Astrodome [in the 1980s] so my loyalty is unwavering."

The tropes here were the familiar misogynistic binaries of elite male sports culture. To leave, even for moral reasons, was a sign of feminized weakness. True fans were strong, with the tough, honorable masculinity that implied. They stuck with their team through thick and thin, even if that team cheated. It was okay to be disappointed, but only if your loyalty did not waver. To keep loving the team was the right and principled thing to do. As one poster castigated 1BIGFandyPackler, "GTFO [Get the fuck out] with this shite [of ditching the Astros]. . . . That's not how being a fan works."

These responses also hinted at one of the complexities in the relationship that many fans have with their beloved team. Yes, the fans were bound to the team, but the team was something abstract or ideal.[17] Fans were not necessarily defined by the current players, management, or owners. These were invariably temporary. True fans outlasted them. As another poster on the "Ditching the Astros" TigerDroppings thread explained, "I was an Astros fan before current ownership, and I'll be one after current ownership. My fandom exceeds the current players, managers, or ownership."[18]

The Australian novelist Peter Temple captured something of this with regard to Australian Rules football. In his book *Dead Point*, the main characters are silent as they drive away from a miserable loss:

Very little needed to be said. A supporter near us had screamed most of it at the coach at three-quarter time, two sentences: *Look-at-the-scoreboard-ya-fucken-mongrel. See-what-ya-fucken-done-to-us.*

Us. Done to us. The coach wasn't one of us. Coaches were transients and carpetbaggers. And only a few players in any era in any club ever became one of *us*.

The supporters were *us*. They were the investors. Gave the club their hearts, dreams, they expected a return. Every game was an annual general meeting.[19]

Yet in giving the Astros their hearts and dreams, the fans were still associated with the particular players and front office staff that cheated. They might want to deny the association, to point to the way their fandom exceeded these players, managers, and owner. But the baseball world repeatedly brought up the cheating. Astros fans were deemed guilty by association. Their love was tainted by what had occurred.

Rob Sellers wrestled with this dilemma in a guest column for the *Waco Tribune-Herald* as the (original) start date for the 2020 MLB season neared. "I did not cheat," Sellers notes over and over in his column: "Yet, when I talk to my Texas Rangers–supporting friends, the first thing they reference is the cheating. I have to listen to it. I have to read about it in the newspaper, on Facebook, on Twitter and on Reddit. I have to hear about it on the local news, on ESPN and on the local sports stations."[20] For Sellers it seemed like he had to pay "the price of being an Astros fan. Even though I didn't cheat, my team did." Any announcement of his fandom led to ridicule. Astros caps and T-shirts lead to laughter and scorn. "I have to hear about it."

Nevertheless, Sellers noted, "I still love the Astros." The first part of his column detailed the history of his Astros fandom. He had followed them when they were the worst-performing team in baseball. He had delighted in the turnaround that took place as the team became a powerhouse. He felt indebted to the work of the team in assisting Houston citizens recover from Hurricane Harvey, which devastated the city in August 2017. The World Series victory that followed was "a dream experience."

But "what do I do when they cheat?" asks Sellers. "Do I turn my back on them? Do I deny they did anything wrong, or at least say that they didn't do anything that other teams haven't done, but just got caught?" His answer was a resounding "No." Baseball journalist Ryan Fagan received a similar response from five of the six Astros fans that he interviewed through Twitter direct messages.[21] All were distraught; one even noted being heartbroken. The other five stated that their love for the team was unchanged. In an emblematic statement, @Miguelg1984 summed it up with the following analogy: "I always have my team's back. It's like if your kid ends up getting arrested for selling drugs . . . do you hate him? No, it's your job to always love them and defend them and that's how I feel about my Astros. It's ugly, but have to ride or die with your loved ones."[22]

Even the heartbroken fan was still supporting the Astros, although only in "thought," "not via the wallet."

In early 2020, with the scheduled start of the MLB season on the horizon, a New York Yankees fan set about the task of trying to find former Houston Astros supporters. They figured that "a good chunk of their fans would become fans of other teams," and that the most logical team to change to gain the affections of former Astros fans was the Texas Rangers. So they asked the Rangers sub Reddit if anyone there had previously supported Houston.[23] No one responded affirmatively.

The presumption that Astros followers would—or at least should—leave the team en masse also meant that those who remained Astros fans have been continually asked why they didn't leave. Even those who did not feel the need to reckon with their fandom have frequently had to defend their decision to stay. Such questions are not going away anytime soon. As Bryan C. Parker noted in *Texas Monthly* in the aftermath of the 2020 season, "Like the team they love, Houston fans live in the shade of the Astros' mistakes."[24] Indeed, Parker was one of the many Astros supporters who had spent much of 2020 responding to people wanting him to "explain my fandom of the team."

Such questions are indicative of a strange disconnect around the passions of sports fandom. Spectator sports are one of the most powerful forms of popular culture. And this power remains largely shaped by the fans who obsess over the teams (and athletes) that they follow. Yet the forms of love that frequently drives this obsession remain largely underexplored by scholars and fans alike. Many of those who were surprised that so many remained committed to loving the Astros in spite of the clear cheating by players, managers, and the front office, would likely have remained tied to their own sporting loves in the face of a similar scandal.

The sign stealing by Houston players in concert with management broke CKuno's heart. It felt like a "betrayal" of fandom and tested their love for the Astros.[25] Teams are supposed to uphold the commitment to fair play, even though baseball playing fields are far from level in the major leagues. William Metzger, the managing editor at The Crawfish Boxes, was similarly heartbroken.[26] The triumph of 2017 had felt akin to David triumphing over Goliath. But now the purported "Davids" had been revealed as "wicked Goliaths."

Yet like so many Houston fans, both CKuno and William Metzger would recommit to supporting the Astros. For CKuno, although the experience was "akin to a crisis of faith," their decision to remain was made with an awareness of what their love of the Astros gave them access to:

> When I really think about it, what I want most is to experience the crack of the bat, the thrill of running the bases, and athletes performing at the top of their craft again. The years of emotion and enjoyment poured into the team haven't been swept away yet even though their hold is more tenuous than it once was. I guess that, after all of this, I've discovered that that purity of emotion is the core of my fandom, and everything else is just noise, even though it has grown a little louder. For good or for ill, I'm a fan of baseball and the Houston Astros still.[27]

Fans like CKuno love the Astros in a way that makes the team feel part of them. When a player got a hit, ran the bases, and performed feats of amazing athleticism, it somehow felt like CKuno had done the same. They were part of it all. Hence the many emotions of being a baseball fan: the anticipation, the agonizing tension, the subsequent intense pain or delight. And as the baseball world laughed, mocked, and scorned the multitudes who remained Astros fans, the waves of outrage, indignation, and righteous shaming started to bind together those who were reviled. The fans had not cheated. They were guilty by association. Many felt their love had been tainted or even betrayed. They grieved for what they had lost. But a consensus started to emerge that they were being overly targeted. That all the hatred directed at Houston was becoming unfair. Unexpectedly, the gloriously seductive sporting narrative of the underdog battling against all odds became available. The fans of the Houston Astros could bond together as a David facing Goliath all over again.

Notes

1. CKuno, "A Return to the Limits of Fandom," Crawfish Boxes, January 15, 2020, https://www.crawfishboxes.com/2020/1/15/21065436/a-return-to-the-limits-of-fandom. (Social media noms de web are placed in quotation marks in the first instance and then used without quotation marks.)

2. Mike Axisa, "Astros Hear Boos, Confiscate Fan's Sign in First Spring Training Game Since Cheating Scandal," CNN, February 23, 2020, https://www.cbssports.com/mlb/news/astros-hear-boos-confiscate-fans-sign-in-first-spring-training-game-since-cheating-scandal/

3. Hunter Felt, "Is MLB Right to Let the Cheating Houston Astros Keep Their Title?," *The Guardian*, January 24, 2020, https://www.theguardian.com/sport/2020/jan/24/is-mlb-right-to-let-the-cheating-houston-astros-keep-their-title.

4. Scott Allen, "Angry about the Houston Astros? Now You Can Follow Their 'Shame Tour' on Twitter," *Washington Post*, February 29, 2020, https://www.washingtonpost.com/sports/2020/02/28/angry-about-houston-astros-now-you-can-follow-their-shame-tour-twitter/.

5. 2020 Shame Tour, "Featured Products," https://2020-shame-tour.creator-spring.com/.

6. David P. Hedlund, Rui Biscaia, and Maria do Carmo Leal, "Classifying Sport Consumers: From Casual to Tribal Fans," in *Handbook of Research on the Impact of Fandom in Society and Consumerism*, ed. Cheng Lu Wang, 323–356 (Hershey, PA: IGI Global, 2020); Daniel L. Wann and Jeffrey D. James, *Sport Fans: The Psychology and Social Impact of Fandom*, 2nd ed. (New York: Routledge, 2019).

7. Matthew Klugman, "The Passionate, Pathologized Bodies of Sports Fans: How the Digital Turn Might Facilitate a New Cultural History of Modern Spectator Sports," *Journal of Sport History*, 44, no. 2 (Summer 2017): 306–321.

8. Steven A. Riess, *Touching Base: Professional Baseball and American Culture in the Progressive Era* (Urbana: University of Illinois Press, 1999), 23–25.

9. Simeon Strunsky, "The Game," *Atlantic Monthly*, August 1914, 248–249.

10. Edgar Forrest Wolfe, "Dementia Americana," *Pittsburgh Press*, May 26, 1907, 22.

11. Clare Briggs, "The Conservation of Lunacy Is the Life of the Baseball Business," *Chicago Daily Tribune*, September 23, 1911, 10.

12. Matthew Klugman, "Loves, Suffering and Identification: The Passions of Australian Football League Fans," *International Journal of the History of Sport* 26, no. 1 (2009): 21–44.

13. Klugman, "Loves, Suffering and Identification."

14. Bryan C. Parker, "Being a Houston Astros Fan in 2020 Is Complicated," *Texas Monthly*, October 13, 2020, https://www.texasmonthly.com/arts-entertainment/being-houston-astros-fan-2020-complicated/#comments.

15. 1BIGFandyPackler, "Ditching the Astros," TigerDroppings, February 26, 2020, https://www.tigerdroppings.com/rant/more-sports/ditching-the-astros/88782823/.

16. These and the following comments can be found in the three page thread on "Ditching the Astros," TigerDroppings, https://www.tigerdroppings.com/rant/more-sports/ditching-the-astros/88782823/.

17. Klugman, "Loves, Suffering and Identification."

18. "Ditching the Astros," TigerDroppings, https://www.tigerdroppings.com/rant/more-sports/ditching-the-astros/88782823/.

19. Peter Temple, *Dead Point* (Sydney: Bantam, 2000).

20. This and the following quotes are from Rob Sellers, "Guest Column: Astros Fans the Real Losers in Team's Cheating Scandal," *Waco Tribune-Herald*, March 2, 2020, https://wacotrib.com/sports/guest-column-astros-fans-the-real-losers-in-teams-cheating-scandal/article_f3caf8cc-1bea-5f0e-9d82-3bf01b12b865.html.

21. Ryan Fagan, "'I Feel Like I've Been Duped': Astros Fans Battle Range of Emotions Amid Cheating Scandal," *Sporting News*, February 20, 2020, https://www.sportingnews.com/us/mlb/news/astros-fans-battle-range-of-emotions-amid-cheating-scandal-i-feel-like-ive-been-duped/1n2dol182q4rj1houxtvwwyvy6.

22. Fagan, "I Feel Like I've Been Duped."

23. u/Mattp11111 2020, "Any Former Astros Fans?," Reddit r/Texas Rangers, February 2020, https://www.reddit.com/r/TexasRangers/comments/ftp2i6/any_former_astros_fans/.

24. Parker, "Being a Houston Astros Fan in 2020 Is Complicated."

25. CKuno, "A Return to the Limits of Fandom."

26. William Metzger, "Houston Astros: You Reap What You Sow," Crawfish Boxes, January 13, 2020, https://www.crawfishboxes.com/2020/1/13/21064786/houston-astros-you-reap-what-you-sow.

27. CKuno, "A Return to the Limits of Fandom."

CHAPTER 10

"To Learn Baseball": A Transatlantic Dialogue on the Astros and the American Ways of Winning

MICHAEL HINDS AND JOSEPH RIVERA

Editor's note: Michael Hinds is from Omagh, a small town in Northern Ireland. Joseph Rivera is from Webb City, a small town in Missouri. They both work at Dublin City University. Hinds teaches American literature; Rivera, philosophy Their offices are about one hundred feet apart, and Rivera often has to pass Hinds's office. There is often a pause for conversation, and it moves customarily to sports, not least because it allows them to talk about something other than work.

That said, this still means that they have to find words to work through differences in perception that arise out of their backgrounds, cultural contexts, and academic specializations. Rivera is exiled in Ireland, a country where practically nobody (apart from the odd expatriate like himself) either plays baseball or talks about it. Hinds originally learned about the game almost by accident, as a by-product of a three-year stint living in Japan at the end of the 1990s. His perception of the great American game has necessarily been altered by that experience. Never having played the game does not diminish Hinds's appetite for knowing more about it, not least because of its lore and rich literary history. He tends to have questions, while Rivera has answers. The phenomenon of the Houston Astros scandal therefore presents them with a problem of mutual acculturation, in trying to figure out whether it is uniquely American or symptomatic of broader trends in sport and culture. To understand each other and reckon the importance of what happened, to find the right idea or reference through which to explore the ancient art of cheating, they performed the Socratic art of dialogue, exploring the relationship between European football scandals and the Astros imbroglio, the literary and language components of scandals, the connections between cultural and national identities and cheating, as well as what Robert Frost, a baseball fan and American poetic icon, might have thought about the scandal.

José Altuve

Hinds: I remember talking to you in 2018 about José Altuve, Joe. He seemed so good to me that it almost felt like cheating. Watching Chris Sale pitch for the Red Sox around the same time felt like something similar. Both of them seemed to be practically unplayable, in the sense of the word as I understand it. They seemed almost too adept at the game they were playing.

Altuve's excellence in particular seemed so singular, though, because it seemed as if he was built for resilience rather than dominance but turned out to have both. Aside from Diego Maradona or Leo Messi, he seemed to me to be the best sportsman (I think we have a language gap to negotiate, would an American say athlete?) I ever saw who was under five and a half feet (he's officially listed by Major League Baseball as five-six). So he undermined all sorts of assumptions about modern sport requiring an increasingly typical uber-physicality, ballplayers who were at least a foot taller like Sale.

Altuve was one in the eye for sports eugenicists; in fact, above all what he seemed to represent was defiance, both of the opposition and the odds. So when the news of the malfeasance of the Astros organization emerged, it was not so much that it was hard to comprehend, because I assumed that things like sign stealing are more or less a constant in the game. Rather, it seemed that a player such as Altuve did not seem to need any help. He gave off a vibe that he had never got much of that from anyone. And, as it turns out, the analysis by Tony Adams seems to show that Altuve did not avail much of the sign stealing, if at all. Yet this seems to be the kind of scandal that may well taint people by association anyway. If the organization is perceived to be dirty, then the player is seen as symptomatic of that.

Rivera: Hitting a baseball coming at you in excess of ninety miles an hour represents not just an athletic skill only some of us are lucky enough to master but perhaps the skill with the highest degree of difficulty in all of sports. The repertoire of the pitcher can overwhelm the hitter so much that even the best sit down in the dugout and take notes on each pitcher (Albert Pujols is famous for keeping a detailed notebook on pitching styles, counts, etc.): the curveball, the splitfinger, the knuckleball, the cutter, the slider, the fastball with natural movement, and not least the changeup; even the all-powerful Pedro Cerrano in the 1989 movie *Major League* could not find the patience to hit the changeup. He could hit the ball a mile when he connected, but he simply could not connect most of the time!

Even Altuve, however small in stature he may well be, cannot cheat himself into the kind of athlete who can hit for a historically high average, and short players in baseball's lore are plentiful, from Joe Morgan and Pete Rose to Ozzie Smith and Kirby Puckett—to name a few. In 2017, the year Altuve won the MVP, he hit .346 and had just over two hundred hits. His twenty-four home runs do not even reach the widely regarded low-water mark of thirty for a slugger to be considered a power hitter.

His statistical line, too, matched what he had produced since 2014—this is not to include his base stealing prowess stretching back to 2012. Altuve is simply an excellent athlete who might have exploited some sign stealing in service of a few more base hits. If he had hit sixty home runs or hit .400, then I would like to challenge the notion that Altuve morphed into something he's not, like José Canseco or Mark McGwire after steroids. I was genuinely shocked by the revelation of the complex mechanism involved in sign stealing conducted by the Astros, but I was equally shocked to see so much outrage, as if it constituted a massive advantage of some sort. Sign stealing is not tripling one's strength (and size) through use of human growth hormone.

The Scandal in American Context

Hinds: So do you think this is a peculiarly American thing? Does the American way of winning have a particular character of its own, whether it be ugly or beautiful? How does the victory culture of European soccer, with its hegemonic big clubs that dominate despite the complexes of promotion and relegation, compare to that of the United States, where systems try to foster competitiveness while protecting the investments of owners? The phrase "financial doping" gets used in European soccer to decry the influence of big clubs over the others, and their ability to dominate transfer markets. I doubt if anyone would ever use that phrase to describe how the Yankees operate, even if their dominance would be comparable.

What seems most remarkable about American sports is its protectionism; the European way in which clubs get promoted and relegated seems too terrifying to contemplate. It has me asking whether the European model is emulating the chaos of free-market capitalism or rather allowing for social mobility. At different moments in history, it might look like either.[1] But by contrast, Major League Baseball, the National Football League, National Hockey League, and National Basketball Association look to a European like four closed loops, where the same teams follow the same course, year on year, and yet this apparently structural anticompetitiveness does actually guarantee competitiveness. The Royals, with a much lower payroll than the Yankees, won the World Series in 2015, not the Dodgers or the Yankees. What the

Astros did was perhaps offer an expression of this particular version of competitiveness; the kind of solution they offered to the problem of trying to read the opposition's intentions was particularly calculating but maybe appropriately so. In an environment where the teams are so familiar with one another and there is so much scouting and scrutiny of the opposition, getting some kind of an edge over the other team must be especially hard.

Rivera: This topic could open out into an endlessly ramified set of speculations about the nature of American sports, not least American culture and exceptionalism. My instinct, in light of the Astros scandal, is to say that American sports is tightly regulated and hemmed in by a deep sense of what is "fair" in a way (only by complexion or intensity) that remains impossible for pan-European sports to emulate. The conceptual, political, and metaphysical framework of what constitutes "fair play" or "justice as fairness" lies at the heart of American culture; certainly political philosophy attests to this.[2] Preoccupation with "fairness" may well simply be a uniquely American emphasis and thus constitute an American expression of what it means to lay down rules, procedures, and policy. Once a consensus is reached, it may also be American to insist that hard discipline befalls those who do not abide by them rigidly. Sports commissioners, like politicians, are visible, public figures who hold enormous cultural (and legal) power.

Hinds: I wonder if there is a more thorough American belief in fairness, or rather if there is less cynicism about it than elsewhere. There is not really a direct equivalent to the likes of Adam Silver (NBA commissioner), Roger Goodell (NFL commissioner), or Rob Manfred (MLB commissioner) in European sports. National leagues have chairs or presidents, and there is a supremo of European soccer (UEFA is the governing body), and a head of FIFA (international soccer's governing body), but the people who hold those positions nearly always seem to be embroiled themselves in financial scandal, as if the office itself tainted them by association. FIFA has become notorious for serving its own financial interests, even as it presents a veneer of promoting the game globally as a force of progress. I know that not everybody loves the American commissioners, but it does seem as though their offices are respected. By contrast, soccer administrators across the world generally are regarded with suspicion, not least because the allocation of World Cup tournaments is a notoriously grift-ridden business.

I recall that the head of the team behind the failed American bid for the 2022 tournament, Don Garber, was astonished by how Qatar succeeded and genuinely shocked by how other countries conducted themselves: "It's not just soccer fans who took a little shot in the head today."[3] Distrust of FIFA for its business ethics manifests as exasperation with it in other ways too, such as when they change the offside law or alter the game in other ways. They are regarded as entirely venal and cynical in terms of soccer as a business, then regarded as meddling and incompetent in terms of reviewing the rules of the game on the field. Either way, they never seem to be associated with fairness, for all that they preach "fair play."

It feels paradoxical in a way. The baseball commissioner is chosen by the owners of the ball clubs, so he serves their interests, not those of the sport as a whole as such. Is that right? FIFA and UEFA bosses are independent of the soccer clubs, yet they are usually regarded very skeptically. Nobody really thinks they have anything to do with "fair play." Is it that the American structures are at least transparent in that the interests of the owners are evidently paramount, and so the commissioners enjoy at least some degree of trust?

The Scandal in European Context

Rivera: And why does fairness, strictly conceived and regulated, manage to occupy such a discernible atmosphere of virtuousness and honor in the American imagination, especially in sports commentary and culture? Why did the steroids scandal of the 1990s in Major League Baseball require political intervention in the form of staged congressional hearings? I think the sheer cultural, linguistic, and religious diversity of Europe renders uniform expectations about fair play simply so unlikely as to make the American rigidity concerning "fairness" unimaginable for European football or rugby. The European mindset, by force of cultural diversity, invokes a set of rules so that the game can be played, but its application and interpretation remain dynamic and fluid (at least more so than in American sports). The media coverage, childhood habits of play, interpretations of time, and "what's important" about style of play, what constitutes an aspirational work ethic, etc., all of this differs in a discrete manner according to country, from Italy and France to Ireland and Germany, not least Romania, Russia, Sweden, and so forth.

We could enumerate other queries here (also economic in nature): what role do sports play in European unity-in-difference, especially the Champions League in football? Differences in all those categories, including sports, emerge in America too, according to area (the football-obsessed South versus the Pacific Northwest's focus on outdoors and a variety of sports, basketball in the Carolinas and East Coast, and the like), but nothing to the degree they are visible in Europe.

Hinds: That is interesting. You have probably noticed that Irish people use the phrase "In fairness" a lot in conversation. What it really communicates is a passive-aggressive "no," but such overt refusals are not really part of our vocabulary. I do not think that this is a concept of "fairness" that an American would recognize. It is also true that European sports keeps mutating, as does its culture and its language. Nearly all the refs in the Champions League use English as their mode of communication. It used to be that international soccer was the highest expression of the game, and that the World Cup and European Championships were truly exceptional events in which distinctive cultures faced off against one another. The vast majority of players belonged to clubs in their own countries of birth, and only one club from each country got to play in the European Cup, the forerunner of the Champions League.

As a fan, you hardly ever got to see a player from another country, even within Europe. The downside of this was the building of fundamentally racist assumptions about cheating. Fans and media commentators from North European cultures often liked to denigrate teams from the South and other Latin countries for their perceived skullduggery and violence, for example. You still hear vestiges of these attitudes, but reality shows them to be inherently ridiculous. Everyone dives, everyone whines to referees, nearly every club side in European soccer consists of a league of nations. Every club is internationalist, or rather globalist, and, as such, they reflect the history of the European Union, and how it has moved away from the idea of the nation. It is fascinating to see the displays of nationalism in the NFL and MLB, and the recurring deference to the military; you might get that to a degree in international games in Europe but not in matches between clubs.

This also manifests anxieties about identity that go along with that. Lots of European national teams now feature players who have acquired eligibility through being immigrants; nearly everyone has a Brazilian on their club. That is the shape of our globalized reality; at its best, unity-in-difference is realized at the local level, and even the smallest club side has an inbuilt diversity. In this context, national conceptions of fair play must become contested or negotiable. I wonder how many nations or cultures present themselves as having invented fair play. Britain certainly does it; they talk about things "not being cricket" when they are apparently unfair. Yet it was an American, Grantland Rice, who said it was "how you played the game" that counted.

The Language of Sports

Rivera: Sports, while literally a game, lies within the philosophy of language as just one more cultural product among others, wholly conditioned by cultural cues and the many implicit social norms those involve. Sports, like a cultural institution, is derivative of a form of life. Wittgenstein famously observed that if "a lion could talk, we wouldn't be able to understand it." Of course we may well apprehend some of the words, terms, and syntax, but we would not have the cultural competence of "being a lion" or hermeneutical forestructures (or assumptions already in place that facilitating understanding readily a statement) of "lionhood" that would give us the aptitude to grasp the speech of a lion, at least not without endless interpretive labor.[4]

More broadly, we can say that baseball's form of life, that its framework within which agreement about what counts as an "out," a "home run," a "double," and so forth, also invokes a broader form of life we may call sports and sporting culture. No doubt this "sporting culture" grounds our ability to communicate, to inquire, and to argue about sports at all, including the boundaries of what counts as fair play, as in the example of the Astros cheating scandal.

Here, to reinforce the function of baseball's unique form of life, we imagine the following scenario. Try to watch baseball with someone who is not from a culture that loves baseball (baseball cultures are, for example, Venezuela, Japan, the Dominican Republic, and of course the United States). It remains, for myself, impossible to convince the person, say from Ireland, about the pleasures of playing and watching a baseball game. (The same would be true in trying to get an American to understand a cricket match.) They do not have sufficient mastery of its form of life, and only once that individual enters into the form of life can the phenomenon of baseball be understood and, maybe, enjoyed. They must, in other words, share my world of baseball in order to understand, not least enjoy, the game of baseball. Michael, you had to live in Japan to experience (or suffer) its wonders. One may extrapolate: only once one enters into American sports culture can one then, after time, grasp and thereby internalize the rules of fair play, which consist so often of implicit norms that can be made explicit only when they are violated!

Hinds: So even though I do love watching baseball, I am not really at home within it, or at home within its language. So I inevitably cannot grasp the full dimensions of what the Astros did. Yet it would be misery for you to have to watch a baseball game with me, because there would be a burden on you, the American, to be available to translate. For friendship's sake, better to leave me in my ignorance. Funnily enough, I would also venture that I enjoy feeling like an alien with regard to baseball, that is a happy enough form of self-definition for me. One mysterious thing I remember from Japan was the endless bunting; I wondered where it had gone whenever I started to watch baseball from America, which also became available on Japanese TV as the pitcher Hideo Nomo caught fire with the Dodgers. It really did seem like a different game in Japan. Then Ichiro came on the scene in Japan for the Yakult Swallows, and he seemed to blow apart the playbook of Japanese ball, which was extraordinarily boring and cautious at times (which does not mean it was uninteresting). Other teams could not cope. I think they were relieved to see him go to the United States.

More curiously, my wife told me how she was teaching an English class to some undergraduates at one of Tokyo's many private universities, an elite school for women with three specializations: international relations, Christianity, and horticulture. In class one day, she gave baseball as an example of a word that had come into Japanese from elsewhere, and the usually polite students objected in unusually stringent terms. They argued that Japanese had its own word and kanji for baseball, 野球 (pronounced *yakyu*, literally meaning fieldball); therefore, baseball was as Japanese as samurai and sushi. If baseball was an imported thing, they would have used katakana to phonetically re-create the word "baseball."[5] I wonder to what degree this is a positive matter of using a sport to assert Japaneseness, or rather a way of saying that baseball is not American (or not exclusively so). This was not a controversial idea to Japanese sports fans of my acquaintance, but it was to me, an ignorant Irishman who did not know any better about either the Japanese or the American conceptualizations of the game.

I grew up going to football matches in Northern Ireland in the 1970s, where away fans would sometimes come to your stadium and tear out seats and chuck them on the pitch. Japanese fans on away trips (especially if they are following the international team in soccer) famously tidied up after themselves, bringing brushes and bin bags with them to the game to collect garbage. This is not so much a mark of respect, necessarily; rather, it is a refusal to look bad in the eyes of the other. In European soccer, you actually want to look bad in the eyes of the other supporters, as bad as possible—without doing any lasting harm to anybody, of course.

This is a long way back to the Astros, but if I am being honest, the banging of the trash cans is the most vital part of that phenomenon for me, the flagrancy of their offense. In the early years of the Northern Irish Troubles, women from Catholic sections of cities like Belfast and Derry would bang their metal dustbin lids on the street to let locals know that British troops were beginning to search the area, effectively summoning youths out onto the street to resist them. To my trash can–hardened ears and eyes, the Astros were not only cheating but doing so riotously, effectively telling the opposition that they were doing it, and that there was nothing they could do about it. Was this the real problem, that they were announcing the brute reality of cheating as an intrinsic part of the sport? Were they hooligans, announcing a threat to baseball law and order by proving how easy it was to succeed by transgressing against it? Riotousness is public disorder, and even if fans were apparently unaware of their stratagems, banging the can was effectively making their transgression public.

Cheating: Normal or Riotous?

Rivera: I am uneasy with the term "riotous." Injecting steroids, corking bats, or even arguing with an umpire vigorously (or riotously) embody a set of practices proper to the definition of riotous. When it comes to the Astros' unique scandal of detecting signs and pitch selection, they were ingeniously nonriotous, in that the players carefully disguised it, right? If by "riotous" we intend to mean the sheer level of planning and overt inclinations to cheat on display, as if there is no question they were deliberatively and meticulously violating the rules of the game, then yes, it was riotous! The Irish may depict the Astros event, its form of life, as a "bold" speech act; a child in Dublin is "bold" when he is being naughty. The Astros assumed the status of naughty, not riotous, I would think.

Hinds: I will not say "in fairness," but they were definitely naughty, and they certainly sounded riotous. The funny thing to me is how what begins as a technologically sophisticated stratagem finds its ultimate expression with the banging of a bin. That is what seems so calculatedly egregious here, the gesture, not the cheating. The trash can was not only speaking to Astros batters but also to the opposition, a declaration of "Hey, we're cheating!" But isn't cheating actually a normal part of playing a game? Aren't the Astros' bins also saying, "Game On!"? I was reading Johan Huizinga's *Homo Ludens: A Study of the Play-Element in Culture*, and he points out that it is a spoil-sport rather than a cheat whom we most tend to deplore, the kid who takes the ball away altogether in a huff in adversity: "The spoil-sport is not the same as the false player, the cheat; for the latter pretends to be playing the game, and, on the face of it, still acknowledges the magic circle." The problem with the spoilsport is that he or she "robs play of its *illusion*," "threatening "the existence of the play community."[6]

Nobody would argue that the Astros brought the entire sport into jeopardy. Larger forces, if anything, will do that. So were the Astros spoilsports? You could definitely say that they robbed the game of its illusion, and noisily.

Rivera: Surely yes. Cheating inhabits the inner world of any sport or game. The Astros were manipulating the sport for an informational advantage. They did not deflate the ball (or juice the ball here) or cork the bats. Instead, the Astros stole information and then used it to their advantage, almost like reconnaissance in a wartime scenario, or how the Patriots would film the opposing team's practices.[7] Intel gathering about the style and tendencies of play of the opposition constitutes the heart of many sports, from basketball and soccer to football and baseball. Hence the import of film sessions and scouting.

Rules and implicit norms in sports are also boundaries against which the sport can rebel, and in this process, cause the sport to adjust those norms. For example, pitchers have used all kinds of tricks, many illegal (Vaseline or pine tar on the fingers), to harness their throwing skill. Eventually the mound was raised to fifteen inches above the field of play in order to help pitcher and batter attain equilibrium. The higher the mound, the better the pitcher: the high or steep angle (coming down from fifteen inches) generated so much momentum that the offense (that is, hitting home runs) came to a halt. Indeed, the mound would sometimes be secretly raised above fifteen inches, and the Dodgers in the 1960s were famous for building up the dirt mound to height above the legal limit, giving an even greater advantage to power pitching. Finally, the rule changed: in 1968, after so many offenses struggled to generate statistically compelling offense, the MLB lowered the height of the mound to ten inches above the field, where it stands today.[8]

What about bats? Differences in wood and density, in weight and length, each of those physical characteristics affect the play. Imagine if professionals could use metal bats! In college and Little League ball we use metal bats, and it takes little imagination to see how striking a baseball with a piece of metal could be dangerous to the health of the infielder!

Hinds: The alleged conduct of Tom Brady in Deflategate, in which team employees at the New England Patriots deliberately deflated footballs to the specifications he requested, seemed more spoilsportish to me than what the Astros did in a way, because it was an attempt to effect a result before a whistle blew. It also seemed very difficult to establish the actual advantage that was being achieved and seemed strangely petty. Then again, it also seemed petty to pursue Brady for it so rigorously. Since it was preemptive, it seemed sneakier than something occurring in the course of the game itself. It is obviously not a big deal, but it *appears* worse, because it is puncturing the illusion of the game as something where things could be taken for granted. Like the ball. Yet messing with bats and apparatus strike me as absolutely intrinsic to the game; people adapt to try to get a material edge over the others, and they will do that until someone tells them to stop. That is where the commissioner comes in, I suppose, and that is why he exists—to establish what is cheating and what is not.

In "Birches," Robert Frost wishes for a boy "too far from town to learn baseball."[9] This suggests that the potential for disrepute is there in baseball, and that to learn how to play the game is also to learn how to cheat at it. He seems to think of it as an inevitably corrupting activity, something that will bring about a fall from innocence. Frost wrote elsewhere that he never felt "more at home in America than at a ball game be it in park or in sandlot. Beyond this I know not. And dare not."[10] He attaches a curious and careful ambiguity to what primarily appears as folksiness, almost as if the game reveals something pleasurable and terrifying at the same time.

If there is an often-heroic strain in the literature of baseball, we also persistently come across the allegation that someone is fixing or trying to fix the game, whether the players or the umpires. Like in "Casey at the Bat". "'Fraud!' cried the maddened thousands, and echo answered fraud."[11] Games are legal systems; they need to exist only because illegality is potential. To heroize players is in fact a part of this overall logic; we have to generate heroes because there will always be cheats and cheating. Sometime this all takes place within the same individual. The greatest hero of Greek literature, Odysseus, is not the biggest guy, but the most clever and cunning: maybe that is how we should read Altuve.

The Laws of Baseball

Rivera: I concur with this assessment. True, baseball is exemplarily a legal system; however, the legal system of baseball could be restated better as a form of life.

Hinds: Sure, and the first- and third-base coaches almost look like lawyers for the batting team; there is something of the courtroom in all that side-of-the-hand whispering. Inside knowledge seems to be everything in baseball;

it is not just about the bat and the ball but also the transfer of information pertaining to the bat and ball. Code-keeping and code-breaking are an overt part of what we see. It is a unique game in this regard; it practically seems to ask for cheating, or at least to see cheating as an acceptable risk of the game, because the information you might glean is so potentially precious. Maybe this is what Frost means by "too far from town to learn baseball." Playing the game is one thing, but "learning" it takes you out of the domain of play and into strategy, cunning, and deception.

Rivera: Yes, it takes "inside knowledge" of baseball's implicit norms to understand that those hand gestures are communicating a specific strategy to the batter, namely, not to swing on 2–1 count, or to the base runner to steal second base on a 3–0 count, and so forth. The rules of the game are only properly understood once you get to know the game. So when a pitcher "hits" the batter, it is necessary that when the batter's team is pitching, that he retaliate and "hit back" one of their hitters. How would I know that retaliation is necessary? One would think such retaliation is illegal, and it is according to MLB rules, and the umpire has every right to eject the pitcher or the manager from the game. The retaliation is acceptable because it constitutes social "scorekeeping," and baseball teams hold each other accountable in these implicit kinds of ways.[12] Fans expect retaliation and understand it as part of the normal implicit or "unspoken" internal consistency of the baseball game as *this* form of life and not some other form of life. Baseball brawls (like hockey fights?) reflect, too, a necessary mode of holding teams accountable to fair play. If one baseball team is out of line, for whatever reason, the opposing team may charge the pitcher and literally attempt to fight him on the mound. The clearing of both benches ensues, and often, but not always, a full-scale brawl is born as spectacle to behold on the television. No one really gets hurt in the brawl, but the posturing of the spectacle, while illegal, is an implicit norm in baseball. So I would say violating some formal rules in favor of implicit rules constitutes a central part of any sport and especially baseball. Again, one may infer this as a way of "being a baseball player and fan" once one undergoes inauguration into its form of life.

Hinds: Baseball fights in Japan were interesting in this regard, organized skirmishes in which nobody should get hurt. My favorite player over there, a sullen pitcher named Balvino Galvez, hilariously failed to understand that this was the script. He would casually thump people, at least it looked casual, and their astonishment when he did so was palpable. It seemed as if nobody could figure out what his problem was. Whenever he played, there was real trepidation in the air, a sense that norms were going to be violated. I loved him, not least because he satisfied the idea that a palpable level of transgression is necessary to the experience and pleasure of sport. In some respects, it is what makes it most enjoyable and memorable. Apologies for using soccer as my reference point again, but Maradona's "Hand of God" goal in the 1986 World Cup is easily as memorable and great as anything else he did. The Astros did not spoil baseball, therefore; if anything, they made it newly interesting. Look at the pleasure fans took in booing them in the 2021 playoffs. Carlos Correa was a magnificent heel.

Cheating involves some of the grandest designs of sport, even on its most modest stage. In order to secure the cancellation of a forthcoming game, a lower league Irish soccer team pretended to league authorities that one of its players (incidentally, he was from Spain and had already moved to another team) had died. In reality, all of the players were going to a bachelor party.[13] Nobody died, so there should not be too much outrage, and nobody was ever sign-stolen to death either. Yet the Irish scandal was quickly forgotten, and the Astros remain under intense scrutiny. I do not know if decoding a series of hand gestures is worse than faking a death. Maybe American cheats are less forgivable simply because there is so much more invested (literally) in their games. Yet maybe nobody would have cared at all if the Astros had lost.

Ireland, Fiers, and Back to Altuve

Rivera: As an American living in Ireland, I chuckle to myself because it is true to a chief difference between American and Irish culture. Irish culture, much like their Mediterranean counterparts, enjoy a fluid sense of time, and with this comes a more relaxed interpretation of rules in general, rules about sporting events, drinking, eating, attending lectures at university, banking regulations, and so on. This anecdote about the Irish soccer team feigning the death of a teammate would probably never happen in American sports. Perhaps the players know that American media machine, famous for its journalistic scrutiny, would unveil the horrors of the truth and, in turn, mercilessly moralize the affair as shameful. Obviously the Irish public found out about the stunt, and yet, while it is memorable (you raise it here and still remember the event fondly), it is recalled as an event of humor and clever manipulation, for the sake of lads celebrating each other at a bachelor party.

Life is a party, of course, and the parties serve to function as a cathartic release for whole cultures. America could improve its party instinct. That is: I do think, while outdated, the distinctly Protestant work ethic of American capitalism (and German capitalism) proposed and defended by Max Weber more than a century ago, and critically updated by Kathryn Tanner in a recent set of Gifford lectures in Scotland, means that American sports culture makes winning the telos, the ultimate object, of sports. One can hear the tortured focus on winning a championship in most professional male athletes, for the competitive nature of a Michael Jordan, a Kobe Bryant, a Tiger Woods, or a Tom Brady is legendary. LeBron James is chasing championships as we speak, and he looks haggard for it. Yet, this haggard, if tireless, focus on winning is valued by the American public. Only those who sacrifice everything will be champions, and what nobler trait can one develop than being a champion? Who does not want to be a winner? Catholic culture, according to Weber (however outmoded his reasoning is), produces a more holistic approach to life, where winning is enjoyed but is not the bottom line or telos of one's vocation. It follows, therefore, that an Irish soccer team need not ensure that production (or winning) is maximized at all costs. One could say that the overly Protestant cultural norms (often implicit) could learn the joy of a broader definition of winning harbored in Catholic Ireland. Such a comparison remains pregnant with possibilities of cultural and historical analysis and offers little more than a suggestive framework for future considerations of fair play, sports, and a sense of vocation.[14]

Hinds: I don't know. We take some sport very seriously in Ireland, especially at the international level. That is a reflection of the smallness of the country, maybe, and the anxieties over prestige that come with it. Perhaps, if Ireland was more economically powerful, then it would care less about losing to England or France. As the Irish nation evolved out of British rule, the Gaelic Athletic Association invented sports in which they would not have to compete against other countries, hurling and Gaelic football. A smart move in terms of nation-building, perhaps. These are amateur games, but they are cutthroat and highly competitive. A faked death would be a massive scandal, as would drug use or any form of perceived illegality. Even if such things happened, you would more than likely never hear about it. Nobody would talk.

Which brings us to Mike Fiers, the pitcher who revealed the scheme to *The Athletic*. In some eyes, he might be viewed as the supreme spoilsport. He communicated an inconvenient truth, and many people would maybe rather he said nothing—including the commissioner. I am sure we could go on for hours about the peculiar status of whistleblowers in Western culture, and Fiers can be compared as a whistleblower (guardedly) to figures like Edward Snowden. But what was especially striking about Fiers was that he was not simply some kind of splenetic malcontent, operating out of resentment against a former team, but that he was highlighting how the Astros' cheating compounded other injustices that were generated by the peculiar labor market that is attached to pitching. This brought the case into a different sphere altogether and exploded the idea of team unity in such a culture. In the original piece in *The Athletic*, he made it transparently clear that this was a problem for the game as a structure, and not just the Astros:

> I just want the game to be cleaned up a little bit because there are guys who are losing their jobs because they're going in there not knowing. Young guys getting hit around in the first couple of innings starting a game, and then they get sent down. It's B.S. on that end. It's ruining jobs for younger guys. The guys who know are more prepared. But most people don't. That's why I told my team. We had a lot of young guys with Detroit (in 2018) trying to make a name and establish themselves. I wanted to help them out and say, "Hey, this stuff really does go on. Just be prepared."[15]

This is peculiarly consequential thinking and is a manifestation of the context of precarity within which so many people, especially young people, experience employment in the twenty-first century. The biggest reason to feel cheated in such a context is that you work as hard as the Protestant work ethic demands and end up with very little in return. Sports is a gig economy in extremis, where for every LeBron (although there is only one) there are thousands of expendable individual contractors who play ball and get relatively little in return. Europeans still have their social protections, and you can tolerate cheating when you have such a safety net. The most notorious transgressions center on match-fixing and on-field violence, but these are global and transhistorical issues. Occasionally there is a really egregious outrage, as when Spain won the Men's Intellectually Disabled Basketball Gold at the 2000 Sydney Paralympics, but many of their team had falsified their disabled credentials.[16] Yet that case seems so bad that it almost becomes pathetic. Imagine wanting a medal so badly that you would steal one from an intellectually disadvantaged person. But now you can not only imagine it, you can even see how it was done! The rules seem almost irrelevant.

The sport that most closely resembles baseball in its form, cricket, has its issues, such as ongoing cases of "ball-tampering" and "sledging" (verbal abuse of opponents), but cricket is not really a European game, rather a colonial one, played wherever the British Empire was most hegemonic. Like cricket, baseball has never caught on as a participation sport in Europe. Maybe we are not prepared to work (and cheat) hard enough? The Astros scandal would not play out in the same way in Europe, largely because the major sports there are not as susceptible to the kind of dynamic and real-time info cheating which happened on-field in Houston and on the road. As such, to European eyes, what happened there remains intriguing but fundamentally unfamiliar, nothing to get too worked up about.

For Americans, perhaps this scandal does not admit such a tolerance. The Astros are guilty of something simultaneously profound and meaningless. And whether he cheated or not, Altuve is still great, if just a little bit more mortal. Do we agree?

Notes

1. At the time of writing (April 2021), this issue dramatically intensified with the announcement by many elite football clubs in Europe that they wanted to form a breakaway league, without promotion and relegation. Many of the English teams involved (Arsenal, Liverpool, Manchester United) were owned by American interests.

2. For example, on fairness see the classic work of Rawls, *A Theory of Justice*, rev. ed. (Cambridge, MA: Harvard University Press, 1999), chapter 1; also Rawls, *Political Liberalism* (New York: Columbia University Press, 1993), lecture V.

3. Stuart James, "World Cup 2022: 'Political Craziness' Favours Qatar's Winning Bid," *The Guardian*, December 10, 2010, https://www.theguardian.com/football/2010/dec/02/world-cup-2022-qatar-winning-bid.

4. For more on the conception of form of life and language game, see Wittgenstein, *Philosophical Investigations*, trans. G. E. M. Anscombe, P. M. S. Hacker, and Joachim Schulte, 4th ed. (Malden, MA: Wiley-Blackwell, 2009), §23.

5. Thanks to Michael Parke for his clarifications over these language issues.

6. Johan Huizinga, *Homo Ludens: A Study of the Play-Element in Culture* (1938; repr., Brooklyn: Angelico Press, 2016), 11.

7. Dan Bernstein, "Spygate Revisited," *Sporting News*, April 2, 2019, https://www.sportingnews.com/us/nfl/news/spygate-revisited-how-patriots-scandal-false-rams-connections-impact-legacies/ypdo4i8h1uov1xbp9u38mxhho.

8. "Pitcher's Mound," *Baseball Reference*, https://www.baseball reference.com/bullpen/pitcher%27s_mound#.

9. Robert Frost, "Birches," in *Collected Poems, Prose, and Plays* (New York: Library of America, 1995), 117.

10. Robert Frost, "Perfect Day-A Day of Prowess" in *Baseball: A Literary Anthology* (New York: Library of America, 2002), 263.

11. Ernest Louis Thayer, "Casey at the Bat," in *Baseball: A Literary Anthology*, 13–15.

12. Robert Brandom, *Making It Explicit: Reasoning, Representing, and Discursive Commitment* (Cambridge, MA: Harvard University Press, 1994), 180–198.

13. Emmet Malone, "Dublin Soccer Club Fake Player's Death to Get Match Called Off," *Irish Times*, November 17, 2018, https://www.irishtimes.com/sport/soccer/dublin-soccer-club-fake-player-s-death-to-get-match-called-off-1.3712590.

14. Max Weber, *The Protestant Ethic and the Spirit of Capitalism*, trans. Talcott Parsons (New York: Routledge, 2001). For a modern reformulation of Weber and

thus for a testament to the enduring significance of Weber's work, see Kathryn Tanner, *Christianity and the New Spirit of Capitalism* (New Haven, CT: Yale University Press, 2019).

15. Ken Rosenthal and Evan Drellich, "The Astros Stole Signs Electronically in 2017—Part of a Much Broader Issue for Major League Baseball," *The Athletic*, https:// theathletic.com/1363451/2019/11/12/the-astros-stole-signs-electronically-in-2017 -part-of-a-much-broader-issue-for-major-league-baseball/.

16. Michael Pavitt, "Official Sanctioned Over Sydney 2000 Paralympics Scandal Denies Knowledge of Cheating," insidethegames.biz, September 21, 2021, https:// www.insidethegames.biz/articles/1113226/sydney-2000-paralympics-scandal-boss#.

PART IV

THE SCANDAL AND
ITS ETHICAL DILEMMAS

Houston Astros starting pitcher Mike Fiers delivers during the first inning of the team's game against the New York Mets, Sunday, September 3, 2017, in Houston. Fiers, later a pitcher with the Oakland A's, told *The Athletic* about the Astros' cheating scandal. (AP Photo/ Eric Christian Smith)

CHAPTER 11

Baseball Has No Love for Truth Tellers

MITCHELL NATHANSON

Before her lame sorry, not sorry in the immediate aftermath of the revela-tion, Jessica Mendoza expressed loud and clear what pretty much everybody in baseball was saying under their breath about Mike Fiers, the former Astro who spilled the beans on his old organization to *The Athletic* in November 2019: that irrespective of the truth of his allegation, it was the act of speaking out, of exposing the truth, that was the real sin. For baseball has no love for truth-tellers. They're rats, turncoats, lowlifes, for violating the *omertà* of the clubhouse. If baseball has a problem—and yes, of course it does—it's not so much this sign-stealing incident, which will percolate through the next few months and then go the way of the steroid crisis. Instead, it's the persistent belief that there is something sacred about a Major League clubhouse. That misguided assumption has been dragging baseball down for decades and shows no sign of letting up.

As she highlighted repeatedly during her tour of the ESPN glue factory yes-terday morning, she'd been in clubhouses as a player; she'd been a teammate. Therefore, she knew that—above anything and everything else—one team-mate should never "rat out" another. No matter what. No matter that these teammates were making a mockery of the idea of competition, of sportsman-ship, of all those things we tell ourselves are important as we plunk down the hundreds of dollars it costs to sit in the stands nowadays to watch what we blindly assume to be a fair fight. No, it's more important to protect the guilty. Why? Because of the perceived sanctity of the clubhouse.

If this makes no sense to you, congratulations, consider yourself a mem-ber of the human race. If it does, it's probably because you're a professional ballplayer and have been acculturated to believe that down is up, that wrong is right. You also kept your mouth shut as your teammates grew to cartoon-ish proportions a generation ago. You might not like Barry Bonds but the real villain in your eyes is José Canseco, who not only did what Bonds did but had the temerity to write a book about it. In other words, you're screwed up.

Baseball has always made a practice of punishing its truth tellers, even if the truths they're telling are relatively benign. In 1960 a relief pitcher named Jim Brosnan published a charming book called *The Long Season*. It let fans into the cloistered world of the baseball clubhouse just a little. And Brosnan paid for it with his career.

Brosnan's book showed fans what the game looked like from the inside: the personal struggles, the doubts, the pettiness of management, and the quirks of his teammates. After reading it fans understood a little more about what it was like to spend an entire game in the bullpen, attend a meeting with a pitching coach, and take a road trip to Chicago. People loved it, with one reviewer calling it "probably the best look ever at baseball as seen through a mature mind." No matter, other players soon began looking at Brosnan with suspicion, particularly after he released his follow-up, *Pennant Race*, the next year. At that point even management began to give Brosnan the stink eye. With two books, popularly referred to as "tell-alls" (even though they were far from it), Brosnan had made himself a marked man. He'd better be a top-level performer on the field if he wanted to stay in baseball after that. He wasn't, and he was out of the game by the end of the '63 season.

In 1970 Jim Bouton published *Ball Four*. It revealed a bit more of the locker room than Brosnan's books did. Accordingly, the blowback he received from the game's insiders was both swifter and harsher. Bouton wrote about pill-popping teammates, skirt-chasers, and worst of all, a drunken Mickey Mantle. It was an instant sensation, spending seventeen weeks on the *New York Times* bestseller list, ultimately selling more than five million copies. Fans loved it; critics loved it. Baseball hated it. Upon its release one critic saw the writing on the wall. *Ball Four*, he wrote, was "a wry, understated, honest and memorable piece of Americana, by a good man they will clobber because of it." And clobber him they did.

"Fuck you, Shakespeare," Pete Rose yelled at Bouton when he took the mound the day after an excerpt of his book was published in *Look* magazine. As Bouton liked to say later, once the book came out, he was "persona non grata in big league clubhouses, emphasis on the non grata." He was out of baseball within two months.

Mike Fiers walks in the imprints of these footsteps. Of players who were shunned by those on the inside not for telling lies but for telling too much of the truth. Unlike the ones told by Brosnan and Bouton, the truths Fiers told were hardly benign, as were those told by Canseco. They impact the game on the field in significant ways. The legitimacy of the 2017 and '18 World Series has been shattered because of them.

If history is any guide, while "Astrogate" might be bad for baseball, it promises to be much, much worse for Mike Fiers. He'll be thirty-five years old next season; his best years are probably behind him. He was a solid pitcher for the A's in 2019, but not that solid. Which means that just like those who came before him, in the insular world of baseball, he's toast.

This article originally appeared in Sports Talk Philly, January 17, 2020.

CHAPTER 12

Bad Apples or Bad Astros?
Collective Responsibility and
the Perils of Team Loyalty

ERIN C. TARVER

The Astros' sign stealing was a scandal of greater significance than most in sports because it was both deliberate and collaborative, individual and institutional. These features ironically made it both more shocking than other instances of cheating and more difficult to sanction. The dominant ideology of moral failing and punishment in the United States is highly individualized: moral violations are almost definitionally, for Americans, the actions of specific individual "bad apples," and justice demands penalty for these individuals. Faced with a situation in which an entire team collaborated to subvert explicit league regulations, Major League Baseball responded with sanctions that seemed at once too harsh and too lenient: managers who may or may not have known about the cheating were suspended and ultimately lost their jobs, while the team was allowed to keep the World Series title it won while breaking the rules, and the players escaped any sanction at all.

Beyond concerns about the justness of Major League Baseball's actions, however, the Astros scandal is worth our attention—not merely because it was a cheating scandal nearly without equal in modern sport, but more important because of what it reveals about moral and political life in the United States. Here I analyze both MLB's and fans' responses to the scandal and argue that each exposes key problems in contemporary moral frameworks for understanding and addressing wrongdoing by groups, particularly those with which we identify. The Astros scandal illustrates the need for better moral resources to understand and respond to collective wrongs, as well as the moral dangers that follow loyalty to and identification with groups like teams. Many fans' loyalty to the Astros, after all, led them not only to resent the judgment of the Astros' collective responsibility for cheating but to alter their moral outlook in ways that preserved both their judgment of the Astros' fundamental goodness and their own self-image. When we consider the deep resonances between team loyalty and political loyalty in the contemporary United States, it is all the more urgent to take seriously the dangers of such moral shifts.

The Uniqueness of the Astros Scandal
and the Challenge of Adequate Response

Cheating is not new in sports or in broader American life. The expectation of rule breaking is a central feature of any system that seeks to deter it by the imposition of penalties. Major League Baseball, for example, eventually implemented a complex system of testing and penalties for players who were found to have used banned substances after the steroid investigations of 2003 revealed that the rules against their use had been largely ignored.[1] Indeed, as Astros fans were quick to point out, the trash can scandal was hardly MLB's first instance of widespread cheating, and as scholars of baseball's history have noted, various forms of cheating are arguably part of "the fabric of the game."[2] What, then, made the Astros' cheating so offensive to baseball fans and players, and at the same time so difficult for the league to punish? We will understand this more fully if we recognize what made the scandal unique and how it diverged from typical patterns of intentional rule breaking. Its uniqueness, I will argue, has less to do with intentional rule breaking as such and more to do with the collective nature of the rule breaking and the complex causal web in which it existed.

As philosophers of sport have argued, what makes a particular instance of rule breaking "cheating" rather than, say, "gamesmanship" or merely conduct subject to in-game penalties is a rather difficult question to answer.[3] I will not attempt to articulate a theory of cheating here, but virtually all instances of rule breaking that are (1) deliberate, (2) concealed, and (3) undertaken for the purpose of competitive advantage are generally acknowledged as cheating, even if cheating need not necessarily involve all three of these characteristics. More important for the purposes of this essay, however, it is worth noting that the regulatory bodies that govern sport have established methods to sanction such violations—provided that they are undertaken by individual agents or have clearly identifiable outcomes. When individual players are found to have violated the banned substances policy, for example, there are clear sanctions imposed on those players, including suspension. This is true even if the specific effect of their cheating is unclear.

The provision of such penalties, even in cases when we cannot be certain of the precise effect that rule breaking has on the game, is worth considering for a moment, since penalties in sport are often thought of as mechanisms to correct wrongs. For example, when Sammy Sosa's RBI in a 2003 game against the Tampa Bay Devil Rays was found to have been achieved with a corked bat, the run was disallowed, the base runner sent back to third base, and Sosa was out, in addition to being ejected from the game.[4] This penalty and others like it that reverse particular outcomes on the basis of their having been achieved via prohibited means have the goal of ensuring that athletes and teams get what they rightly deserve—namely, what they earn within the scope of the agreed-upon rules—and nothing more.

Achieving this goal is more difficult when the effect of a violation is more complicated than a single RBI. This complexity was tacitly cited by MLB commissioner Rob Manfred as a reason not to strip the Astros of their World Series title even after the trash can scheme was discovered: How could anyone know what would have happened in the absence of the illegal sign-stealing scheme? Yet, the causal complexity of this question is hardly sufficient to render punishment impossible. Indeed, it is more often than not the case that we cannot know the precise advantage conferred by an instance of cheating. Given the complex causal interaction of player training, skill, and the performance of opponents (among other things) that contribute to any one game's outcome, determining what would have happened if the cheating had not occurred is usually an exercise in futility. Accordingly, the type of penalty imposed on cheaters in such cases necessarily differs from the type of penalty imposed on Sosa and the Cubs: they are aimed at affecting a team's future prospects rather than past achievements. Such punishments are forward-looking in the sense that they function to deter future rule breaking, rather than to right the wrongs of past rule breaking.[5] Such forward-looking penalties may not in fact satisfy those players or fans who feel that they have been wronged by the rule breaking, of course. But they exist as widely accepted mechanisms for punishing and deterring rule breaking when corrective action is not possible.

The bodies that govern sport are less adept at responding to rule breaking engaged in collaboratively by the members of a team. There are obviously provisions for collaborative rule breaking when it can be isolated within a specific game—as, for example, when teams are penalized for using illegal formations in football, or when regulations like the infield fly rule are instituted to prevent infielders from working together to turn an intentionally dropped ball into a double play. But a system of collaborative rule breaking that spans much of a season and which involves active participation by the majority of a team is not the sort of cheating that contemporary sport is well equipped to handle.

The nearest analogues to the Astros scandal arguably occurred in the NFL: the Patriots' "Spygate" and "Deflategate" scandals, each of which involved deliberate, apparently coordinated rule breaking by multiple members of the organization. Spygate similarly involved the use of video to steal hand signals, this time of coaches on the opposing sideline. Yet, the Patriots did not seem to use the information gained from their illicit filming during game play; moreover, the collaboration involved members of the coaching staff rather than members of the team itself. And given the swiftness with which the Patriots' illegal taping was discovered and stopped, it was unclear that the scheme had much effect on games at all. The Deflategate scandal, in which the Patriots were found to have slightly underinflated the balls they played with on offense, thus making them easier to grip, did involve active, in-game participation by players. However, it was unclear that this participation went beyond Tom Brady, the quarterback—and even Brady's intentional participation remains in doubt in some quarters, given his consistent denials that such a scheme existed.[6] In both of these cases, the ultimate punishments reflected the NFL's judgment that it had identified the specific individuals responsible for rule breaking, even as the team as a whole might have benefited from it: they included, in other words, penalties directed both at the individuals judged responsible (Belichick and Brady) as well as the franchise as a whole. Whether because the rule breaking involved identifiable individuals who were visibly punished (as in Deflategate) or because its effects were negligible (as in Spygate), neither of these cases elicited the same level of indignation or prompted the same challenge for punishment as did the Astros' trash can–based sign-stealing scheme.

MLB's Response, Collective Wrongs, and the Ideology of "Bad Apples"

MLB is hardly alone in lacking the resources to respond adequately to wrongs done by groups. Indeed, mainstream US moral discourse tends to presume that wrongs (legal or moral) are definitionally the responsibility of individual moral agents with nefarious motives. Despite efforts by advocates of racial justice to address systemic differentials in the treatment of black and white citizens by police departments across the country, for example, regular high-profile killings of black people by white officers are routinely portrayed as the actions of individual "bad apples." According to such discourse, racial bias is conceptualized—if it is admitted to exist at all—as a problem in the hearts and minds of specific individual racists. The problems of the league's response to the Astros scandal reflects a larger shortcoming in broader American moral discourse: in general, we lack adequate resources to conceptualize or respond to wrongs done by groups.

On the rare occasions when we are forced to acknowledge that a collective acted wrongly—the paradigmatic case being corporate malfeasance—we have quite limited means of responding. Notwithstanding the US Supreme Court's *Citizens United* decision, because corporations are not literal human persons who could be subject to the full range of penalties to which individual offenders are vulnerable, monetary fines are the primary means by which they are punished for wrongdoing. Corporations that, for example, pollute a public waterway may be required to pay fines to the government under whose jurisdiction the waterway falls. Sometimes such fines may be paid as a form of financial restitution to specific individuals or groups particularly harmed by the corporation's action.

Despite their ubiquity, the usage of fines as the principal means of addressing collective wrongdoing is both ethically fraught and frequently unsatisfying. First, conceiving fines as restitution for wrongs done often requires the dubious (or in some cases, morally repugnant) task of financially quantifying the damage done by the wrongdoing. It is difficult to know where to begin to quantify, say, the harm suffered by a community whose water is filled with carcinogens. If, alternatively, we conceive the fine as a deterrent to future such action, the unequal financial context of such penalties makes them more challenging than it might appear to have the desired effect. The reason for this is that, as political philosophers Johannes Himmelreich and Holly Lawford-Smith note, the "punishment effects" of such fines are likely to be "disproportionately distributed" within the group being punished.[7] For example, if a major corporation is fined millions of dollars for corporate malfeasance, higher-ranking employees and shareholders may lose some value in their stock prices or in their previously substantial salaries, but lower-ranking employees may be laid off entirely or have cuts to their salary that are more likely to result in their suffering. Regardless of the structure of staff layoffs or pay cuts, however, it is quite likely that any negative effects of corporate fines will disproportionately harm those least well paid. The fact that such employees' status at the lower end of the corporate hierarchy also compromises their abilities to refuse to participate in collective wrongdoing exacerbates the ethical concerns that fines thus raise as a means of corporate punishment.

Of course, one might argue, as Himmelreich and Lawford-Smith do, that the injustice of such a disproportionate distribution of punishment effects is a separate question from whether the punishment is justified.[8] Indeed, one might well argue that the responsibility for such unjust distributions falls to the collective being punished (which typically has control over the distribution of such effects in ways that the legal system does not), and not of those doing the punishing. While this might be true, it hardly addresses the larger concern of whether our typical modes of responding to wrongs are up to the task of confronting collective wrongdoing. If our most frequently used method of addressing such wrongdoing is so easily manipulated to ensure that only comparatively disempowered members of collectives suffer consequences for wrongs done by the group, this speaks to the need for better or different responses.

Now, one might respond that we can circumvent this problem by targeting penalties at the top of the corporate ladder—as happens when specific executives are charged with wrongdoing committed "on their watch." In fact, this often seems the appropriate response, particularly for hierarchically organized groups where the wrong action is entirely directed from above. But we should notice two things about this strategy: first, it concedes entirely the possibility of responding to collective wrongs, reconceiving the wrong it punishes as the action of specific individuals, whether they be "bad apples," scapegoats, or nefarious masterminds. Second, such a response will be inadequate if and when we are confronted with cases of genuinely collective responsibility for harm—a possibility, we should note, that exists even in some cases of hierarchically organized groups.

The Astros scandal, in fact, offers a particularly striking illustration of the inadequacy of this strategy. A baseball team is certainly a hierarchically organized group: players report to managers, who report to general managers, who report to the owner. Key terms of players' employment as well as their day-to-day activities are organized and regulated by those who operate above them in the hierarchy. Accordingly, MLB's targeting of punishment to the Astros manager and general manager reflected the judgment that their positions (nearly) atop the Astros hierarchy made them uniquely responsible for the team's activities. Yet, it is hardly clear that the hierarchical structure of the team ought to entail that players bear no responsibility for the actions in which they collaboratively participated, or even that they bore less responsibility than those to whom they reported. Indeed, given the unique status of professional baseball players as compared with typical employees of a hierarchically organized corporate workplace (their fame commands much more significant market power, for example, and the strength of the players' union offers them protections unheard of for most workers), it is arguable that any mitigation of responsibility that might typically accompany lower status in a hierarchical group should be effectively canceled out in this case.

A professional baseball team is obviously a unique sort of collective, but it does offer an important example of the moral limitations of punishing group wrongs by targeting specific individuals within that group. Even in hierarchical groups where there is an identifiable leader, unless that leader exerts fairly extreme levels of control over the group's actions (in which case it is arguably a case of individual rather than collective wrongdoing), this strategy of response will quite simply fail to address the collective wrongdoing.

Beyond fines and individually targeted penalties, the remaining strategies for responding to collective wrongdoing are aimed at preventing the group from continuing to operate *as* a group. A corporation in violation of criminal statutes or antitrust law may have its license to operate suspended (as occurred with the accounting firm Arthur Andersen in 2002 when it was convicted for destroying documents related to Enron's illegal accounting practices) or be broken up (as Standard Oil was in 1911 for violating the Sherman Act). In the corporate world, penalties like these often function as an effective death sentence for the corporation: their effect is to prevent the collective from engaging in further wrongdoing by compromising or eliminating the collective to act *as* a collective at all.

Although these last strategies have the virtue of clearly targeting the collective as such and are arguably the best option in the most egregious cases of corporate malfeasance, the scope of their viability is quite limited. Given their serious (and often irrevocable) consequences, they seem inappropriate as a response to less egregious instances of collective wrongdoing. Moreover, in some cases (like that of a police force or other government agency), breaking up or eliminating the collective is impossible or undesirable because its larger functions are still thought to be necessary. Finally, we might question whether such punishments are truly effective in deterring future wrongdoing—again, the primary purpose of most collective punishments—if the individuals who make them up are permitted to reconstitute new collectives later (as in fact occurred in the case of Standard Oil).

The lack of a satisfactory response by MLB to the Astros scandal, then, was hardly unique to baseball. The league's response—which seemed to scapegoat individual managers while leaving the team unscathed, and which could muster only a forward-looking fine for the institution itself, leaving its ill-gotten gains intact—was largely aligned with broader US approaches to punishing collective wrongdoing. Conceptualizing moral or criminal violations as the province of individual bad actors and restricting our understanding of collective wrongdoing and punishment to the domain of corporate capitalism have left us without adequate moral resources to respond when groups commit wrongs for which specific individuals cannot be blamed or whose harms cannot be enumerated on a balance sheet.

Fan Response and the Perils of Team Loyalty

The response of many Astros fans to the scandal was revealing and disturbing in a second way. Faced with the condemnation of their team by the league, by players from opposing teams, and by other fans (who most frequently described them as "cheaters"), many Astros fans reacted with a seemingly contradictory mixture of remorse, minimization, defensiveness, and defiance. Some seemed willing or even eager to revise their moral outlook in order to maintain their positive view of the team. These responses, I argue, reveal both a lack of ethical resources regarding how to react to wrongdoing on the part of collectives to which we are loyal, and (by extension) the social and moral dangers that accompany such loyalty. Highly identified fans predictably felt criticism of the Astros as an unwarranted attack to be defended against—especially against those who claimed the scandal tainted the World Series victory—even when they wanted to admit disappointment, shame, or acknowledgment of the club's violations.

Before turning to specific examples, it is worth noting that Astros fans' reactions to the scandal were largely consistent with the types of reactions that social scientific research on fan behavior might predict. Specifically, social scientists who study highly identified fans have found that such fans experience negative outcomes for their teams—whether via shocking defeats or off-the-field setbacks—as personal attacks.[9] Such negative experiences, which are referred to in the fan literature as "identity threat," prompt a range of responses from fans as they attempt to cope with the negative emotions involved. Because fans are typically not in a position to alter the facts of their team's situation, these coping strategies often involve deliberate attempts to "alter their perception of the stressor." To do so, fans employ a range of strategies, including "distancing oneself from the team, forming biased perceptions of the issue, or being optimistic about future performances."[10] Fans also engage in "derogating outgroup members," focusing their negative emotions on rivals in a way that allows them to maintain—and perhaps even increase—positive associations with their own team.[11] The revelation that their team was engaged in a collective cheating scandal that would be punished by MLB certainly constituted a case of identity threat, and Astros fans responded accordingly.

Although a minority of Astros fans expressed such extreme disappointment in and disapproval of the team that they effectively withdrew their identification as fans,[12] the majority of fan responses chronicled by media outlets and observable in online discussion reflected the challenge of maintaining team loyalty while disapproving of the team's collective actions. In many cases, fans' navigation of that challenge seemed to involve, as one analyst put it, "cognitive dissonance," with fans and local Houston commentators "vacillating between 'see, they apologized!' and 'they have no reason to apologize because everyone else was cheating and no one else is talking about that, are they?!'"[13]

Indeed, it is striking how frequently in highly identified fans' responses that acknowledgment of the Astros' wrongdoing was followed by a rhetorical pivot to minimization, hostility to rivals, or the reassertion of loyalty to the team. What follows is a representative sample of such responses by fans who were interviewed by various media outlets:

They shouldn't have done it but there was no rule against it, it wasn't a law.[14]

I'm a die-hard Astros fan. I'm sorry that this has happened, I feel that it does taint, you know, the 2017 World Series just a little bit . . . but the bottom line is I think that starting in grade school most people at some level cheat, whether it's kids cheating on the test at school, or people cheating on their income tax, or people driving down the highway and breaking the speed limit, it's human nature to cheat a little. I'm not in support of it and I wish they wouldn't have done it, but I will continue to support the Astros and I believe that their hometown is going to support them through this.[15]

When the report finally came out and I read it, it was like your uncle bought you every Christmas present you ever wanted and then a year later you find out they were all stolen. But with all of the pile on and pile on that's been coming about things that there is no evidence or proof of, it's all speculation, and now I feel like all I'm doing is defending the team every time I turn around.[16]

This team obviously did something that they should not have done, but we know the players, we have seen all the good that they do for the community, and we will not let this define them. We will support them.[17]

Other fans resolved the "cognitive dissonance" by refusing negative judgments of the team entirely. Most fans accomplished this by repeating the assertion that all teams cheat, and suggesting that the real outrage was the Astros' being singled out for punishment. In a taped interview at Astros spring training, a woman named Jan, wearing earrings in the shape of Alex Bregman's face, typified this strategy: "We didn't do anything anyone else didn't do," she argued. "We just got caught. Simple as that." A woman interviewed at the Astros Fan Fest in Houston told the local reporter, "I think they've suffered enough, with the penalties and losing coaches. I think that's enough. I think it was more than enough. I think we're being made an example out of."[18] Another fan named Catherine told the *Houston Chronicle*, "I don't think the Astros were the only team doing it,"[19] and then expressed hope that equal punishment would befall the other teams also engaged in illegal sign stealing.

Still other fans engaged in the rhetorical strategy sometimes called "whataboutism," in which criticisms are deflected by the assertion that others are engaged in comparably bad or worse activities. In a video shot at spring training, Astros fan Jan and a friend named Donna recounted stories of being subject to harassment in local restaurants for wearing their Astros jerseys, suggesting that they were wrongly victimized by rival fans.[20] Separately, a fan named Amanda cited death threats against Astros players as the development that most affected her feelings about the scandal, juxtaposing her horror at such a response with the comparatively insignificant violation that precipitated it: "yeah, we know the facts: they cheated, they did. And they've admitted to it so OK, let's play baseball." While acknowledging that she was not herself the target of such vitriol by rival fans, Amanda seems to experience it as an attack. "It becomes, I don't want to say personal," she explains, without choosing an alternative word to describe it.[21] Engaging in a similarly vicarious experience of outrage was Kelly, the fan who previously opined on humans' natural propensity to cheat, who ended her remarks by speculating that in the coming season, pitchers from opposing teams would throw at Astros players in retaliation, a scenario she was concerned to condemn in advance of its occurrence.[22]

Online, many fans employed a similar strategy when discussing Mike Fiers, the former Astros pitcher who first confirmed the trash can scheme to *The Athletic*. Fiers was "a rat," whose reputation, they speculated, would be ruined by his failure to "keep that shit in the locker room." Multiple fans suggested that Fiers was in fact a hypocrite for accepting the World Series ring he won with the team in 2017, or that he was dishonorable for waiting to speak up about the scheme while it was happening, or for giving further interviews on the subject after the story broke.

The final strategy adopted by Astros fans was the most extreme in its defiance: some fans embraced the team's newfound reputation as cheaters, choosing to "alter their perception" of the situation by reframing the anger of rival fans and players as a badge of honor. A fan named Butch at Astros spring training recounted with a smirk the experience of being approached by a fan of a rival team who noticed his Astros hat: "He asked me what my opinion was—where do I stand on the issue? And I said, 'well I was the guy banging on the trash can!'"[23] We can get a sense of the prevalence of a view like Butch's in the widespread sale of Astros T-shirts featuring slogans with similarly unapologetic sentiments. The *Houston Chronicle* published two separate articles months apart in 2020 about the surge in sales of T-shirts designed to mock "haters." The first article, in February, featured a shirt that read simply, "Hate Us," with the Astros' H-star logo standing in for the first letter of "hate." The shirt, which debuted in February, the first week of 2020 spring training—only a month after MLB's official report—was sold out in a matter of hours.[24]

Seven months later, the *Chronicle*'s subsequent T-shirt collection (in an online feature titled "Silence the haters with these in-your-face Astros shirts") included a more extensive set of trolling slogans. All set in the backdrop of the Astros' orange and navy team colors, these included "Haters Gonna Hate," "Houston vs. All Y'all," "Kiss My Astros," and the newly re-stocked "Hate Us" shirts. Alongside these, a new offering made the connection between Astros fandom-as-trolling and the political ethos of the Republican Party under Donald Trump: a shirt reading "Bregman/Altuve '20: Making Houston Great Again."[25] The design and typeface of the shirt's slogan celebrated two of the Astros' most visible star players by visually echoing shirts from the 1984 Reagan presidential campaign, which read "Reagan/Bush '84." Reagan/Bush shirts have recently experienced a revival, with reprints sold as "vintage" T-shirts in stores with conservative clientele, particularly in the South.[26] The addition of the "Making Houston Great Again" slogan offers a deliberate homage to the Trump campaign's ubiquitous "Make American Great Again" refrain, drawing a clear line between conservatism in the Trump mold and unapologetic Astros fandom. In each case, the swaggering bravado and the fixation on "haters" purport to show an unconcern with others' disapproval, but ironically they stake their identity on the reactions of others.

The strategies Astros fans employed to cope with identity threat illustrate a second major problem faced by contemporary Americans confronting collective wrongdoings: the difficulty that arises when we attempt to make sense of wrongs done by collectives to which we are loyal or with which we identify. This is no small matter, and its consequences extend far beyond the context of sports. For a great many people, indeed, loyalty to some group, party, team, or religion is paramount in their lives. As the Bregman/Altuve '20 shirt suggests, such identifications may be felt just as strongly in politics as they are in sports—and in both cases, the identifications predictably result in fans' feeling criticism or sanction of their side as a threat to be defended against rather than new information to be processed. Accordingly, many such fans would rather reframe their perception of the moral issues involved rather than accept a reality in which "their" collective does not confer an entirely positive self-image. The danger of this strategy is obvious: if "we" are good, then whatever "we" do is, by definition, right—and the possibility of legitimate critique is conveniently eliminated.

At the same time, as we have seen, these same Americans remain broadly committed to an individualized system of moral judgment that cannot speak to wrongdoing by collectives at all. Faced with this situation, fans are left with few choices: they can blame specific members of the team as "bad apples" to be scapegoated and withdraw their identification only from those individuals; they can alter their perception of the issue by minimizing it, blaming others, or attacking rivals; they can reframe their moral judgments by embracing the behavior wholesale and adopting the troll persona; or they can withdraw or temper their identification with the team as such. As we have seen, fans engaged in each of these strategies, and some seemed to vacillate between more than one, resulting in cognitive dissonance and the appearance of genuine moral struggle. The trouble, of course, is that none of these strategies seem fully adequate to the task of responding morally to wrongdoing by collectives of which we are a part. Each strategy evades either the wrongdoing *or* the collective identification.

When the collective wrongdoing is that of a baseball team, this state of affairs may not be great cause for concern. It provides fodder for sports pundits and motivation for future ticket sales. But as we have seen, the issue goes far deeper than sports. When we lack the resources to conceptualize how groups might do wrong, we lack the ability to achieve (or even seek) justice. When this lack is coupled with a strong sense of collective identification, its consequences can be morally devastating as group members take wild steps to preserve the group's positive self-image—from fixating on the supposed wrongs of their enemies to reconceiving which behaviors are worthy of praise or blame. The consequences of such moral shifts in domains like politics and sports may be perilous indeed. The Astros case, in sum, shows why it is so crucial that we begin to develop a robust sense of collective action and collective responsibility—and helps explain why much contemporary moral and political discourse about groups, wrongs, and justice is so unsatisfying.

Notes

1. Associated Press, "A Timeline of MLB's Drug-Testing Rules," *USA Today*, March 28, 2014, https://www.usatoday.com/story/sports/mlb/2014/03/28/a-timeline-of-mlbs-drug-testing-rules/7024351/.

2. David Luban and Daniel Luban, "Cheating in Baseball," in *The Cambridge Companion to Baseball*, ed. Leonard Cassuto (Cambridge: Cambridge University Press, 2011), 186; "Houston Astros' Fans React to the Cheating Scandal," *Palm Beach Post*, February 19, 2020, YouTube video, https://www.youtube.com/watch?v=HiRUINA5Flk.

3. Philosopher of sport J. S. Russell argues that there is no normatively distinct concept of cheating. See Russell, "Is There a Normatively Distinct Concept of Cheating in Sport (Or Anywhere Else?)," *Journal of the Philosophy of Sport* 41, no. 3 (2014): 303–323. Others are less skeptical about the possibility of distinguishing cheating from other forms of rule breaking but recognize the difficulty of the question. See, for example, Leslie Howe, "Gamesmanship," *Journal of the Philosophy of Sport* 31 (2004): 212–25; and Robert Simon et al., "Ethics in Competition: Cheating, Good Sports, and Tainted Victories," in *Fair Play* (New York: Routledge, 2015), 59–80.

4. Damon Hack, "Baseball: Sosa Ejected for Using Corked Bat in a Game," *New York Times*, June 4, 2003, https://www.nytimes.com/2003/06/04/sports/baseball-sosa-ejected-for-using-corked-bat-in-a-game.html.

5. A significant exception to this forward-looking approach to rule breaking with difficult-to-determine effects exists in NCAA athletics, where backward-looking penalties are more common. The NCAA has, in several cases, "vacated" the wins of institutions found to have engaged in some significant rule breaking—though, puzzlingly, this does not have the concomitant effect of reversing the losses in the records of such teams' opponents. The NCAA argues that such penalties are necessary because the structure of intercollegiate athletics means that individual rule violators have often moved to professional athletics by the time their violations are discovered, and thus that they and their institutions would otherwise escape sanction. See Greg Bishop, "NCAA Penalties Erase Wins But Not Memories," *New York Times*, August 1, 2011, https://www.nytimes.com/2011/08/02/sports/ncaa-penalties-erase-the-wins-but-not-the-memories.html.

6. Dan Bernstein, "A Timeline of Patriots Scandals: Spygate, Deflategate and Other Controversial Incidents under Bill Belichick," *Sporting News*, January 4, 2020, https://www.sportingnews.com/us/nfl/news/patriots-spygate-deflategate-bill-belichick-timeline/ovkdjh8ny5qb1fnns9grat5mk.

7. Johannes Himmelreich and Holly Lawford-Smith, "Punishing Groups: When External Justice Takes Priority Over Internal Justice," *Monist* 102, no. 2 (2019): 135–136.

8. Himmelreich and Lawford-Smith, "Punishing Groups," 148.

9. Highly identified fans identify so strongly with their team that they feel their team's successes and failures as their own, as typified in the sentiment, "We're number one!" The positive feelings associated with such successes are known in the literature as Basking In Reflected Glory, or BIRGing. See Robert B. Cialdini et al., "Basking in Reflected Glory: Three (Football) Studies," *Journal of Personality and Social Psychology* 34, no. 3 (1976): 366–375.

10. Elizabeth B. Delia, "'You Can't Just Erase History': Coping with Team Identity Threat," *Journal of Sport Management* 33 (2019): 204.

11. Delia, "You Can't Just Erase History," 203, 209.

12. Examples of this reaction are stark but limited. One fan wrote a letter to the organization demanding an apology and claimed that "all of our Astros' gear has gone to clothing donations; all posters, decals, and the MLB championship video have been thrown in the trash; and we do not plan to attend games nor watch you on TV for the foreseeable future." See Craig Calcaterra, "Anger, Apologies, Incompetence and the Chaos Surrounding the Houston Astros," NBC Sports, February 17, 2020, https://mlb.nbcsports.com/2020/02/17/anger-apologies-incompetence-and-the-chaos-surrounding-the-houston-astros/. A few fans filed lawsuits against the team for deceiving them. See David Barron, "Another Fan Sues Astros over Sign-stealing Scandal," *Houston Chronicle*, September 14, 2020, https://www.houstonchronicle.com/texas-sports-nation/astros/article/Another-fan-sues-Astros-over-sign-stealing-scandal-15565507.php.

13. Calcaterra, "Anger."

14. "Houston Astros' Fans React to the Cheating Scandal."

15. "Houston Astros' Fans React to the Cheating Scandal."

16. Hannah Keyser, "The Pen: How Astros Fans Feel about the Sign-stealing Scandal Rocking MLB," Yahoo! Sports, February 24, 2020, https://www.yahoo.com/lifestyle/the-pen-how-astros-fans-feel-about-the-sign-stealing-scandal-rocking-mlb-144541799.html.

17. Ryan Fagan, "'I Feel Like I've Been Duped': Astros Fans Battle Range of Emotions amid Cheating Scandal," *Sporting News*, February 20, 2020, https://www.sportingnews.com/us/mlb/news/astros-fans-battle-range-of-emotions-amid-cheating-scandal-i-feel-like-ive-been-duped/1112doli82q4rj1houxtvwwyvy6.

18. "Astros Fans Moving on from Cheating Scandal," KHOU 11, January 18, 2020, YouTube video, https://www.youtube.com/watch?v=bJ_MpMlBRa4.

19. Hannah Dellinger, "'I Feel Duped': Fans React to Astros Cheating Scandal," *Houston Chronicle*, January 13, 2020, https://www.houstonchronicle.com/news/houston-texas/houston/article/I-feel-duped-Fans-react-to-Astros-cheating-1497?555.php.

20. "Houston Astros' Fans React to the Cheating Scandal."

21. Keyser, "The Pen."

22. "Houston Astros' Fans React to the Cheating Scandal."

23. "Houston Astros' Fans React to the Cheating Scandal."

24. Sonia Ramirez, "'Hate Us' Shirts Are Just the Ticket for Houston Astros Fans This Season," *Houston Chronicle*, February 24, 2020.

25. Micolette Davis, "Silence the Haters with These In-Your-Face Astros Shirts," *Houston Chronicle*, September 16, 2020.

26. Soon Youn, "As Nation Mourns George H. W. Bush, Millennials Keep Buying up Reagan-Bush Swag," ABC News, December 5, 2018, https://abcnews.go.com/Business/millenials-love-reagan-bush-swag/story?id=59623079.

CHAPTER 13

From Protector to Whistleblower: Being a "Good" Teammate When Cheating Occurs

ALLISON R. LEVIN AND MATTHEW STAKER

The 2019–2020 Major League Baseball offseason was marked by a critical event: the exposure of the 2017 Astros' sign-stealing scandal. Everyone had an opinion, and many boiled down to disbelief that the Astros, who won the World Series that year, had gotten away with such a large-scale scheme for so long. To understand how a scandal can become so large that it now holds a place in American pop culture, we have to start by examining the idea of what it takes to become a professional athlete. While many children dream of playing professional baseball, only a select few make it to the majors. It is clear that talent is crucial to success, but more talented athletes exist than do spots in the majors. Thus, we can argue that it is the most dedicated players that achieve their dream. This dedication opens the path to the majors and fosters a desire to win at any cost. Inherent in the mindset is a willingness to push and test how far the written rules can be bent, which in extreme cases leads to scandals such as what we saw with the Houston Astros.

We argue that this begins with the very identity that athletes assume. The idea of athletic identity, explained by social identity theory, is the individual's knowledge that he belongs to a group that provides him with a feeling of belonging. Social identity theory posits that an individual gains emotional value and significance from acceptance into a particular group.[1] Once somebody feels a connection to a group, they are more likely to be influenced by accepted group behaviors.[2] For some, membership in the group becomes a key aspect of their self-worth, and they are more likely to engage in depersonalization, or conforming to normative group behavior.[3] Accordingly, players whose identities are closely tied to being an athlete are likely to be influenced by the accepted norms of the sport. If that same athlete's identity is also closely tied to being a member of a particular team, he is likely to be influenced by the need for social approval from their teammates and the desire to behave "correctly" by matching the team's beliefs, attitudes, feelings, and behaviors.[4] Of course, this varies by the individual—some will choose the ethos of the sport over the team or make choices more in line with their own ethical compasses.

Becoming a professional athlete means a certain amount of individual overconformity, which means exceeding the expectations society holds for individual behaviors or beliefs. Professional athletes overconform by pushing past the limits a normal person deems as typical and thus are praised for their accomplishments.[5] On the other hand, athletes are deemed unmotivated or underconforming if they are seen as unwilling to sacrifice everything, trying to avoid risks or refusing to play through pain.[6] Thus, in the context of professional athletes, a level of deviant (or worrying) overconformity is expected and viewed as normal (or normative). It is through this lens that we can begin to understand why players cheat. Because normative overconformity is praised, athletes often want to push themselves harder. They often find new and innovative ways to excel at the game to achieve the goals of wins, championships, and individual records.[7] Some of this can lead to cheating through, for example, game play and body manipulation such as the use of steroids. Pushing these boundaries is so common that it is clearly embodied in the commonly used phrase "you aren't trying if you aren't cheating." As Vivian Chen and Yuehua Wu explain, a desire to cheat to get ahead is part of human nature.[8]

Accordingly, cheating is part of the culture of sports. It is fair to assume that some level of cheating is occurring among players who belong to the same community, since their identity is tied up in behavior that would generally be frowned upon in society but is praised in sport.[9] Athletes learn early in their careers from coaches, other players, agents, and even owners, what is expected of them to be successful—what is considered ethical or normative overconformity. In baseball, these complicated ethics are tied up in what we often think of as the "unwritten rules," which often include acceptable behaviors that exceed normative ethics.[10] If the goal in baseball is winning and the accepted means by which we achieve that goal is through fair play, cheating would include all actions that fall outside that definition. Watching the sport tells us that this is not the case; players constantly go beyond the definition of fair play as defined by the rulebook. Actions that fall outside the game's written rules are overlooked because everyone is doing it, such as pitchers using rosin and sunscreen on the baseball, and calling out one player would mean calling out most players. The game's technical rules are also set aside for the safety of players, such as accepting middle infielders getting in the vicinity of second base without actually touching it during a double-play attempt.

As a result of both normative overconformity and the unwritten rules, there is no bright line that we can point to and determine what is cheating. What we can say is that some forms of cheating are accepted, and others are deemed unacceptable and result in punishment.[11] Because players who make it to the professional levels both overconform and highly identify with the sport, we will define cheating as going beyond the accepted norms or ethics of the game—pushing the bounds from normative overconformity into the realm of deviance. In other words, while some cheating seems an inevitable part of the game, members of the sports community view cheating beyond a certain line, sometimes poorly drawn, as problematic and often unacceptable. To be successful, fans and the players expect greatness beyond what the average person would achieve, but we also expect them to avoid the consequences associated with their efforts when they do so. We expect players to play through pain but are shocked when they overuse painkillers sometimes to their physical detriment; we accept players doctoring the ball to ensure a good grip but decry when they doctor the ball for other reasons (though both can be true at the same time); and in the team context, we explain to non–baseball fans that you aren't trying if you aren't attempting to decipher the other teams' signs, but we call for championships to be nullified when technology is used in that process. As Coker-Cranney explains, the line between normative overconformity and deviance is blurry because the norms of the sports ethic are not equal to the norms of society.[12] Athletes are expected to seek excellence and accept that they should act as if there are no limits to their performance if they want to be the best, which results in their prioritizing the game over everything else—including accepting the need to perform at the highest level even when dealing with pain or injury. As the athlete is placed on a pedestal for their exceptional performance, they are willing to push the boundaries further and further.

Looking at the Hall of Fame, we see this debate raging today regarding the cases of players who have admitted to or are heavily linked to steroids. Voters are split on whether they were engaging in normative behavior—as with the current doctoring of the baseball, since the use of performance enhancing drugs was a widely known secret tacitly accepted by MLB—or if these players engaged in deviant overconformity that should keep them out of the Hall.

Starting from the use of unwritten rules and the role tacit acceptance by MLB plays, we can begin to explore the concept of sign stealing. It has been long established that attempting to decipher the opposing teams' signs is an accepted part of the game; there is a reason that players and coaches talking on the mound cover their mouths and catchers go through a series of signs when there are runners on base. In fact, there have been reported cases of players stealing signs and finding creative ways to signal them to their teammates for more than 120 years.[13] Players and teams have long come to accept this as part of the game or, by our parlance, as normative overconformity. A familiar quote by managers demonstrates how ingrained sign stealing is in the ethics of the game: "If your signs are getting stolen, maybe it's time to change your signs."[14] We learned in the 2019–2020 off-season that the fans, players, coaches, and MLB believe this normative overconformity crosses over to deviant overconformity when technology is used. The rules against using technology to steal signs were made clear in 2000 when Sandy Alderson, then an MLB executive, strictly warned that no club should use electronic equipment "for the purpose of stealing signs or conveying information designed to give a club an advantage."[15] MLB's line was drawn: the traditional means of stealing signs was still within the ethical norms of the game, but the use of technology crosses over into deviant behavior. As others have put it, something that constitutes cheating is acceptable (within the normative ethics of the game) when everyone does it, so long as they do it equally well.[16]

When it came to the Astros scandal, this technology use seems to be the crux of the issue. Even if stealing signs is generally accepted, the Astros were using technology in the form of cameras and monitors fueled by record keeping enabled with spreadsheets with macros, and apparently doing it better than anyone else, with the support of everyone from the clubhouse staff to the players and the front office.[17] The level of organized deviant overconformity, a group of players all working together to exceed the normative ethics of the game, makes cases like this rare. To further understand how the Astros as a team unit were able to bond together as teammates in a manner to achieve and then maintain this level of deviant overconformity, we must look at how team identity forms.

For players, peer social approval is contingent on following team norms; they feel a oneness or sense of belonging to the team.[18] How they achieve this is dependent on their level of identity with the team. For some overconformity is part of being a professional athlete, and for others it is the means to the ends of being socially accepted by a team.[19] For the former, these players identify with the game and act out of their own self-good while understanding the importance of the team to meeting their goals; they will protect their teammates and try to be a voice of reason within the clubhouse. Team chemistry can easily develop between these players because of the united goal of winning they share, but their own belief structures and desires will prevent them from being drawn into deviant overconformity. For the latter, they identify with being members of a team as much as, if not more than, broadly being an athlete who plays the game. In these situations, if the majority of the team comprises players who are highly identified with the concept of team, a risk of a "toxic culture" developing or the pressure for those athletes to engage in deviant overconformity is high. This occurs because when a large group of athletes defines their self-worth as being part of and being accepted by a team, they are willing to push each other farther and farther to gain acceptance and prove their worth.

While it takes a group of players who are highly identified with the concept of team, or for simplicity, a highly identified team to perform collective deviant behavior, not all cohesive, highly identified teams will cross over into deviant overconformity—behavior that goes beyond what is morally accepted in the pursuit of victory. So, what makes a team prime for such action? These players are highly identified with the sport and need to be seen as successful baseball players as part of their identity, thus leading to individual overconformity prime to cross over into deviant overconformity. When you put a large number of these players on one team, they frequently bond together and become highly identified with not just the sport, but the idea of being on the team. According to Barrie E. Litzky, Kimberly A. Eddleston, and Deborah L. Kidder, who studied deviant behavior in the workplace, when you have a large number of people who are prone to deviant overconformity, and you have leaders or managers who engage in or tolerate the deviant behavior, it leads to a team that collectively engages in the deviance.[20] A baseball team structure with a manager and team leaders dovetails nicely with their example, and thus it is easy to see how strong leaders and managers that encourage or ignore the deviant overconformity can foster an environment where the deviant behavior becomes accepted team behavior. More specifically, when players who act as team leaders and coaches and managers engage in or accept this behavior, they model its validity. As a result, other players who are highly identified with the team but reticent about the ongoing deviance can rationalize the behavior.[21] As indicated by Jim Crane, the owner of the Astros, this is what happened when it came to the sign-stealing scandal. While the system named "Codebreaker" began in the front office, a system in which Astros personnel charted the signs of opposing pitchers into a spreadsheet, the data was used by a groundswell of players who participated in or were complicit with the process. This new system involved watching the game feed from a monitor near the dugout and banging on a trash can to communicate what the hitter should expect from the pitcher.[22] The system evolved to the point that everyone knew about it, but the culture was such that nobody was willing to speak out.[23] It was the culture of the Astros, a team made up of players who were highly identified with and who firmly believed that team and team culture were sacred,[24] that led to a prolonged period of collective deviant behavior that continued unchecked. A highly identified team culture, by rationalizing deviant behavior, leads teammates to feel as if their bond is unbreakable, and as a result they have a duty to protect the secret. This need to support the deviant overconformity is built upon the idea that the approval of their teammates roots their social identity.

To understand how teamwide deviance can continue over time and what it takes for it to dissolve, it is important to look at how players punish each other for deviant behavior in different situations. When we have a team made up of individual players who are not highly identified with the team or a highly identified team with leadership that does not accept the deviant behavior, team leaders will stop individual players who are engaging in the action. In both cases the players will model the team leader's response, because in the former case it protects their best interests, and in the latter because it is what the team culture indicates is best.

Since most Astros players viewed being on the team as part of their identity, we will focus on how one would expect individual punishment to be handled. Surprisingly, the players who are most likely to be punished by such a team are those that are the most highly identified with the concept of team. When that player crosses the line from normative overconformity to deviant overconformity in a manner that is not accepted by the team, the benefits of the group identity or favoritism falls to the side. In this case the group is "apt to display harsher treatment towards one of their own whose actions bring negative attention to the group."[25] This is referred to as the black sheep effect, the tendency of the group members to evaluate unfavorable behavior by conforming highly identified group members more harshly than those on the outside.[26] In other words, on a team consisting of a majority of players who highly identify with the team concept, leaders will police those who demonstrate identification harsher than they do those on the outside. They do not want one individual's behavior to reflect poorly on the bond they have built through team identification, whereas somebody on the outside can be dismissed as never fully conforming to the team norms and ethics. Players who are part of the in-group need to see the harsh punishment to reconcile the deviant behavior since they see the team as part of themselves; they have developed a coping mechanism to ensure that the group integrity is not threatened. They must feel as if the leaders were also affronted by the behavior and that the punishment fits the incident. Then the deviant player is viewed as an anomaly and different from the rest of the group. If, on the other hand, there is no black sheep to blame, the entire team could be viewed in an unfavorable light.[27] The players with strong ties to the team have a greater need to have the actions of individual players explained and contained in the clubhouse by the leaders in order to continue to feel like a part of the team. If the leadership justifies the actions of the deviant player, the message is sent to the highly identified teammates that such deviance is accepted as part of team norms and ethics, while a rebuke lets them know the behavior is unacceptable. On the other hand, if players who are not highly identified with the team and are part of the out-group engage in deviant behavior, it often goes unchecked by team leadership because it is unlikely to be modeled by the team. An out-group player engaging in deviant overconformity has not demonstrated that they are worthy of the protection given to group members because they have not shown that they have fully bought into the system. As a result, any punishment by the League or disclosure in the media will not have a significant effect on the morale of the team; the majority of the team does not view the player as being part of the in-group that carries and decides the norms and ethics the team follows.[28] Teammates can explain away that player's actions and behaviors as going against the belief structure of the in-group.

Since players who make it to the major leagues are highly identified with the game regardless of their level of team identification, they understand that they will need to be a member of and work with a team to meet their personal goals. Therefore, it is expected that when a player moves teams, he will share instances of deviant overconformity on his last team to help his new team be more successful. In other words, a new teammate will share the strengths and weaknesses of their old team, including any special techniques they use to identify signs, catch pitchers tipping pitches, and the like, with the new team. This expectation, which stems from identification with the game, explains why most players and coaches have supported Fiers moving to the A's and telling them what was going on with the Astros.

The difference lies in the response to his interview in *The Athletic*.[29] While most people associated with baseball accepted him talking to a new team, many were unhappy with him taking the sign-stealing scandal outside of the clubhouse. Keeping team information, even deviant overconformity, inside the clubhouse is part of the ethical norms, and players who violate normative behavior are often ostracized. Teammates view players who speak to the press and take information outside the clubhouse as not supporting the concept of a team. These players are deemed deviant because they break the norms of the game, but rather than being deviant overconformers, they are labeled as deviant underconformers—players who engage in actions that are subnormal to the point that they have negative consequences and violate general expectations.[30] Because it is very difficult to make it to the majors and succeed while not at least being willing to overconform to the sport ethic, we would ordinarily not expect to see a current player go to the press with a story like the Astros' cheating while active on the team. What Fiers did was in a gray area since he was no longer a member of the team.

The feelings of people in MLB about Fiers going to the media when no longer a member of the Astros is a subject that will always be debated. How one feels about the issue comes down to whether that person's identity is strongly tied to that of a team. That Fiers spoke to Ken Rosenthal and Evan Drellich once he had left the Astros bubble is called "whistleblowing" by those who are highly identified with the game and "snitching" by current and former players who are strongly identified with the concept of team. It is important to note that Fiers did not stand alone; he was joined by then recently retired pitcher Danny Farquhar and three anonymous sources.[31] Fiers's name is the one associated with the story, and he faced scrutiny by fans, players, and media for speaking out because he was still in the game and playing for another team in the same division. Players who would likely be classified as identifying with the game, such as current players like Cody Bellinger and J. D. Martinez and former players like Dan Haren, think that what Fiers did was brave.[32] Furthermore, players who were teammates of Fiers on the Astros but have moved on to other teams, such as Charlie Morton, Marwin Gonzalez, and Dallas Keuchel, came out after the fact applauding him for speaking out and indicating they wished they had said something sooner.[33] While it is easy to be skeptical about the timing of their comments, it remains true that they saw what he did as something that fit within the confines of normative behavior. Their statements also fit with those of a player who identifies strongly with the game. They respect what Fiers did because it called out deviant overconformity, which they see as hurting the game. Not speaking out themselves also makes sense, since it may have been more important for them to continue to focus on what they sacrificed to make it to the majors rather than jeopardize their reputation by reporting their former teammates.[34] Whistleblowers have to risk their own self-worth, identity, and years of sacrifice in order to try to preserve the spirit of the sport.[35] These obstacles explain why we see so few public whistleblowers despite the amount of deviant overconformity that has gone on over the history of the game.

Meanwhile, players who were still a part of the Astros, a team with what MLB described as a toxic culture or, from our perspective, engaging in team-wide deviant overconformity, could not fathom the breaking of ranks. Carlos Correa speaks to this directly when he expressed shock at Fiers saying anything "because we were a team. We were a team. We were all together, and we had a bond."[36] Another anonymous Astro put it much more succinctly when he called Fiers a "freakin' punk ass bitch." The common consensus was that he should "give his ring back,"[37] showing that they believed that they were just doing what it took to win, even if it crossed the line into deviant behavior. Even after they were caught and given immunity, the Astros' rhetoric demonstrates how highly identified the team was and how ingrained the deviant overconformity was as it went unchecked (and endorsed) by the team leaders and upper management. These players demonstrate the mentality of being part of the in-group. They are unable to grasp how a player who played on the team could share what they think of as private information; they view being part of a team as a crucial part of their identity. This thought process, of course, led to the original deviant overconformity, marked by the toxic culture of the Astros but also the fierce loyalty they still felt in 2020.

The normative or acceptable action for Fiers—who likely identifies with the game but is not a member of the highly identified in-group—while he was on the Astros was to voice his concerns behind the closed doors of the clubhouse. Knowing that, some former players are engaging in interesting rhetoric. Included in this group are former players such as David Ortiz and Pedro Martinez, who demonstrate through their comments that they highly identified with their former teams. While we do not know if the Red Sox teams Ortiz and Martinez played on engaged in teamwide deviant overconformity, their takes were very clear: Fiers abandoned his team even though he was no longer a part of it or its culture. They are joined by others such as LaTroy Hawkins and Ron Washington, who came out with statements that sounded good upon first glance but actually criticized Fiers for violating the norms and ethics of today's game.[38] Hawkins explained that he would have respected Fiers if he "would have done it when he was on the Astros and not when he left. That would have more integrity. You win a World Series with them, go away and now you talk about it? If you had integrity, why didn't you talk about it while it happened?"[39] Ortiz agreed, saying, "After you make your money, after you get your ring, you decide to talk about it. . . . You look like you're a snitch. Why you gotta talk about it after? That's my problem. Why nobody said anything while it was going on?"[40] Because the norms of the game establish that players do not publicly share what is happening in their team's clubhouse, it is clear that if Fiers had taken this approach, these critics would have been outraged. Players and fans, who put these athletes on a pedestal leading to normative overconformity in the first place, would have seen Fiers as engaging in deviant underconformity if he had exposed the team while still on the roster. A cynical fan might conclude that these prominent baseball names felt pressure, as MLB was cracking down on the Astros, to say something about the controversy. Upon more in-depth analysis, what they advocated saying goes against the normative ethics of the game—a current player taking private clubhouse information public.

The issues of overconformity have surrounded sport since their inception with players striving to play harder and be the best. It is no surprise that the Astros' cheating scandal hits at the center of how players view the game. On one end of the spectrum, we have players who identify with the game and strive to be the best but do not push the boundaries beyond expected normative overconformity and the ethical norms of the game. They may not have gone as far as Fiers but can accept his reasons and simply refer to him as a whistleblower. On the other end of the spectrum there are the players who are highly identified with their team(s). They follow, and at times influence, team culture and can get caught up in teamwide deviant overconformity like what occurred on the Astros. They call Fiers a snitch because for them the concept of team lives on well after you leave a team.

It is clear that Fiers was needed to expose the Astros scandal and reestablish clear normative ethics surrounding the use of technology, as demonstrated by the strong statements about technology and sign stealing issued by MLB. His actions will likely be remembered by popular culture and historians as being brave/positive. But the question remains: How long will using technology to steal signs be verboten? It will be interesting to revisit this topic in the future and see where the "unwritten rules" have moved and what is deemed normative overconformity. Teams will likely continue to try to find ways to improve the methods they use to steal signs. As a result, as technology becomes more ubiquitous in baseball, if teams can move forward on equal footing we might see a form of sign stealing similar to what the Astros pursued as part of the normative ethics of the game—this time with MLB's tacit approval.

Notes

1. Matthew J. Slater, Pete Coffee, Jamie B. Barker, and Andrew L. Evans, "Promoting Shared Meanings in Group Memberships: A Social Identity Approach to Leadership in Sport," *Reflective Practice* 15, no. 5 (2014): 672–685, https://doi.org/10.1080/14623943.2014.944126; Vivian Hsueh Hua Chen and Yuehua Wu, "Group Identification as a Mediator of the Effect of Players' Anonymity on Cheating in Online Games," *Behaviour & Information Technology* 34, no. 7 (2013): 658–667, https://doi.org/10.1080/0144929x.2013.843721.

2. Barrie F. Litzky, Kimberly A. Eddleston, and Deborah L. Kidder, "The Good, the Bad, and the Misguided: How Managers Inadvertently Encourage Deviant Behaviors," *Academy of Management Perspectives* 20, no. 1 (2006): 91–103, https://doi.org/10.5465/amp.2006.19873411.

3. Scott A. Graupensperger, Alex J. Benson, and M. Blair Evans, "Everyone Else

Is Doing It: The Association Between Social Identity and Susceptibility to Peer Influence in NCAA Athletes," *Journal of Sport and Exercise Psychology* 40, no. 3 (2018): 117–127.

4. Leslie R. Hawley, Harmon M. Hosch, and James A. Bovaird, "Exploring the Social Identity Theory and the 'Black Sheep Effect' among College Student-Athletes and Non-Athletes," *Journal of Sport Behavior* 37, no. 1 (March 2014): 56–76.

5. Ashley Coker-Cranney, Jack C. Watson, Malayna Bernstein, Dana K. Voelker, and Jay Coakley, "How Far Is Too Far? Understanding Identity and Overconformity in Collegiate Wrestlers," *Qualitative Research in Sport, Exercise and Health* 10, no. 1 (2017): 92–116.

6. Jay Coakley, "Drug Use and Deviant Overconformity," in *Routledge Handbook of Drugs and Sport*, ed. John M. Hoberman (London: Routledge, Taylor & Francis Group, 2017), 379–392.

7. Coker-Cranney et al., "How Far Is Too Far?"

8. Chen and Wu, "Group Identification."

9. Coker-Cranney et al., "How Far Is Too Far?"

10. Mark G. Vermillion, Clayton Stoldt, and Jordan R. Bass, "Social Problems in Major League Baseball: Revisiting and Expanding Talamini's Analysis Twenty Years Later," *Journal of Sport Administration & Supervision* 1, no. 1 (April 2009): 23–38; Coker-Cranney et al., "How Far Is Too Far?"

11. Vermillion, Stoldt, and Bass, "Social Problems."

12. Coker-Cranney et al., "How Far Is Too Far?"

13. Tom Verducci, "How MLB Handled Sign Stealing Before Punishing the Astros," *Sports Illustrated*, January 23, 2020, https://www.si.com/mlb/2020/01/23/sign-stealing-history-astros-red-sox.

14. "If Stealing Signs Is Part of the Game, Why Do Teams Get So Upset?," Jugs Sports, August 18, 2018, https://jugssports.com/blog/if-stealing-signs-is-part-of-the-game-why-do-teams-get-so-upset/.

15. Verducci, "How MLB Handled Sign Stealing."

16. Rob Arthur, "October 2, 2020," Baseball Prospectus, October 2, 2020, https://www.baseballprospectus.com/date/2020/10/02/.

17. Arthur, "October 2, 2020."

18. Coker-Cranney et al., "How Far Is Too Far?"; Janet S. Fink, Heidi M. Parker, Martin Brett, and Julie Higgins, "Off-Field Behavior of Athletes and Team Identification: Using Social Identity Theory and Balance Theory to Explain Fan Reactions," *Journal of Sport Management* 23, no. 2 (2009): 142–155.

19. Coker-Cranney et al., "How Far Is Too Far?"

20. Litzky, Eddleston, and Kidder, "The Good, the Bad, and the Misguided."

21. Graupensperger, Benson, and Evans, "Everyone Else Is Doing It."

22. Jared Diamond, "'Dark Arts' and 'Codebreaker': The Origins of the Houston Astros Cheating Scheme," *Wall Street Journal*, February 7, 2020, https://www.wsj.com/articles/houston-astros-cheating-scheme-dark-arts-codebreaker-11581112994.

23. Bob Nightengale, "Astros Owner Jim Crane Opens up on Sign-Stealing Scandal: 'It Weighs on All of Us Every Day,'" *USA Today*, July 31, 2020, https://www.usatoday.com/story/sports/mlb/columnist/bob-nightengale/2020/07/31/astros-owner-jim-crane-sign-stealing-sorry/5544673002/.

24. Joshua Iversen, "Mike Fiers Did the Right Thing Blowing Whistle on Astros'

Cheating," Athletics Nation, December 13, 2019, https://www.athleticsnation.com /2019/12/13/21011864/mike-fiers-whistleblower-astros-cheating.

25. Hawley, Hosch, and Bovaird, "Exploring Social Identity Theory."

26. Hawley, Hosch, and Bovaird, "Exploring Social Identity Theory."

27. Fink, "Off-Field Behavior."

28. Hawley, Hosch, and Bovaird, "Exploring Social Identity Theory."

29. "Boston's JD Martinez Understands Why Mike Fiers Spoke up about Astros," NBC Sports, January 19, 2020, https://www.nbcsports.com/bayarea/athletics /bostons-jd-martinez-understands-why-mike-fiers-spoke-about-astros; Kathcrine Acquavella, "Jessica Mendoza, Mets Adviser, Calls out Sign-Stealing Whistleblower Mike Fiers," CBSSports.com, January 17, 2020, https://www.cbssports.com/mlb /news/jessica-mendoza-mets-adviser-calls-out-sign-stealing-whistleblower-mike -fiers/; Paul Newberry, "Whistleblower Mike Fiers Deserves Kudos, Not Criticism, for Exposing Astros' Cheating," *Times Reporter*, January 19, 2020, https://www .timesreporter.com/sports/20200119/whistleblower-mike-fiers-deserves-kudos-not -criticism-for-exposing-astros-cheating.

30. Graupensperger, Benson, and Evans, "Everyone Else Is Doing It."

31. Iversen, "Mike Fiers."

32. Ryan Fagan, "MLB Needs More Whistleblowers like Mike Fiers If It Wants to Clean up Sign-Stealing Mess," *Sporting News*, January 22, 2020, https://www .sportingnews.com/us/mlb/news/mike-fiers-astros-whistleblower-sign-stealing -scandal-pedro martinez-comments/1gl/ltqn1wzs413vet77v1v1sz; "Boston's JD Martinez Understands Why Mike Fiers Spoke up about Astros."

33. Jason Kelly, "MLB Players Look Like Hypocrites for Attacking Mike Fiers and Commissioner Rob Manfred," Baseball Essential, February 23, 2020, https:// www.baseballessential.com/news/2020/02/23/mlb-players-look-like hypocrites-for -attacking-mike-fiers-and-commissioner-rob-manfred/.

34. Coakley, "Drug Use and Deviant Overconformity."

35. Coakley, "Drug Use and Deviant Overconformity."

36. "Boston's JD Martinez Understands Why Mike Fiers Spoke up about Astros."

37. Iversen, "Mike Fiers."

38. Nightengale, "Former MLB Players, Coaches Have Mixed Feelings toward Mike Fiers, the Whistleblower in the Astros' Cheating Scandal," *USA Today*, January 18, 2020, https://www.usatoday.com/story/sports/mlb/columnist/bob -nightengale/2020/01/17/mike-fiers-whistleblower-houston-astros-cheating/450128 2002/.

39. Nightengale, "Former MLB."

40. Kelly, "MLB Players."

PART V

TECHNOLOGY AND THE SCANDAL

Billy Beane and Brad Pitt at the Columbia Pictures premiere of *Moneyball* on September 19, 2011, in Oakland, California. Beane was the general manager of the Oakland A's when author Michael Lewis wrote his book *Moneyball. The Art of Winning an Unfair Game*, which explored the efforts by the A's, among other teams, to use statistical analyses to make up for payroll disparities. Pitt played Beane in the movie. (Photo by Eric Charbonneau/ Invision/AP Images)

CHAPTER 14

Stealing Signs: Technology, Surveillance, and Policing inside and outside the Game

DAIN TEPOEL AND EILEEN NARCOTTA-WELP

The sports world erupted late in 2019 because of the Houston Astros' sign-stealing scandal. Will Leitch, writer, founding editor of the former sports blog Deadspin and a fellow contributor to this book, suggested that the controversy was "glorious and freeing," in contrast to other debates in baseball circles (e.g., steroids, labor issues, race and ethnicity, sabermetrics, the unwritten rules) which have become politicized, polarizing, and taken too seriously.[1] Admittedly, the Astros' scheme and its subsequent ballyhoo generated plenty of amusement and astonishment. The stakes were enormously high, with the Astros winning the World Series in 2017 and contending again for the championship during the following seasons. It is remarkable that a cheating scandal in one of the world's most successful professional sport leagues, on its biggest stage, boiled down to something as rudimentary as banging a trash can. Elite sport and athletic performance has become so thoroughly commercialized, routinized, monitored, and controlled that there is an element of subversive, rebellious pleasure in the Astros' skirting of the rules.

Moreover, information and communication technologies (ICT) such as laptops, smartphones, the internet, wireless networks, and social networking made the scandal an interactive playground for fans and internet sleuths. As Fernanda Bruno states, "participation has been understood as the defining principle of digital culture, having consolidated itself as one of the most important models for action, sociability, communication, and content production and distribution, especially on the internet."[2] The participatory impulse and ethos of engagement in digital culture was a core part of the public response to the Astros scandal. As Leitch observes:

> There are literally thousands of hours of footage of baseball games going back decades, footage that is publicly available for fans to sift through at

their leisure. So a cottage industry, led by an enterprising and incredibly entertaining baseball YouTuber named Jimmy O'Brien and his growing Jomboy Media empire, has sprung up, attempting to find every example of the Astros' cheating in 2017 . . . not only could you capture the garbage-can bangs in an audio chart, the bangs actively tracked, on a near-perfect basis, to off-speed pitches thrown. A Jomboy Media video detailing precisely how the scheme worked has more than 1.6 million views on YouTube.[3]

Amid these fun details of the controversy, however, are issues that deserve scrutiny for their social significance. While pundits and fans debated the implications of the electronic sign-stealing scandal for the purity of the sport and integrity of the Astros' 2017 World Series victory, others, such as Major League Baseball Players Association (MLBPA) executive director Tony Clark, interpreted the stakes differently. Clark stated that this scandal is "only a microcosm of greater issues facing baseball that have been caused by the game's technology revolution," including, he claimed, abuses of the injured list, the manipulation of player service time, the evaluation of players, and the type of game being played on the field.[4] "The backdrop of that technology being unchecked," he argued, "is how we develop this culture of it's okay to do all these things."[5] Essentially affirming Clark's claims, Seattle Mariners general manager Kevin Mather sounded off to the Bellevue Breakfast Rotary Club in February 2021, openly admitting to manipulating player service time during the pandemic-shortened 2020 season.[6] He has since resigned.

In this chapter, we follow Clark and consider our examination of the scandal a modest "check" on the corporate managerial culture of Big Data surveillance that forms the backdrop of the Astros' sign-stealing shenanigans and the broader concerns with unrestrained use of Big Data in sport. For our purposes, we employ Big Data as a reference not only to the increasingly large and diverse sets of data that are collected, processed, analyzed, and stored at unprecedented speeds and capacities, but also the experts, businesses, organizations, and industries that create such data. The entities turn data into actionable items for personnel decision making, revenue generation, marketing, sales, and product development and distribution. As many popular news and trade articles demonstrate, professional sports organizations—including and perhaps exemplified by MLB teams such as the Astros—may be construed as "Big Data" for their high level of integration and synthesis with data-driven statistical experts and companies.[7]

Digital technologies and surveillance capacities were at the heart of the

Astros' cheating strategy and the public's consumption of it. We view the scandal, and MLB's tepid response to it, as a canary in the coal mine for how deeply enamored, intertwined, and invested professional sport has become with digital surveillance evaluation of athletes. As reported by *USA Today*, one of the reasons for the MLB lockout before the 2022 season stems from the MLBPA disputing an "over-reliance on analytics."[8] The Astros' coaches and players, using a system developed and directed by their front office, turned the same tools of surveillance used to measure and evaluate their own performance against their opponents.

What are fans, observers, and scholars of sport to make of the fact that MLB refused to punish the Astros as harshly as precedent might suggest, when Commissioner Kenesaw Mountain Landis banned eight Chicago White Sox players for life following the accusations that they had thrown the 1919 World Series? Or more recently, in light of MLB's continuous refusal to re-admit Pete Rose to the game, or in the handwringing about what became of baseball in the 1990s and 2000s because of performance enhancing drugs? Note that our concern is not with the morality or ethics of the players' conduct, then or now. In this imbalanced power relationship, players are interchangeable and disposable laborers in management's efforts to maximize winning percentage and organizational profits. We aim instead to interpret responses from the commissioner's office, owners, and front office executives, who govern the game's finances, policies, and structure.

The Astros' use of technology to steal signs broke one of MLB's written rules, but they used the same intrusive technologies that have come to dominate baseball teams' decision making on and off the field. One might posit that commissioner Rob Manfred had no interest in making an example of the Astros by banning players or taking away their 2017 championship, because doing so would have fueled greater attention to Clark's point about the unchecked culture surrounding the implementation and use of new technologies. As noted, acceptable use of digital surveillance and data analytics were among the key issues that drove the collective bargaining agreement standoff between MLB and the players association before the 2022 season. In some cases, such as the Astros' transformation into one of the best teams in baseball in the late 2010s, the implementation of data analytics is heralded as a "sign" of an elite front office. In others, such as when the Astros players used tools of digital surveillance to steal opposing teams' signals, the use of the very same technologies is interpreted as a "sign" of violating the integrity of sport. As Clark stated, the Astros' cheating scheme provides an entrée into larger issues and concerns the digital revolution has brought to MLB.

Neoliberalism, Governmentality, and the Rise of Market-Based Decision Making

In *Discipline and Punish: The Birth of the Prison*, Michel Foucault explains how modern surveillance systems grew out of the historical development of disciplinary institutions. Foucault focuses on panopticism—or an "unequal gaze"—inherent to the possibility of constantly being observed within the prison system. Prisoners internalize this unequal gaze, creating "docile bodies" capable of self-regulation in accordance to institutional rules.[9] Surveillance scholars have used Foucault's theories of panopticism and docile bodies broadly to understand not only the historical construction of the governance of a state but also the specific technologies employed to maintain civil order in ever-changing societies.[10] Sport scholars have also incorporated Foucault's concepts of panopticism and disciplined bodies within the hierarchical coaching-athlete power relationship or the ideological disciplining of female bodies in media representations.[11] However, in later writings, Foucault acknowledges that self-governing technologies of surveillance are entrenched in a larger and more complex political and economic apparatus: neoliberal governmentality.[12]

Neoliberalism is a slippery concept in academia, for scholars "invoke it to describe a dizzying array of recent economic, political, and cultural developments."[13] We define neoliberalism first as an economic theory that structures US society and then as an ideological apparatus that teaches, guides, and influences individual values and actions. According to David Harvey, neoliberalism is "a theory of political economic practices that proposes that human well-being can best be advanced by liberating individual entrepreneurial freedoms and skills within an institutional framework characterized by strong private property rights, free markets, and free trade."[14] Following Henry Giroux, we agree that neoliberalism must be understood as both an economic theory and "a powerful public pedagogy and cultural politics."[15] We do not see neoliberalism and governmentality as singular and distinct forces working autonomously in society; rather, we understand neoliberalism and its economic and ideological properties as mutually constitutive entities that affect and are affected by the other. According to the theories and critiques of neoliberalism we have outlined, a central focus of government, outside of providing basic services and infrastructure, is to invest in private entrepreneurial activities, provide expertise in equipping corporations and institutions with new technologies for financial success, and deregulate the economy.[16]

Over the last two millennia, the liberal democratic state has been founded upon an agreeable dialectical assumption. First, liberal democracy embodies Plato's *Homo politicus*, a political individual capable of self-rule and self-governance. Second, the liberal democratic state is constructed as a collective relationship of governance, whereby the ruling class is morally bound and ethically obligated to be aware of the resources, services, and needs of others within their social sphere.[17] The accumulation of wealth and goods is only desirable as it benefits the collective, particularly those who are less fortunate, culminating in a socially governing body instead of a collection of individual actors.[18] However, Foucault's neoliberal political subject *homo oeconomicus* breaks this social contract. *Homo oeconomicus*, who is defined by a market rationale and a narrow self-interest, is in pursuit of maximum utility (profit) whether they are a producer or consumer. As such, neoliberal subjects struggle to imagine the need for a collective and the welfare of all. There is scant room for liberal democracy in neoliberal spaces, for *homo oeconomicus* cannot conceive of a moral imperative beyond itself.

In post–World War II America, the US government matured into a nexus of strategies, techniques, and procedures through which experts were anointed as authorities in order to govern the masses without destroying the government's existence or autonomy. The advent of Ronald Reagan's presidency in 1980 marked a stark economic and cultural shift in US politics as neoliberalism subtly infiltrated the US political landscape. Urban sport historian Sean Dinces explains that neoliberalism has operated in the United States since the mid-1970s through "exclusionary capitalism," the "political-economic system responsible for the upward redistribution of resources and power."[19] The political economy was now engaged with a conservative model of governance that excluded most people from the benefits of economic growth in terms of denying them access to certain physical spaces, economic markets, and previously allocated public resources.

Political rhetoric and discourse increasingly labeled the government as burdensome and oppressive. The strong commitment to a collective society began to diminish as politicians and political pundits circulated messages of individualism. These messages framed citizens as having a choice to actively maximize their own quality of life or allow the government to dictate their future prosperity. Reaganomics justified the reduction of the federal government through the privatization of many social welfare programs along with the various tax cuts for US corporations. At the same time, competition via capitalism was reproduced as a natural human process that heralded victories as proof of one's ability and moral worth. Capitalism was celebrated, especially during the Cold War, as a system that allocated rewards through meritocracy, viewed as the only fair way to distribute resources.

Sport is a cultural institution—a site of public and political pedagogy—that, in the United States, exists within and cannot be understood outside of these neoliberal ideologies. According to David Andrews and Michael Silk, corporate sport formations

> unselfconsciously acknowledge their corporatized institution structure, management hierarchies, profit-driven focus, and economically-driven rational efficiency. Moreover, the sport industry has become a self-sustaining and regulating phenomenon, constituted by undergraduate and graduate programs, professional conferences and organizations, and a thriving publications sector, all of which reproduce what are tantamount neoliberal corporate sport orthodoxies.[20]

Professional corporate sport formations such as MLB are considered to be the height of expertise where only the most talented and gifted are allowed to participate. As Jay Coakley notes, corporate sport "become[s] the 'ideal' and a standard against which other sports [and teams] are compared and evaluated."[21] MLB's economics reproduce and value the myth of meritocracy. As such, capital does not flow equally. Those MLB franchises with a history of success are highly valued and receive significant corporate sponsorship while others that do not conform to this image have lesser value, as they have not fulfilled a cultural and economic ethos of success.

Moneyball and Sabermetrics as Neoliberal Governmentality

While the commercialization of sport pre-dates this corporatized ideology, late capitalism has constructed professional sport as a space to reproduce and normalize neoliberal governmentality.[22] Take the Oakland Athletics as a case in point. Oakland's general manager, Billy Beane, was lauded and recognized for using data analytics and experts to reimagine the A's roster and on-field strategy within the constraints of a small market budget.

Scouts, managers, and coaches have historically been included in the expert regime of baseball knowledge. However, in 2003, Michael Lewis's book *Moneyball: The Art of Winning an Unfair Game* focused on Beane and his unconventional but analytical sabermetric approach to assembling a competitive baseball team. Lewis argues that the collective wisdom of baseball insiders was outdated and subjective, part of a flawed system. He posits that Beane's use of statistical analysis permitted the Athletics to outsmart the richest MLB franchises in acquiring productive players.[23]

While successful, Beane's sabermetric approach embodies the ideals of Foucault's neoliberal subject: *homo oeconomicus*. As Foucault notes, *homo oeconomicus* is someone who accepts reality, "pursues his own interest . . . [and] responds systematically to modifications in the variables of the environment."[24] Beane recognizes that he is part of a system in which financial capital plays an outsized role in the success of MLB franchises, and he attempts to earn, through the statistical cost-benefit calculations of player production, a space to maximize the value of the Athletics organization. Sabermetrics allows small market organizations to compete first by reducing players to numbers and statistics. Beane's strategy produced financial and on-field success. This success validates the "rational" actions of Beane (*homo oeconomicus*) to maximize franchise value.

From the view of a spectator or front office manager, sabermetrics posed a massive shift in the way that baseball and many other sports evaluate athletes. Sabermetrics initiated much more than a new evaluation strategy. Thought leaders like Beane constitute a new way of conducting oneself in society, for they are able "to lay claim to legitimacy for their plans and strategies because they are, in a real sense, *in the know* about which they seek to govern."[25] Beane laid the groundwork for a new economic and ideological structure in baseball as baseball's most valued franchises (e.g., New York Yankees, Boston Red Sox, Los Angeles Dodgers) began to utilize the sabermetrics system. His methodology and the subsequent cultural circulation of *Moneyball* in the early 2000s entrenched a market rationale within a corporate sport space but also validated and endorsed this neoliberal ethic as the "right" way to succeed. While sports franchises have always had a business side that balanced expenses—including player salaries, revenues, and competitiveness as often competing values—Beane used the economic language and concepts of management—the business side—in pursuit of sporting success.

The Houston Astros took it even further. In 2011, the organization hired Jeff Luhnow, a former McKinsey and Company consultant, as general manager to implement sabermetrics into their overall player recruitment and production strategy. Between 2007 and 2014, the Astros were abysmal, managing to climb above the .500 mark only once, in 2008. Their lowest winning percentage of .315 was recorded in 2013, the first year after their transition from the National League to the American League. The hiring of Mark Fast, a highly sought after tech engineer with a physics degree, as a front-office analyst in 2013 helped to shift the Astros' fortunes. In a few short years, the Astros became a poster child for the successful integration of data and analytics as a strategy for transforming a team from perennial basement dwellers to a model franchise.[26] Over the next nine years, the Astros rose to the top of the American League with first-place finishes in their division in 2017, 2018, 2019, 2021, and 2022; American League championships in 2017, 2019, 2021, and 2022; and World Series championships in 2017 and 2022. During this time, the Astros witnessed a meteoric rise in franchise value. According to *Forbes*, Houston ranked No. 26 in franchise valuation in 2015 with a value of $800 million. In 2020, they were the eleventh highest valued franchise in MLB at $1.85 billion.[27]

As the Astros' value soared to the top of MLB, the front office and their commitment to winning at all costs resulted in the abdication of their social and collective responsibility to the league, fans, and the integrity of the game, through their violation of MLB Regulation 1:1, which states: "No club shall use electronic equipment, including walkie-talkies and cellular telephones, to communicate to or with any on-field personnel, including those in the dugout, bullpen field and—during the game—the clubhouse. Such equipment may not be used for the purpose of stealing signs or conveying information designed to give a club an advantage."[28] In August 2017, the Boston Red Sox were caught using smart watches to steal signs, and the commissioner's office provided notice to all teams shortly thereafter, reiterating the rules regarding the use of electronic equipment to steal signs. Then, a March 2018 memo from MLB further emphasized that "electronic equipment, including game feeds in the Club replay room and/or video room, may never be used during a game for the purpose of stealing the opposing team's signs."[29]

These memos detailing the expansion of MLB's prohibitions and punishments for the use of electronic sign stealing are significant because MLB teams continued to allege the Astros were cheating in 2018 and 2019. The Oakland A's filed an official complaint with MLB in September 2018, while the Cleveland Indians (now Guardians) and Red Sox shared their concerns publicly during the 2018 playoffs. *The Sporting News* reported that a man associated with the Astros named Kyle McLaughlin was caught taking photos of the Cleveland dugout with his phone in game 3 of the ALDS and game 1 of the ALCS, against Boston.

In the 2019 playoffs, the New York Yankees levied their own public accusations against the Astros.[30] Yet, *homo oeconomicus* ruled the Astros' self-governing space. Accountability and commitment to ethical standards were replaced with calculated decision making based upon a market rationale. The cheating scandal brings neoliberal governmentality and *homo oeconomicus* into stark reality. As Leitch mentions, "Baseball teams have been stealing signs and clawing for every competitive advantage as long as they have been adjusting their cups and spitting. The Astros introduced new technology into it, and they make for convenient villains with their data-driven, win-at-all-costs, hedge-fund-bro-asshole mentality."[31]

In describing what makes the Astros "convenient villains," Leitch identifies several hallmarks of neoliberal economic and cultural aims: the dominance of quantified, individualistic, and profit-driven masculinity.[32] Toward the end of the 2016 season, Derek Vigoa, an intern at the time, showed Luhnow a presentation featuring an Excel-based application that the team's high-tech front office had programmed with an algorithm that could decode opposing catchers' signs, called "Codebreaker." During the 2017 season, the front office staff laid the groundwork for the electronic sign-stealing schemes to be implemented on the field, even though Luhnow maintained that he had no prior knowledge of any misconduct. Vigoa, who had been promoted to the Astros' senior manager for team operations, stated that Luhnow not only knew of the "codebreaker" system, but also wanted it to be used in live games because that is "where the value would be." Other Houston Astros employees agreed. Matt Hogan, the Astros' current director of player personnel, said there was no reason to hide the codebreaking system, for Luhnow told them, "It would have been something to show we were working and get validation from our work." The team's director of advance operations told MLB investigators that Luhnow would visit the Astros' video room and ask, "You guys codebreaking?" In short, despite Luhnow's obfuscation, the codebreaking system was fully integrated and embraced in the organization.[33]

The value of winning at all costs over league regulations was prevalent not only in the Astros organization but also in other top franchises. As mentioned, in September 2017 the Red Sox and Yankees were fined, the former for using Apple Watches to steal signs, and the latter for improperly using the replay review room phone. These incidents indicate that a technological arms race had emerged among teams to capitalize on the increasingly ubiquitous presence of digital surveillance technologies in the game. Yet, despite the public accusations and official complaints in 2018 and 2019, it was not until November 2019, when the website *The Athletic* published a detailed report on Houston's cheating with on-the-record quotes from former players, that the MLB launched an investigation into the matter. A one-month investigation resulted in minor punishments: a one-year suspension for Luhnow and manager A. J. Hinch, a $5 million fine for the owner, and the loss of a first- and second-round pick in the 2020 and 2021 MLB drafts.[34]

Punishments for players who executed the cheating scandal on the field were noticeably absent. While Commissioner Rob Manfred offered players immunity in return for their honest testimony, Collective Bargaining Agreement (CBA) negotiations with the powerful MLBPA were looming on the horizon. While unions remain a strong antidote to neoliberal power, MLB's CBA has not caught up with the changes the technology revolution has brought to the game, which Clark so deftly points out, and which the Mariners' former general manager's candid statements laid bare. Leitch suggests Manfred may have avoided strong punishments for players in anticipating tense negotiations and a potential strike that would devastate MLB's bottom line.[35] Instead, Manfred allowed the shame and anger directed at the Astros by fans and MLB players to stand in as retribution.

MLB's ability to profit from Houston's success and increasingly lucrative revenue streams from athlete biometric data is lost in discussions of the weak punishments.[36] In 2017, the year the Houston Astros won the World Series, the MLB gained 8 percent in sponsorship revenue.[37] Manfred's statement that the cheating scheme was "player-driven and player-executed" amounts to a public shaming of the players for undermining the integrity of the game. This shaming is Janus-faced. MLB has institutionalized and profited from a successful neoliberal governmentality production model. Ramy Elitzur notes, "By 2013, more than 75 percent of MLB teams were using [the Moneyball approach]."[38] Therefore, shaming players and coaches for utilizing a system the MLB created is hypocritical. As Tyler Kepner explains, Manfred "took no responsibility for failing to recognize the temptations in the spread of technology to the dugout. Baseball did not acknowledge that the sign-stealing epidemic almost certainly extended well beyond Houston and stopped short of establishing clear boundaries that could stop the problem for good."[39] As neoliberal corporate managers, they have no incentive to do so. More important, this logic highlights the "unprecedented disconnection of power from obligations," obligations MLB dismissed that uphold an ethical social contract within a liberal democratic society.[40]

Surveillance, Big Data, and the Exploitation of Athletes

Surveillance studies have proliferated since the terrorist attacks of 9/11.[41] This makes sense given that surveillance practices manifest in numerous cultural and political spaces ranging from the obvious sites of law enforcement agencies and border security to popular culture, consumerism, and moral regulation. Scholars in a variety of fields, including sport sociology, sport history, and sport law, have examined "the importance of information-gathering and data-sharing techniques" and documented "the changing character, and some of the consequences, of surveillance practices around the globe."[42]

These practices are related to a "diverse set of political and social problems" well beyond the scope of this chapter, but surveillance entails much more than power in the hands of a few attempting to control the unsuspecting masses. Surveillance is not just a "form of one-way observation carried out for purposes of law enforcement and state security." In its contemporary forms, surveillance is situated in networks of "searchable databases, networked computing, high-speed communication, and an array of technical gadgets." Many play a role in their own surveillance, while the release of personal information online and through social-networking sites enables hierarchical and peer-to-peer forms of surveillance. In short, understandings of surveillance that only emphasize techniques of control and disempowerment belie spaces, sites, and technologies that have made surveillance "more than a mode of domination."[43]

The Astros' use of new technologies to capture live in-game video feeds of their opponents, and the fans who jumped on YouTube to pore over countless hours of video and audio data, cannot be divorced from broader political and social problems stemming from the intersection of society, technology, and surveillance. The scandal emerges within a particular neoliberal context in which advanced new digital technologies adopted for surveillance are not well understood, contain significant flaws, and are highly intrusive.[44] This appraisal of troubling surveillance trends provides a structure for examining the Astros scandal and the responses to it as something that matters with echoes in the "real world."

danah boyd and Kate Crawford define Big Data at the intersection of three phenomena: technology, analysis, and mythology.[45] In terms of technology, Big Data experts and companies aggregate, harness, and connect large data sets through the mechanisms of maximal computer power and the algorithms that provide these machines their instructions, in addition to the advanced forms of computing and increased capacity to store information digitally that make Big Data possible. The real-time monitoring of objects, being tracked in ways unimaginable in previous historical contexts, is also part of what makes Big Data "new." This data can also be correlated with data in other databases. In short, this amounts to the collection and processing of massive amounts of information through new technologies. For analysis, Big Data allows certain kinds of claims to be made via the location of patterns within large sets of data. Algorithms parse the pieces for connections through deep and dynamic analysis of massive heterogeneous and multiscale data anytime, anywhere. Analytically based connections then serve as the ground for claims about matters that would have otherwise remained beyond the limits of human perception. Big Data thus enables new perspectives on the world that can alter what and how decisions are made, and the techniques used to make new claims. Third, Big Data enacts a new mythology, one attached to the notion that sets of large data can produce previously inaccessible knowledge that is presented as truthful, objective, and accurate. The analytics associated with Big Data are given a status of "elevated intelligence." Those who fail to tap into Big Data are derided as "partial and subjective in one's decision-making" or simply as falling behind.[46]

The application of Big Data to sport presents several concerns for athletes. Mainly, athletes have been and continue to be on the outside looking in regarding the predominance of Big Data as a form of knowledge. Some may argue that many athletes have welcomed analytics. Aggregated personal data can be used to gain a deeper understanding of health and athletic performance and to aid in maximizing their earning potential. These athletes attempt to shift control over the data being generated from corporate-scientific to individual ownership by hiring personal data analysts or statisticians. However, as Andrew Baerg notes, scant evidence exists to suggest that agents have been successful at the negotiating table as teams "may simply ignore any data players and agents bring in."[47] Further, sports organizations marginalize player-agent data, and perhaps more damaging, the athlete who commits to personalized Big Data collection reinforces the divide among athletes themselves. Without the same kinds of tools and access as professional sport franchises valued in the billions of dollars have, athletes are subject to a new manifestation of the digital divide as the statistics in analytics data sets have become enmeshed in commercial sport capital. This divide separates those with access to proprietary data from those who do not. It privileges the insider and those with capital to pay for access and makes disputing claims very difficult to challenge if not impossible to confront. In sum, for athletes, Big Data leads to further economic and structural disadvantages on one hand and a turn against previous forms of knowledge, and those who adhere to it, on the other.[48]

Professional sport has embraced Big Data. Denver Nuggets front office executive Pete D'Alessandro issued one of the most extreme statements in favor of biometric tracking of athletes, stating in 2014 that teams "need to be able to have [an] impact on these players in their private time" and through "sequencing and understanding the genome. And how that relates to pro athletes on an injury basis and who's naturally good at certain sports."[49] Despite this statement, the monitoring of athletic performance via intensive forms of quantification is not new and may be as old as organized modern sport itself.[50] However, the concern with monitoring and quantification of athletes today lies with the ownership, security, privacy, access, and exploitation of Big Data.[51]

Since the 2013–2014 season, the National Basketball Association (NBA) has partnered with SportVU to collect more data than ever possible before. Initially, its systems had six cameras tracking and aggregating data of player movements twenty-five times per second, capturing 72,000 unique movements each game, such as the number of dribbles, proximity to other players, miles run, and passes prior to an assist. Over a whole season this amounts to eighty-eight million data artifacts fed to a league server where teams can access and deploy the knowledge in coaching and personnel decisions.[52]

GPS and biometric tracking devices are also embedded in players' equipment during practices, gauging player energy exertion and modifying physical demands on players. The NBA partnered with Catapult and STATSports to have D-league players wear GPS and biometric devices during games, tracking a variety of measurements such as speed, distance run, and more sophisticated data points like acceleration, deceleration, force of jump and landing. This can reveal whether players favor particular movements, allowing coaches and trainers to tailor workouts to prevent injury from perceived biomechanical flaws. They could also uncover which players give maximum or lesser effort.

MLB also employs a camera and a radar system, Statcast, that collects information on a baseball's spin rate after a pitch, as well as a batter's launch angle. A pitcher's spin rate represents the rate of spin on a baseball after it is released and is measured in revolutions per minute. Launch angle refers to the vertical angle at which the ball leaves a player's bat. These terms are among the new Big Data stats that represent the collection of data in baseball that was not possible in the past. The amount of spin on a pitch changes its trajectory, and launch angle relates to where the batter hits the ball. Each has a "commonsense" application to playing the game of baseball that is now intensively quantified and measured. As biometric data collection of players' heart rate, skin temperature, and sleeping patterns increases, however, so do the commercial and investment opportunities.

There are many more examples of collecting and storing vast amounts of information via optical tracking cameras and/or wearable devices across multiple sports. The data serve a variety of constituencies, including sport leagues, organizations, and sport media. In sport, statistics are typically a public record, even some of the data produced by Big Data firms such as SportVU and STATSports. Yet most of this new data remains under the control of ownership. It is important to note that the algorithms that generate the numbers are not available to athletes, leading to issues of access and the issue of who is allowed to do what with the metrics. For instance, professional athletes have concerns over ownership rights of the data and how it may affect their current and future contracts. As Sarah Brown and Natasha Brison write,

Wearable technology enables access to intimate, sensitive data, particularly an athlete's physiological analytics, and without clear delineation of ownership and the athlete's ability to restrict others' access, an athlete's privacy is at risk because the athlete has no control over the data. Of particular concern are the wearables that athletes wear 24 hours a day, in which GPS is tracking the athlete's location. This type of data goes beyond the athlete's health and training and into the athlete's private life. Therefore, it is critical for there to be a clear understanding of the intended purpose(s) of the data collection.[53]

The problem here is not secrecy as much as surveillance of the athletes and the lack of agency in having this data collected in the first place. Baerg questions whether athletes can overcome this Big Data digital divide and possess some control over the conditions of their surveillance. Or, he asks, "Is subjecting oneself to corporately controlled surveillance a necessary condition for participation in 21st-century professional sport?"[54]

Numerous popular articles before the cheating scandal touted the Astros for their data and analytics prowess. In 2018, the *Wall Street Journal* referred to the "Astros and the Transformative Power of Analytics."[55] In 2019, The Ringer, a sports, pop culture, and tech website, claimed the Astros "disrupted player development" and became "the model MLB franchise."[56] That same year, the *New York Times* proclaimed that the Astros were MLB's "Happy Place" with their "sophisticated use of analytics" and "culture of frankness."[57] Therefore, the Astros' players and front office used the same tools to cheat as the ones that afforded their organization such unequivocal praise in pursuit of their competitive and economic interests. Or, stated more pessimistically, the Astros' front office and players, in a Big Data culture that had been gaining steam in professional sport for nearly a decade, simply employed the shrinking privacy boundaries, employee monitoring, and extreme commodification of athletes characterized by normalized surveillance to their fullest extent.

Brown and Brison demonstrate that Big Data generated through wearable technology provides new revenue streams for leagues, teams, and athletes through fan engagement and the creation of competitive advantages. Though wearables have become ubiquitous in the five major professional sport leagues in the United States, the "leagues' understanding and protection of the data is still very limited," indicating a less than effective management of ownership, access, privacy, and security of such data, let alone agreements with players' associations on "suitable uses."[58]

Per the MLB CBA that went into effect in 2017, players are allowed to wear devices in-game, but teams and players cannot access that data until imme-diately afterward. According to Brown and Brison, the players' use of wear-ables is "strictly voluntary," and teams must provide players with "a written description of the technology and a list of individuals who will have access to the data collected." While the CBA provides for the creation of a Joint Committee on Wearable Technology, with equal representation between the MLBPA and Commissioner's Office to discuss player safety, data manage-ment, privacy, confidentiality, and other relevant topics, MLB may still col-lect data that "cross the line from health and performance to personal life-style."[59] And while the CBA bans commercial use or exploitation of players' data, use of such biometric information in contract negotiations remains un-clear. In short, the CBA reveals a lack of specific security protocols, clarity on ownership of data, guidelines for data protection, and recourse for ath-letes to bring claims for unwanted disclosures and compromised data. While the CBA provides some direction for MLB moving forward, as Baerg states, "the boundaries on different forms of data and what can be done with them appear hazy."[60]

More pointedly, no CBA can mitigate the fact that Big Data collects more intimate and personal data on athletes than ever before, and that the contin-ual collection of such information on and off the field "allows for the athlete's performance and effort level to be constantly compared, creating a risk for the athlete" that did not previously exist.[61] The precariousness of a profes-sional athlete's career and sport's adoption of Big Data practices that exacer-bate an athlete's vulnerability provide a context to grasp why Astros players may have embraced the in-game video feed system of cheating. They could situate it within a system of hierarchical and peer-to-peer surveillance al-ready flourishing throughout MLB. The Astros' "dark arts" disrupts, but also fits neatly within, popular celebratory narratives of their organizational "el-evated intelligence."

Conclusion: Policing Individuals

Incidents that transpired during the summer of 2020 fueled concerns about government surveillance in the United States heading in a dangerous di-rection. In particular, these include the government's heavy-handed target-ing of Black Lives Matter protesters, media reports of extensive aerial sur-veillance carried out by law enforcement, and increased police reliance on AI-powered social media surveillance. Steven Feldstein and David Wong of the NYU School of Law note that biometric technologies (e.g., facial recognition) have been rapidly embraced with little oversight. Facial recognition systems—a massive and intrusive form of data collection—are "designed to facilitate the widespread collection and mass monitoring of sensitive personal data without individualized suspicion."[62] The New York Police Department has made almost three thousand arrests based on the technology in the first five years of its use. Florida law enforcement conduct an average of eight thousand searchers per month using facial recognition, and a 2016 report from Georgetown's Center for Law and Technology claims that half of American adults are searchable within a law enforcement facial recognition network.

Flaws are inherent in these applications. A 2019 study by the National Institutes of Standards and Technology found that certain algorithms were more likely to misidentify African American or Asian individuals than white males by factors of ten to beyond one hundred times. Technologist Roger McNamee argues that these flaws are cultural in the disregard for the technology's impacts and a lack of adequate consideration of due process rights. The design logic of ICT (e.g., smartphones, laptops) is oriented toward maximizing the collection of user data with little oversight or transparency. Smartphone apps and phone carriers accumulate information on a user's physical location and activity on their device, facilitating what Shoshanna Zuboff describes as a "'surveillance capitalism' ecosystem of commercial exploitation."[63] This ecosystem makes it possible for governments to acquire such data for surveillance and investigative purposes.

Feldstein and Wong argue for a need to develop appropriate frameworks to guide use of new tech in ways that strike a correct balance between citizen rights and law enforcement needs. This will take a lot of time and effort, but they believe it can start with a simple standard for digital surveillance tools: "technology known to contain structural flaws or biases should not be used for any decisions that meaningfully affect people's lives until those issues are rectified." Or, as Will Douglas Heaven commands: "fix them or ditch them."

The Astros' sign-stealing scheme reveals much about the use of digital surveillance tools that are flawed, not fully understood, and have inequitable negative consequences. Several issues arise out of the scandal that have not been thoroughly debated, analyzed, and evaluated prior to the adoption of new technologies in sport. It would be worth fixing or ditching Big Data in sport, too, as athletes must have rights and protections against teams and league bodies surveilling their on- and off-field activities. We acknowledge that this chapter asks more questions than it answers. For instance, what is the level of transparency and accountability between players, teams, and leagues who gather such data? Which tools have the leagues adopted, and how well understood are they? What are their flaws? What consideration has been given to their impacts and effects on those being monitored? Will teams with weak accountability and histories of questionable ethical standards and practices take a leadership role in driving Big Data in sports, as the Astros have? Moreover, fans and other enterprising individuals played with and embraced the Astros' sign-stealing, trash can–banging antics through an online media culture environment that fueled more surveillance, although of a more transparent and visible kind. Monitoring footage posted on You-Tube with the same quantitative and analytical fervor as Big Data to track and document the Astros' transgressions elicits important questions about shouldering accountability and regulation onto active citizens.

Granted, stealing signs in baseball for a competitive advantage and steal-ing citizen data for law enforcement purposes are not intersecting issues. We are not writing about the government turning federal agents on its cit-izens. However, the mechanics of the Astros' sign-stealing operations, and the public reactions to them, raise concerns that parallel the troubling sur-veillance trends. They are reproductive of a maturing neoliberal surveillance capitalism, and they emerged within the cultural and political climate of the Donald J. Trump administration, which adopted an attitude of authoritarian empowerment to use whatever technology and surveillance tools were avail-able without regard for legality. It may be fun to laugh at the Astros' hedge-fund bro assholes who were caught with the smoking gun, or therapeutic to take out some anger on José Altuve. But the scandal is troubling when con-textualized alongside MLB's growing culture of unchecked surveillance and the mythology of Big Data's superior intelligence that produced it.

Notes

1. Will Leitch, "Finally, a Fun Baseball Scandal," *New York Magazine*, Novem-ber 19, 2019, https://nymag.com/intelligencer/2019/11/the-houston-astros-cheating -scandal-is-fun.html.

2. Fernanda Bruno, "Surveillance and Participation on Web 2.0," in *Routledge Handbook of Surveillance Studies*, ed. Kirstie Ball, Kevin Haggerty, and David Lyon (London: Routledge, 2012), 343.

3. Leitch, "Finally, a Fun Baseball Scandal." As of August 2022, the video has over 7.4 million views.

4. Andrew Cohen, "MLBPA Executive Director Wants to Examine Technol-ogy in Baseball Beyond Astros' Scandal," Sporttechie.com, February 25, 2020, https://www.sporttechie.com/mlb-mlbpa-executive director-tony-clark-baseball -technology-houston-astros.

5. Cohen, "MLBPA Executive Director."

6. Dan Cancian, "What did Kevin Mather Say? Full Transcript of Seattle Mari-

ners CEO's Controversial Speech," *Newsweek*, February 22, 2021, https://www.news week.com/kevin-mather-seattle-mariners-mlb-comments-transcript-1570976.

7. Ryan Ayers, "How Big Data is Revolutionizing Sports," Dataconomy.com, January 24, 2018, https://dataconomy.com/2018/01/big-data-revolutionizing-favorite -sports-teams/; Abhas Ricky, "How Data Analysis in Sports Is Changing the Game," *Forbes*, January 31, 2019, https://www.forbes.com/sites/forbestechcouncil/2019/01 /31/how-data-analysis-in-sports-is-changing-the-game/?sh=56604ce33f7b; Darian White, "How Analytics is Changing the Game for Sports–and Academia," Insidebig data.com, February 13, 2020, https://insidebigdata.com/2020/02/13/how-analytics-is -changing-the-game-for-sports-and-academia/.

8. Gabe Lacques, "MLB Lockout Inevitable on Dec. 1: What Is In Dispute and How Long Will It Last?," USAToday.com, November 29, 2021, https://www.usatoday .com/story/sports/mlb/2021/11/29/mlb-lockout-imminent-whats-dispute-and-how -long-last/8794626002/.

9. Michel Foucault, *Discipline and Punish: The Birth of the Prison* (New York: Random House, 1995).

10. See David Wood, "Foucault and Panopticism Revisited," *Surveillance & Society* 1, no. 3 (2003): 234–239; Bart Simon, "The Return of Panopticism: Supervision and the New Surveillance," *Surveillance & Society* 3, no. 1 (2005): 1–20; Majid Yar, "Panoptic Power and the Pathologisation of Vision: Critical Reflections on the Foucauldian Thesis," *Surveillance & Society,* 1, no. 3 (2003): 254–271; Ivan Manokha, "Surveillance, Panopticism, and Self-Discipline in the Digital Age," *Surveillance & Society,* 16, no. 2 (2018): 219–237; David Lyon, ed., *Theorizing Surveillance: The Panopticon and Beyond* (Portland, OR: Willan Publishing, 2006); and John Campbell and Matt Carlson, "Panopticon.com: Online Surveillance and the Commodification of Privacy," *Journal of Broadcast & Electronic Media* 46, no. 4 (2002): 586–606.

11. See Margaret Duncan, "The Politics of Women's Body Images and Practices: Foucault, the Panopticon, and Shape Magazine," *Journal of Sport and Social Issues* 18, no. 1 (1994): 48–65; Laura Azzarito, "The Panopticon of Physical Education: Pretty, Active and Ideally White," *Physical Education and Sport Pedagogy* 25.6 (2009): 19–39; Natalie Barker-Ruchti, "Foucault in Leotards: Corporeal Discipline in Women's Artistic Gymnastics," *Sociology of Sport Journal* 27 (2010): 229–250; Pirkko Markula and Richard Pringle, *Foucault, Sport and Exercise: Power, Knowledge and Transforming the Self* (New York: Routledge, 2006); C. L. Cole, "Resisting the Canon: Feminist Cultural Studies, Sport, and Technologies of the Body," *Journal of Sport & Social Issues* 12, no. 2 (1993): 77–97; Brian Gearity, "Discipline and Punish in the Weight Room," *Sport Coaching Review* 2 (2012): 124–134; Juha Heikkala, "Discipline and Excel: Techniques of the Self and the Logic of Competing," *Sociology of Sport Journal* 10, no. 4 (1993): 397–412.

12. Michel Foucault, *The Birth of Biopolitics: Lectures at the Collège de France, 1978–1979* (New York: Picador, 2008).

13. Sean Dinces, *Bulls Markets: Chicago's Basketball Business and the New Inequality* (Chicago: University of Chicago Press, 2018), 5.

14. David Harvey, *A Brief History of Neoliberalism* (New York: Oxford University Press, 2005), 2.

15. Henry Giroux, "The Terror of Neoliberalism: Rethinking the Significance of Cultural Politics," *College Literature* 32, no. 1 (2005): xxv.

16. Nikolas Rose and Peter Miller, "Political Power beyond the State: Problematics of Government," *The British Journal of Sociology* 43, no. 2 (1992): 197–198.

17. Wendy Brown, "American Nightmare: Neoliberalism, Neoconservatism, and De-democratization," *Political Theory* 34, no. 6 (2006): 690–714; Wendy Brown, *Undoing the Demos: Neoliberalism's Stealth Revolution* (New York: Zone Books, 2015); Plato, *Republic* (New York: Oxford University Press, 1998).

18. Wendy Brown, "Neoliberalism and the End of Liberal Democracy," *Theory & Event* 7, no. 1 (2003), https://www.doi.org/10.1353/tae.2003.0020; Brown, "American Nightmare"; Brown, *Undoing the Demos.*

19. Dinces, *Bulls Markets*, 6–7.

20. David Andrews and Michael Silk, "Sport and Neoliberalism: An Affective-Ideological Articulation," *Journal of Popular Culture* 51, no. 2 (2018): 511.

21. Jay Coakley, "Ideology Doesn't Just Happen: Sports and Neoliberalism," *ALESDE Revista* 1, no. 1 (2012): 78.

22. Coakley, "Ideology Doesn't Just Happen," 75; Andrews and Silk, "Sport and Neoliberalism," 517.

23. Michael Lewis, *Moneyball: The Art of Winning an Unfair Game* (New York: Norton, 2003).

24. Foucault, *Birth of Biopolitics*, 270.

25. Rose and Miller, "Political Power Beyond," 186.

26. Ben Lindbergh and Travis Sawchik, "How the Houston Astros Disrupted Player Development to Become the Model MLB Franchise," *The Ringer*, June 3, 2019, https://www.theringer.com/mlb/2019/6/3/18644512/mvp-machine-how-houston-astros-became-great-scouting.

27. Jack Witthaus, "Astros Value Soars in New Forbes Rankings," bizjournals.com, April 11, 2017, https://www.bizjournals.com/houston/news/2017/04/11/houston-astros-value-soars-in-new-forbes-rankings.html; Mike Ozanian and Kurt Badenhausen, "Despite Lockdown, MLB Teams Gain Value in 2020," *Forbes*, April 9, 2020, https://www.forbes.com/sites/mikeozanian/2020/04/09/despite-lockdown-mlb-teams-gain-value-in-2020/.

28. Tom Verducci, "How MLB Handled Sign Stealing Before Punishing Astros," *Sports Illustrated*, January 23, 2020, https://www.si.com/mlb/2020/01/23/sign-stealing-history-astros-red-sox#.

29. mhatter106, "MLB Commissioner Rob Manfred's Full Statement on the Houston Astros Sign Stealing Investigation," SBNation, January 13, 2020, https://www.crawfishboxes.com/2020/1/13/21064270/mlb-commissioner-rob-manfreds-full-statement-on-the-houston-astros-sign-stealing-investigation.

30. Dan Bernstein, "Astros Cheating Scandal Timeline, From the First Sign-Stealing Allegations to a Controversial Punishment," *Sporting News*, July 24, 2020, https://www.sportingnews.com/us/mlb/news/astros-scandal-timeline-sign-stealing-punishment/zbe6j4yoi1g21iaosay31zv3n.

31. Leitch, "Finally, a Fun Baseball Scandal."

32. Giroux, "Terror of Neoliberalism," xv; Lisa Duggan, *Twilight of Equality: Neoliberalism, Cultural Politics, and the Attack on Democracy* (Boston: Beacon Press, 2003), 12–17.

33. All quotes are from Jared Diamond, "'Dark Arts' and 'Codebreaker': The Origins of the Houston Astros Cheating Scandal," *Wall Street Journal*, February 7, 2020,

https://www.wsj.com/articles/houston-astros-cheating-scheme-dark-arts-code
breaker-11581112994.

34. Bernstein, "Astros Cheating Scandal Timeline."

35. Will Leitch, "The MLB Commissioner's Statement on the Astros Has One
Big Omission. There's a Reason," *Washington Post*, January 15, 2020, https://www
.washingtonpost.com/opinions/2020/01/15/mlb-commissioners-statement-astros
-has-one-big-omission-theres-reason/.

36. Sarah M. Brown and Natasha T. Brison, "Big Data, Big Problems: Analysis of
Professional Sports Leagues' CBAs and Their Handling of Athlete Biometric Data,"
Journal of Legal Aspects of Sport 30 (2020): 63–64.

37. Ken Fang, "MLB Sees Increase in Sponsor Spending while NFL is Trending Negative," Awful Announcing, November 8, 2017, https://awfulannouncing.com
/mlb/mlb-sees-increase-sponsor-spending-nfl-trending-negative.html.

38. "Moneyball Advantage Peters Out Once Everyone's Doing It," Science Daily,
April 8, 2019, https://www.sciencedaily.com/releases/2019/04/190408161654.htm.

39. Tyler Kepner, "Technology, Once the Astros' Ally, Helps Do Them In," *New
York Times*, January 13, 2020, https://www.nytimes.com/2020/01/13/sports/baseball
/astros-mlb-sign-stealing-scandal.html.

40. Giroux, "Terror of Neoliberalism," 11.

41. For example, see Kirstie Ball, Kevin Haggerty, and David Lyon, eds., *Routledge Handbook of Surveillance Studies* (New York: Routledge, 2012).

42. Sean Hier and Josh Greenberg, "The Politics of Surveillance: Power, Para-
digms, and the Field of Visibility," in *Surveillance: Power, Problems and Politics*, ed.
Josh Greenberg and Sean Hier (Vancouver: University of British Columbia Press,
2010), 14; Brad Millington and Rob Millington, "'The Datafication of Everything':
Toward a Sociology of Sport and Big Data," *Sociology of Sport Journal* 32, no. 2 (2015):
140–160; Andrew Manley, Catherine Palmer, and Martin Roderick, "Disciplinary
Power, the Oligopticon and Rhizomatic Surveillance in Elite Sports Academies,"
Surveillance & Society 10, nos. 3–4 (2012): 303–319; David Johns and Jennifer Johns,
"Surveillance, Subjectivism and Technologies of Power: An Analysis of the Discur-
sive Practices of High-Performance Sport," *International Review for the Sociology of
Sport* 35, no. 2 (2000): 219–234; Yago Colas, "The Culture of Moving Dots: Toward a
History of Counting and of What Counts in Basketball," *Journal of Sport History* 44,
no. 2 (2017): 336–349.

43. Quotes from Hier and Greenberg, "Politics of Surveillance," 14–17. See also
Bruno, "Surveillance and Participation on Web 2.0," 343–351.

44. Steven Feldstein and David Wong, "New Technologies, New Problems: Troubling Surveillance Trends in America," justsecurity.org, August 6, 2020, https://www
.justsecurity.org/71837/new-technologies-new-problems-troubling-surveillance
-trends-in-america/.

45. danah boyd and Kate Crawford, "Critical Questions for Big Data," *Information, Communication & Society* 15, no. 5 (2012): 662–679.

46. boyd and Crawford, "Critical Questions," 663–667.

47. Andrew Baerg, "Big Data, Sport, and the Digital Divide: Theorizing How
Athletes Might Respond to Big Data Monitoring," *Journal of Sport and Social Issues*
4, no. 1 (2017): 15.

48. Baerg, "Big Data," 4–5, 15.

49. Pablo Torre and Tom Haberstroh, "New Biometric Tests Invade the NBA," ABC News, October 6, 2014, https://abcnews.go.com/Sports/biometric-tests-invade-nba/story?id=25997467.

50. Allen Guttmann, *From Ritual to Record: The Nature of Modern Sports* (New York: Columbia University Press, 1978), 16, 47–51.

51. Baerg, "Big Data," 8.

52. Baerg, "Big Data," 8.

53. Brown and Brison, "Big Data, Big Problems," 65.

54. Baerg, "Big Data," 9.

55. Irving Wladawsky-Berger, "The Houston Astros and the Transformative Power of Analytics," *Wall Street Journal*, July 20, 2018, https://www.wsj.com/articles/the-houston-astros-a-case-study-of-the-transformative-power-of-analytics-15321021 27.

56. Lindberg and Sawchik, "How the Houston Astros Disrupted Player Development."

57. Tyler Kepner, "The Astros Are Major League Baseball's Happy Place," *New York Times*, August 16, 2019, https://www.nytimes.com/2019/08/16/sports/baseball/houston-astros.html.

58. Brown and Brison, "Big Data, Big Problems," 63.

59. Quotes from Brown and Brison, "Big Data, Big Problems," 70–72.

60. Baerg, "Big Data," 17.

61. Brown and Brison, "Big Data, Big Problems," 65.

62. Feldstein and Wong, "New Technologies, New Problems."

63. Feldstein and Wong, "New Technologies, New Problems."

CHAPTER 15

The Spreadsheet in the Garden: Analytics and the Sign-Stealing Scandal

JONATHAN SILVERMAN

In *The Only Rule Is That It Has to Work*, Ben Lindbergh and Sam Miller tell a story about how they found pitcher Paul Hvozdovic, one of their prize prospects for the Sonoma Stompers, the independent league team those Baseball Prospectus writers somehow finagled to operate for a season. They found Hvozdovic by sorting college baseball statistics on a spreadsheet created by another numbers-oriented baseball writer. When the authors told Hvozdovic how they found him, he replied, "Your spreadsheet's some shit."[1]

His skepticism about spreadsheets echoes through baseball in a variety of ways, but this particular way, the scouting of players by numbers, not by actual experience seeing a player, seems a metaphor for the battle between those who value advanced statistics and those who focus on experience when evaluating players. In the case of Lindbergh and Miller, the spreadsheet took the place of traditional scouting because they had no budget to scout, but baseball has taken a definitive turn to making many of its personnel decisions through these numbers, often shorthanded as analytics.

The Astros scandal *did* involve scouting of a particular sort. Astros staff members recorded the catchers' signs to pitchers and the accompanying pitches to a spreadsheet and then used that spreadsheet, a video camera and console, and a bat and a trash can to send signals to a batter. That spreadsheet and its template was called "Codebreaker," introduced by an intern soon to become an integral part of the Astros' brain trust, Derek Vigoa. For the longest time, spreadsheets and ledgers before them were the province of business, and baseball has been a business for more than a century and a half. Only since the Moneyball era have spreadsheets been an integral part of the sports side of baseball management. Vioga's presentation was to Jeff Luhnow, the Astros general manager, a former McKinsey consultant. Luhnow focused on using numbers-oriented decision-making techniques to first tear down and then build up the team, which would result in a World Series victory in 2017, six years after he took the helm.[2]

That the Astros used analytics and a spreadsheet to fuel sophisticated yet somewhat ham-handed cheating methods seems a metaphor for the awkward interplay between the idealized physical space of the baseball diamond, the wondrous talent of baseball players, and number-crunching statnerds. That this interplay led, perhaps inexorably, to the cheating scandal is what made it weird, if not unprecedented. As Lindbergh and Miller wrote before the Astros scandal, "It's not that cheating is socially acceptable in baseball; the shock and indignation over the steroids era are proof that it is very much not. It's that *certain kinds* of cheating are socially acceptable in baseball and being competitive means engaging in the ambiguous negotiation of the acceptable vs. the unacceptable."[3] In cheating in the manner they did, the Astros violated a number of baseball's unwritten rules, one of which is that the game itself is bigger than the machinations behind it. The move into these new, spreadsheet-driven calculations and the encroachment of technology into the ballfield left many fans cold even before the scandal even broke.

The scandal highlighted the conflict between two different types of games, the one where humans perform miraculous tasks on a carefully manicured field of grass and dirt, and the other where consultants and management make tactical decisions using data to put together the best baseball team. It was one thing to use analytics to scout players. But to use video-captured catcher signs processed in a spreadsheet in the pursuit of a championship in effect transformed the players into part of the second, data-based game, as opposed to the one played on a field, becoming employees as much as players. It's one thing to be a player for a professional team, at the mercy of market forces that directly relate to performance, but it's another to be performance-enhanced and performance-coded as data in a spreadsheet, noting that neither identity is absolute. Fans come to sports for the game on the field, not the one on the spreadsheet, and watching employees play a game is just not the same as watching players play. The way Astros used video to game a game was the culmination of a process that has increasingly moved the game from the field to the computer, violating the notion of baseball's idea of pastorality, and making many fans and traditionalists feel uncomfortable. That is where the line was crossed, and why we still think about the scandal.

In this chapter, I will explore the way analytics evolved from an underground phenomenon to dominant philosophy, the presence of McKinsey in professional sports, and the meaning of spreadsheets in a sports context, before turning my attention to how all this affects our notions of the game as a pastoral phenomenon. In a sense, the statistical landscape of baseball was altered in ways that resemble other landscape alterations when new forms of technology emerge. Leo Marx called this phenomenon "the machine in the garden," mostly writing about the literal and metaphorical ways trains altered the nineteenth-century landscape. More than a century and a half later, the disruption to another type of metaphorical garden—the American baseball diamond—is less noisy and smoky but nonetheless profound, fueled by novel ways of calculating performance, and many of them by a spreadsheet.

Analytics and the New Numbers

Of all the major sports, baseball is the most oriented toward numbers; its numbers are the ones most fans know both in terms of both seasonal and career marks. You say .300 to a baseball fan, and they will know both that's a good batting average and a career milestone for pitching wins as well as a great mark for strikeouts in a season. Say twenty, and the response would be a pitcher's wins and strikeouts in a game; utter five hundred, they say lifetime home runs; and all baseball fans know that three thousand hits means a ticket to the Hall of Fame. But the widespread use of steroids in the 1990s altered the sport's relationship to numbers, particularly its records for home runs in a season, which had long been sixty, achieved by Babe Ruth in 1927. Roger Maris broke it with sixty-one in 1961 (in eight more games, giving him an infamous asterisk).[4] In the storied home-run battle of 1998, Mark McGwire and Sammy Sosa both broke the record: McGwire finished with seventy, Sosa with sixty-five. Barry Bonds broke the record again in 2001 with seventy-three home runs. Bonds holds the record for lifetime home runs as well, 762, edging out Hank Aaron's 755. But Bonds, McGwire, and Sosa either admitted to or were suspected of steroid use, and they do not seem likely to end up in the Hall of Fame despite their prestigious achievements.[5]

Other numbers—salaries, revenues, TV contracts—also play a large part in the baseball world, but these are business numbers, opaque not only because they are complicated but also because ownership hides finances from players and fans alike. The actual value and profit and loss in a season are deliberate unknowns, never to be divulged because with the knowledge of the numbers behind the economics of the game, the players would know the true value of both the franchise and their contribution to it. Without those numbers, players negotiate their contracts with only a partial sense of the business in which they are employed and thus an incomplete sense of their worth.

Other numbers have become more important in the last twenty-five years. Baseball fans, first employing the modern miracle of the copy machine and then the personal computer, began to seek out and construct numbers that they thought better represented what was happening in games in what was labeled sabermetrics, named after the Society for American Baseball Research (SABR), which was founded in 1971. This set of numbers besides player stats and owner money came into prominence in the 1980s and '90s, the set of numbers associated with the process called analytics. They were based on player stats, but they could not be reported or counted by a mathematical formula with two numbers in a simple calculation such as batting average (hits divided by official at bats) or earned run average (earned runs divided by nine). Even something as simple as WHIP, walks and hits per inning given up by a pitcher, a measure used to evaluate pitching effectiveness, required addition before division. Traditionalists can understand batting averages and see the quality of the players through their play. But complicated numbers dilute these qualifications, and abstracting them into spreadsheets dilutes them even further. Of course, one can get those stats anywhere, but the divide between those who find value from what they see and experience and what they read can be culturally significant.

Michael Lewis credits Bill James and Sandy Alderson with popularizing analytics, but the legendary Baltimore Orioles manager Earl Weaver, for example, was an avid user of statistics long before sabermetrics, and SABR had been around for decades before James and Alderson started making inroads from different angles.[6] James wrote a newsletter that explained how currently used baseball statistics were inadequate in explaining what happened on the field and made teams successful, and Alderson, who did not come from a baseball background, saw problems in the way baseball management made decisions. But if it were not those two figures, it would have been others, as Lewis explains in *Moneyball*, which became shorthand for operating organizations, both in and out of sports, based on analytics. (Just Google "the moneyball of.")[7]

The growth of the personal computer and then the internet, the access to more data, the rise of fantasy sports, the expansion of cable television—all of these had an influence of making advanced statistics more available and helping those who were interested in processing them more in touch with one another. Stats-minded writers used blogs and internet message boards to communicate with one another and occasionally the world at large. A lot of the content had to do with how baseball people were making decisions on either incomplete or outdated data and what decision making with better data might look like. Along those lines, *Moneyball* tells the story of Billy Beane and his efforts to remake the Oakland A's, which had a lower payroll than many other MLB teams. Beane focused on finding players using statistics rather than traditional scouting metrics in the name of value. From the fan side, those who believed in analytics were people who loved baseball but who saw irrationality in the way decisions were made by managers and management. But these numbers were really for evaluating players. As Daniel Handler notes, "The figures collected don't simply help settle fan disputes over which player covers more ground as a shortstop; reviewing raw data—as opposed to just video of the plays—can assist baseball clubs in more accurately determining the relative value of different players who play the same position (which is the essence of sabermetrics as displayed in *Moneyball*). When used by clubs, these data can have an enormous effect on player evaluation."[8]

These numbers were generated by a new type of baseball management type. Young white men—and they were almost all men, almost always white—who studied analytics and saw how better, more precise numbers predicted success or failure of players and teams began to work for professional ball clubs. As Lindbergh and Miller write, "Over the past two decades, the sabermetric movement has plowed across Major League Baseball like a glacier, leaving a strange-looking landscape behind: Ivy League–educated twenty- and thirty-somethings with Wall Street experience replacing weather-beaten general managers who came up as players and scouts; precise defensive positioning supplanting guesswork and gut feel; strict pitch counts and swelling bullpens crowding out complete games."[9] It was also about saving money. As Henry Abbott and Yaron Weitzman write, "In baseball, the appearance of advanced analytics is called 'Moneyball.' It's about a lot of things—seeing the strike zone, fielding with range—but, no surprise, it's also about money. [Philadelphia 76ers executive Daryl] Morey, for example, entered the NBA as a consultant, advising Celtics ownership on the bottom line. His annual conference takes place at MIT's *business* school. A lot of the panels are about maximizing ticket revenue or gambling analytics."[10]

Still, writers have documented ways of using analytics that does not eschew the human element. In their work, Lindbergh and Miller not only try to assemble a team but also use the data they collect to try to influence the somewhat old-school manager to make decisions based on it. The problem is that even old-school managers have their own data, based on accrued observations over time rather than the more inscrutable data these authors have, and they find their approach works best when mixed with empathy and patience. In another modern stat narrative, *Big Data Baseball*, by Travis Sawchik, about the Pittsburgh Pirates, career desperation by the general manager and manager led to aggressive use of data in all aspects of the game that turned a team around, and they worked hard to involve all parties involved in the decision making.[11] These books show that analytics does not necessarily lead to rigid, inhumane thinking. It's hard to be nostalgic about a set of inexact decisions being replaced by ones more based in data and logic, but when the logic of a game is altered by outside forces, there are likely to be unintended consequences.

The New Owners

As baseball is governed increasingly by those who value numbers, so are American businesses, whose long slow earners—like regional supermarket chains with profit margins in the low single digits—are often eschewed by asset hunters in established industries like media or lottery-ticket venture capitalists who buy low in promising tech companies. In many sports organizations, including those in baseball, basketball, and increasingly, football, ownership comes from numbers- or tech-based fields, with many of them receiving the same type of degrees—MBAs and finance—as the analytics staffers, whereas many owners in the twentieth century came from the ranks of the real estate, retail, and oil industries. In the finance and technology industries the idea of value is paramount, and risk/reward is also important. Hedge fund managers or private equity investors own nineteen professional sports teams, according to a watchdog group.[12] They are not a monolithic bunch, and there are genres in both hedge funds and private equity firms: for example, Warren Buffett's Berkshire Hathaway is a private equity firm that has bought newspapers and maintained them, and Alden Global Capital is one that has essentially gutted some of the best newspapers in the world.[13] Both have in common an ethos devoted to finding value that others overlooked or to filling a need that was either new or underserved, and tech owners in particular were often obsessed with Clayton M. Christensen's idea of disruption.[14] Because they were rewarded by wealth beyond their dreams and probably comprehension, they believed their work to be indicative of savvy and intelligence that could be translated to other pursuits, including owning a professional sports team.

These owners seem interested in succeeding in this new venture as a type of organizational and intellectual challenge, and they feel comfortable with the numbers aspect of sports ownership: "The lure is no longer just the prospect of owning a trophy asset or hanging out with famous athletes, although that still resonates. These days there's also a cold-eyed appraisal of teams as an increasingly astute financial bet, backed by a mix of real estate, media and technology."[15] In those industries, finding value and efficiency are crucial, for the idea of pure capitalism relies on the idea that an organization should find the best way to make as much money as it can. What is relative are the methods. There are some professional sports teams that have a low payroll and are subsidized by the league to make money. Others see their teams as side businesses to the associate businesses of entertainment and real estate development. But other theories derive business value from having a competitive team that sparks fan interest and associated purchases of television coverage, event attendance, and fanwear. The intangibles of being associated with a successful team or part of a league that provides both competition and camaraderie in the traditionally cutthroat world of American capitalism also can't be denied, as well as the often lucrative public-private partnerships and protection from antitrust violations. These owners are in it to win. But what games are they playing?

Consultants Speak Excel and PowerPoint

Some of these tools for competition are more office than dugout. Owners and their business associates and the new analytics hires both shared the same business-related programs. A spreadsheet embedded in a PowerPoint began the whole process, according to Jared Diamond's account in the *Wall Street Journal*. During a PowerPoint presentation, Vioga showed an Excel spreadsheet detailing the scheme to capture catchers' signals and document them, then transform that to usable information.[16] Vioga was not an intern as we commonly think of interns—college students, primarily—but a former consultant for Wasserman Media Group, a high-profile sports agency. Such was the lure of working for a sports franchise that people with very good jobs often interned for the franchises.

That a spreadsheet and presentation software were involved in a baseball scandal demonstrates that corporate thinking was heavily involved, despite the fact that it ended up with baseball players and coaches banging on a makeshift drum. Excel spreadsheets and PowerPoint presentations are part of the grammar of consultancy. "Value in consulting is derived from a consultant's ability to solve problems for their clients. The vehicle to communicate those solutions is PowerPoint," according to Marcus Adhiwiyogo. "Along with PowerPoint, Excel is something a consultant uses daily. Excel skills are considered 'table stakes' for incoming consultants."[17] (Table stakes means the money to begin play at a poker table—poker also being a particular popular sport among finance and consulting professionals.) "If PPT is how consultants communicate, Excel is how consultants think," according to "Former McKinsey Consultant."[18] Given that Luhnow, a former McKinsey consultant, was the general manager of the team, it's not surprising that the Astros scheme began with the Office suite of Microsoft, the provider of tools to bureaucracies all over the world.

Luhnow came to the Astros through the Cardinals, where he developed a proprietary system of evaluation that he brought to Houston. Before that he started an analytics company and had worked as a general manager for a pet supply company. While the Cardinals job is why he got the position with the Astros, the more interesting part of his background is his time at McKinsey. McKinsey and Company consults with high-level companies and often governments, including that of the United States, to develop strategies for change and success.[19] According to *The McKinsey Mind*, written by former consultants, "McKinsey develops solutions to clients' strategic problems, and possibly, aids in the implementation of those solutions," say authors Ethan M. Raisel and Paul N. Friga. "We hope *The McKinsey Mind* helps you become a better problem solver and decision maker. . . . The ability to frame business problems to make them susceptible to rigorous fact-based analysis is one of the core skills of a McKinsey consultant."[20] Such a description covers a lot of ground, and what is really interesting is that Luhnow was brought in not to reform the business processes of the Astros—but the sport side.

In general, consulting tries to take high functioning businesses in cutthroat competition with others of its kind and use the information to provide a competitive advantage in a capitalist business arrangement, an approach that does not automatically apply to a sports team. To use a gambling metaphor (they are rife in sports and consultancy), the consultancy essentially is the house—the bookie—in capitalistic enterprise, always getting a share regardless of whether their clients succeed. In fact, they almost always show a greater profit, since consultants almost always endorse cost cutting. But it's not the consultants who are getting fired.

McKinsey's presence in a sports organization was not new, and its work didn't always go smoothly. McKinsey partnered with the New York Knicks in 2013, and what the consultants were doing was completely mysterious to the coaches and players, according to shooting coach Dave Hopla, as Mike Vorkunov notes: "He remembers one scene before a game when a McKinsey consultant was sitting courtside, typing, when a basketball ricocheted off the rim and hit his computer. The consultant asked for a heads up. The basketball court's no place for a computer, Hopla remembers [Knicks center] Amar'e Stoudemire saying."[21]

By all accounts, the consultant rollout was much smoother on the Astros.

Luhnow brought in McKinsey in 2016 for the traditional goals of getting an outside perspective on the team's operations: "Since arriving in Houston, the interest in leveraging outside help has continued and intensified, as the baseball operations world has quickly become more complex. We have sought and paid for help in numerous areas across baseball operations, including adoption and rollout of emerging technologies; accessing, developing and retaining the best baseball operations talent; and helping devise strategy and operational approaches in a quickly evolving environment."[22] The language here is instructive: it is not baseball language but the language of a corporation, oblique and almost nonsensical in its insistence on using multiple words to say almost nothing; translated, it might read, "We hired people to help us how to figure out better ways to run our baseball team." Most baseball teams are corporations or owned by corporations or owned by LLCs or holding companies or some weird mix of the above. The most striking phrase in this comment is "devise strategy and operational approaches," which can cover a lot of ground, everything from baseball to marketing. It's a utility phrase, able to be handed out in any situation. It's reminiscent of a scene in *Bull Durham*, where catcher Crash Davis advises "Nuke" LaLoosh on the assorted cliches he must use when talking to the media. Luhnow finished with, "We don't disclose our partners in these areas unless it's mutually desired and convenient. We also do not discuss the specifics of any work [we are not telling you anything about the work we do because we do not want to]."[23]

Here we start getting to the real heart of the strangeness to fans who live in the moment of rooting for players in a live competitive environment, that is, watching very talented people play a game that stimulates all sorts of emotional responses, very powerful ones that leave positive and negative memories. I don't think of New York Knicks' John Starks as a bad employee who neglected his fiduciary duty when he went 2 for 18 against the Houston Rockets in game 7 of the 1994 NBA finals. I think of him as a world-class athlete who had a bad day, one that still haunts me to this day.[24]

Ballplayers are not typically thought of as corporate workers, or if they are, it is pejorative, as in the difference between the love of the game and the high salary are somehow mutually excluding. They are not, of course, which irritates some fans, who claim they would play for the love of the game. A reasonable retort: Not if the person you were playing for had lucrative partnerships within the sport and without it that involved profiting off of your efforts. As corporate workers, ballplayers are now subject to the same market forces as other workers, subject to the data collected about their efforts. Like all corporate workers, they make the choice to engage in this endeavor until they retire or are forced to when no one wants their services or will pay what they think is an appropriate value for them.

Consultant hires from outside the sport seem to violate one of the idealistic laws of sports franchises: the game and business should be separate. Sports franchises are like traditional news organizations in that they are deeply tied to their communities, and their operation relies on a public trust that rooters and readers are deeply invested in. In journalism there are two big lines of division—between business and news gathering, and between news gathering and opinion. The first is to make sure that business interests do not affect the organization's public interest in reporting the news, and the second is to make sure that the opinions of the management are separate from reporting (that many outsiders do not understand this does not impact whether this is the aim of organizations like the *New York Times* and *Washington Post*). In sports, there are two similar lines: one is that financial considerations should not hold perfect sway over the ambitions of the actual sports side, and the other is that sports people should make sports decisions and business people business decisions, both related to the public trust that sports franchises are held in. The first holds that owners must act in the interest of producing a winning team. The second means that owners should not meddle in the everyday business of running the team. So in New York sports history, owners George Steinbrenner of the New York Yankees and James Dolan of the Knicks pass the first test and fail the second—they consistently have interfered in the sports side of team management.

Analytics hires muddled the second line so deeply that sometimes it sometimes felt to players and fans alike they were violating both lines. The best example in sports was "The Process" initiated by former Philadelphia 76ers general manager Sam Hinkie, a Stanford MBA. As the GM, Hinkie traded good players from a decent team to deliberately make the team worse in order to get high draft picks, a process known as tanking. What was different was the degree to which Hinkie did it, based on his analysis that teams only become great with very high-level players. The 76ers have not won the championship since the beginning of the process, but two of those of the players drafted under Hinkie, Joel Embiid and Ben Simmons, were an integral part of the team's success, in first place in the Eastern Conference as of this writing. Hinkie was shunted aside by sport people when his methods seemed slow developing. But it was also true that the payroll stayed the same over time as the NBA cap raised.[25] With Luhnow it was even more stark. In 2011, the Astros had a payroll of about $70 million. In 2013, it was down to $22 million. In their championship year, 2017, it was back up to $124 million, still only eighteenth in the league in total payroll. We don't have access to the conversations between Luhnow and Jim Crane and others, but saving tens of millions a year in salary *has* to be appreciated by an owner.[26]

The presence of people like Hinkie—consultants who are often trained in the Ivy League—in sport decision-making processes remains unsettling to players and traditional sport personnel alike. When McKinsey came into the Knicks orbit, player Cole Aldrich questioned the move. "Aldrich associated consulting companies with businesses, not sports. In fact, McKinsey had reportedly worked with the NBA for a decade by then to help it assess teams' operations, and the company's work helped the league determine how to pay out its luxury tax collection."[27] Fans were mixed in their reaction to McKinsey's presence with the Astros before they won the World Series. "Mathew L." noted in the comments of Evan Drellich's story about McKinsey that while he knew and liked many people who worked for McKinsey ("they were all super smart"), the consultants he worked with seemed more political than analytical:

> I mostly saw McKinsey—in my career—used to validate obvious but politically difficult points (they are not innovators, IMO). I wondered if Lubenow [*sic*] was using them to push through a change the org was resisting (probably to get the backing the owners needed) like laying off scouts. Also, the more I read about the Astros management, the more they seem to suck. I'll take Cashman and Friedman and Theo over these people. I like the embrace of data but not the embrace of the dark side of business.[28]

Spreadsheets and Code

Once consultants and business graduates became involved with the sport side, their use of spreadsheets was inevitable. Spreadsheets are often disparaged for their cold display of data, though to be fair, the ledger, which is centuries old, did pretty much the same duty. One of the creators of the electronic spreadsheet, Dan Bricklin, notes that people have strong reactions to spreadsheets: "There are people who complain about 'spreadsheet thinking' and talk about errors—but if they were doing the same things by hand, do you think it would be better? The spreadsheet doesn't get in the way of you making mistakes. What it does prevent is you making addition and subtraction errors, which we did in the past."[29] Where the objections lie for even those of us who use spreadsheets (hello, fellow Blackboard gradebook users) is the reduction of human experience into abstraction, the raison d'être of spreadsheets. The problem, as researchers note, is that this data is far from complete: "That human experience which cannot be fitted into a particular methodology becomes then by definition nonexistent. . . . The irony is that such a reduction of the human experience creates its own validation."[30] In other words, data entry becomes its own justification—including calculating the signs of opposing catchers, as the Astros did with their Codebreaker algorithm.

One of the most enduring traditions in American baseball is the process by which the pitcher receives a signal from a catcher telling him what type of pitch to throw, supplemented by where the catcher sets his target. Doing so allows the pitcher and catcher to signal to each other where the ball is going and at what speed, which protects the catcher from being surprised and either being injured or letting the ball go past him. There is no rule that this has to be, but it is one of baseball's traditions, one could even say codes. In his fine biography of Yogi Berra, the Hall of Fame New York Yankee catcher, Jon Pessah notes that for the first years of his career, Yankee pitchers and manager Casey Stengel occasionally called the game for Berra. Berra's maturity and development as a catcher led to his calling his games.[31] But trying to find out what that sign is also one of those traditions, because knowing what pitch is coming gives the batter a big advantage.[32]

Signs and codes are among the most loaded of terms for those theoretically oriented. Signs are the things that tell you whether a business is open, where to exit, or to bring your vehicle to a stop. But semioticians—sign studiers—see everything as a sign that can be interpreted. For example, this book is employed in reading the Astros' sign-stealing scandal as a sign, an interpretable text. The catcher's signs are an encoded method of communication between themselves and the pitcher. But the fact that the catcher and pitcher engage in this type of communication itself is a sign—what does such an arrangement say about the relationship between these two entities and the game as a whole?

Then there are codes. Codes are sets of laws governing behavior. They can be formal and specific or unwritten, or they can be fed to a computer. As Katherine Hayles writes, "In the narrow sense in which code operates in computers, code can be defined as a system of correspondences that relate the elements of one symbol set to another symbol set," using as Morse Code as an example as translating symbols in the forms of dots and dashes to alphanumeric texts.[33] Semioticians see human interactions with each other and the physical world as signs as well. Codes are sets of rules, sometimes explicitly, like a dress code, and sometimes not, like baseball's rules about how players should proceed with their behavior when they hit a home run. But there is also computer code, a series of laws that tell the computer how to proceed with its computations or behavior. Code for breaking codes—that's what the Codebreaker was.

And signs and codes are sometimes interchangeable or overlapping. One scene from *Bull Durham* demonstrates this. The pitcher Nuke LaLoosh and the catcher Crash Davis are doing well in a game when LaLoosh, full of confidence, shakes off Davis's sign, meaning he is rejecting Davis's pitch suggestion. He does so twice. Davis accedes to LaLoosh's desire "to bring the heat," turns to the batter and tells him what pitch is coming, and the batter hits a home run. LaLoosh has broken a code, maybe two, by shaking off his veteran catcher—catchers generally have authority for calling a game, telling the pitchers what to throw, and the fact that LaLoosh is a rookie and Davis a veteran magnifies his obligation to respect the sign. Davis breaks a code by helping an opposite player hit a home run but also adheres to another code— his only job is to make LaLoosh better so he can contribute to the organization's success. His success as a catcher will turn on whether LaLoosh has future success.

The scene itself is a sign. As viewers, we can see what the moviemakers are trying to show us, which is to demonstrate that experience and talent of different levels are components that can work well together in balance but fail when that balance is upset (also, always listen to your catcher). An examination of the Astros organization's behavior from the front office to the players suggests that they emphasized the importance of one code—that winning is the most important value for a baseball team—by deemphasizing another code: that some methods of winning are outside the codes of expected behavior by baseball players and officials.

That these rules are not explicit or written down is in concert with so many of our cultural rules, expectations, and traditions, operating by unspoken agreement, what anthropologist Constance Perin calls the "shadow constitution," which she describes as the "implicit ideas constituting the hundreds of systems of meaning and conduct that are American culture."[34] The unwritten rules of baseball, its tacit code, are a part of this constitution, as well as the tradition of having a catcher call a game. This code is often called *The Book*, somewhat reverently by traditionalists and often mockingly by analytics followers as "gospel": "*The Book* . . . is handed down generation to generation through the wisdom and experience of those more learned. . . . *The Book*, the unwritten rules created by generation after generation of baseball followers, was gospel. The preachers did not have quantify and qualify their reasonings, unlike every other multi-million-dollar corporation in the world."[35]

The Book in baseball is a set of rules or codes that dictates actions upon specific circumstances. One of the primary goals of those who practice analytics is reexamine the assumptions behind these rules to see whether they still hold up after statistical analysis. They often do not, and accordingly, those who have believed in them often find this new knowledge unsettling or even hostile. *Moneyball* the movie is particularly good at demonstrating the emotional component behind this type of codebreaking in its ongoing conflicts between Billy Beane and Grady Fuson, the scouting director, on how to find replacements for ballplayers who left during free agency; by runs produced versus traditional numbers; and Beane and the coach Art Howe over who to play, the statistically more adept player or one who has a feel for the game. (That these scenes might be fictionalized is sort of beside the point here.) These fights over inherited wisdom over statistical analysis really hover over many of the conflicts associated with the analytics movement.

In their extreme version of Moneyball, the Astros set up cameras to record signs, activated humans to decode them, and programmed computers to parse the data. The high-tech aspects of baseball sometimes seem incongruous with baseball, which is a game requiring great skill, played on a field, in front of humans, with a long and often romanticized history. The tension among all of these elements—scandal, history, data, skill, and video—make for a particularly interesting matrix of scholarship and expression.

There were no code violations in the Excel spreadsheet. It took the input and processed the request. Other codes associated with this act were violated in one way or another. The use of electronic equipment to gather sign information was probably a borderline code violation; code stealing is as old as the game as is the electronic stealing, though the latter isn't quite as accepted. As contributors have written here, the codes on sign stealing and cheating in general are both well known and often flouted. The organized code relaying definitely broke the code, because . . . well, it was too well planned. A baseball game is supposed to be a combination of play and strategy, impulse and intellect. The balance shifted too far toward intellect. It was an extra beanball after one had already delivered, a closer coming into the seventh inning instead of the ninth. Still, the ultimate goal of any game is to win, and deception is a crucial part of baseball, from base stealing to pickoff moves, fake bunts, and disguised deliveries. A really good pitcher wins often by deception; the Houston Astros won by hiding their deception in plain sight.

Breaking codes in the form of stealing signs seems different because of two elements—the preplanning and the use of in-time, at-the-moment signals conveyed by teammates. With a camera, Astros personnel logged the pitches and the signals. When the data-gathering began and ended, no one has said. The trash can banging began in the spring 2017 and was discovered in September by Danny Farquhar of the White Sox. But the computer and its programmers and data entry began long before that.

The Code of the Pastoral

Using computer processes and video cameras to do so in this matter also seemed to violate a different code, the code of the pastoral. Baseball employs a variety of terms involving both technology and the pastoral, which I define in the way Leo Marx does, as a set of symbolic parameters that relate to the rural and agricultural in the setting of greenery among settled areas (technically, pastoralism has more to do with agriculture). In studying the way nineteenth-century authors such as Nathanael Hawthorne, Henry David Thoreau, and Ralph Waldo Emerson engaged the presence of technological developments like the railroad, Marx writes, "the distinctive attribute of the new order is its technological power, a power that does not remain refined to the traditional boundaries of the city. It is a centrifugal force that threatens to break down, once of all, the conventional contrast between these two styles of life."[36] Substitute "baseball management offices" for city, and you get the same equation—using management techniques to win a game played on a field violates the code of the pastoral experience associated with baseball.

Funnily enough, the language of baseball is rife with both pastoral and technological nomenclature, which makes sense given the universal presence of those concepts in American culture but also suggests a type of divide that perhaps this era's developments have ended up highlighting. Players have tools, they come from a farm system, they have range, they have power, and they have speed. Outfields and infields are farming terms, as is dugout. Baseball is played in a ballpark. Indeed, the "parkness" of baseball is a central force in its aesthetic experience. As David McGimphy notes, "In baseball, there is always the crack of the bat, the slap of the ball in the glove, the roar of the crowd, the smell of leather and hot dogs, the greenness of the freshly cut grass, the smooth infield dirt, and so on."[37] He notes that this Arcadian image is cultivated by the sport's organizers, as a way for people to experience the idea of greenery if not the greenery itself.

Moneyball the movie seems to understand this (the book is far more subtle in its value projecting). The movie is a visual manifestation of all these ideas, but in this movie, the people who evaluate talent by eye are sentimental and seem foolish, while Beane, the A's general manager, and his new analytics hire, Peter Brand (a composite character mostly based on the Beane's employee at the time, the actual future general manager Paul DePodesta), seem like the humane and thoughtful angle players who really understand the game.[38] It's remarkable in the sense that it finds some way to make numbers people heroes and traditional baseball people villains.

After a movie that posits decisions in baseball should be about data, it shows how the joy of Scott Hatteberg hitting a game-winning home run to help set the major league record for consecutive wins and later, the pastoral grandness of Fenway Park in the rain, where owner John Henry seems flummoxed by the personal decisions involving a relationship. See, hedge fund founders are human too! But *Moneyball* can't unmediate itself completely; it ends with a videotape of a catcher hitting a home run, one that Brand and Beane had found through the same types of spreadsheet that the Baseball Prospectus writers had used to find their players. The fact is that these videos are not only celebrations of a catcher's triumph but also of Beane and Brand making a good decision based on data.

In other words, *Moneyball* the movie would like to have it both ways, as a story about the romance of baseball and about the necessity of data to make good decisions. For the most part, fans are often willing to accept both as part of a modern game. Still, the strain of technology in the midst of the pastoral is a historical phenomenon dating back to the Industrial Revolution, about when baseball came into being. Urban growth and technological development associated with the Industrial Revolution was well under way when the casual game of baseball grew into its professional version, and so the pastoral was probably part of the associated symbolic systems of baseball. As Marx notes, Hawthorne, Thoreau, and Emerson were highly aware of the discordance—and yet normalcy—of a train whistle disrupting what was nature. But as Roderick Nash observes, that work had already started when colonists shaped land to their own needs and categorized undeveloped land as wilderness, which they found gloomy and frightening. Development meant security.[39] Humans create parks as a way of simulating nature; what we think of pastoral is already land transformed from wilderness. Land exists first, and humans are the ones who divide it into different types of land: nature, pasture, parking lot, baseball field, and so forth. If nothing else, our ideas of nature are cultivated in response to, in dialogue with, and as part of culture. Bob Bednar notes that "the binary distinction between nature and culture itself is cultural."[40] In that sense, the spreadsheet in the garden only seems strange because it is not living in the way that grass does. Its technological development is as predictable as the turning of wilderness into a park.

The sense of play and relaxation associated with a park remains strong with those who watch baseball in its live and even mediated broadcast state.

The team, the city, the fans, see the game as the game when they watch one. Their own intellectual and emotional processes give meaning to their experiences. They are probably not primarily thinking of OBP or WHIP, but the inherent narrative tension of a game being played. What we love about sports has much to do with this unresolved narrative tension, the fact that we don't know what happens. But narrative tension is no fun for CFOs and hedge fund owners. What technology—and hedge funds and consulting firms—often tries to do is mediate risk or add efficiency or both, which is challenging to do with an art form or sport. This is probably why we seem to see major studios now release mostly superhero and *Star Wars* movies for theater viewing—the risk that these movies will not draw an audience is low. But managing baseball's risk is challenging for a variety of reasons.

Baseball is unique in major American sports in that there is no clock. Pitchers are in a unique position in that they are the instigator of the narrative; they can be hurried along (a pitch clock is in the works), but the pitcher controls the pace of play as well as the pace and direction of the pitch. Knowing what a pitcher is going to throw—well, that changes a fundamental part of the narrative tension, let alone the probable result of the game.

Trash cans are part of this equation in a way. Corralling waste was one of the first hallmarks of urban modernization for both obvious aesthetic and safety reasons.[41] Trash cans allow settled areas to control the chaos and cleanliness of their spaces. Banging on the trash can, itself this symbol of control, transforms it into the vehicle of control, the final step of the algorithm's purpose. Trash removal is undoubtedly an entry on some business spreadsheet in every team, a piece of data to be used to calculate debits that need to be paid. To make it an instrument that helps the bottom line—a winning World Series team unleashes millions of dollars in extra revenue, increases the team's value, and probably guarantees an increase in attendance, as well as viewership on television (teams often own or partially own their own sports networks).[42] Still, it does seem that recording and processing catcher's signs from opposing teams is a line beyond scouting. Scouts and fans document play through observation and study; notebooks seem different from spreadsheets. What's complicated about the Astros' setup is that the closely related scouting operations were legal, even encouraged. In *Astroball*, Ben Reiter describes the admirable behavior of Carlos Beltrán, one of the leaders of the trash can–banging scheme, and his efforts to chart pitcher tendencies, including ones that gave away tipping pitches, by watching videotapes of their performances. He routinely shared such information as a way of helping his teammates become better performers.[43]

In the case of sign stealing, the sign went to the spreadsheet; the calculation went to the Astros' employees and players; the camera picked up the signal game day; it went to the dugout monitor; players hit the trash can, which then became a chemical reaction in a batter's brain and translated into the reactions of a highly trained and skilled athlete, all to reduce the risk of losing. High-tech wizardly and office calculations seem like a weird thing employed in the middle of a game, unless it was part of a larger game the Astros were playing. In the hands of a highly trained employee, a Major League Baseball player, it might have been the difference between winning and losing both games—the one to create a team out of analytically analyzed player outputs and the one on the field itself. In that sense, the consulting project, the spreadsheet embedded in the PowerPoint, embedded in the presentation of an "intern" who had previously worked at a high-level consulting organization, who had attended college as a way of making a living and finding a life, worked. Sort of, anyway. There does seem to be some irony that the team named after a space program that sought the stars found its own version: an asterisk. *

Notes

1. Ben Lindbergh and Sam Miller, *The Only Rule Is That It Has to Work* (New York: St. Martin's Press, 2016), 4.

2. Ben Reiter, *Astroball: The New Way to Win It All* (New York: Three Rivers Press, 2018). *Astroball* is a thoughtful and well-researched account of how Luhnow and other management figures developed their methods and implemented them in the 2010s. It is not critical of the efforts, but its goal is to let the Astros tell their story, and in that it succeeds.

3. Lindbergh and Miller, *The Only Rule*, 49.

4. George Vescey, "Roger Maris: No Asterisk," *New York Times*, December 16, 1985, https://www.nytimes.com/1985/12/16/sports/roger-maris-no-asterisk.html.

5. Tyler Kepner, "McGwire Admits That He Used Steroids," *New York Times*, January 11, 2010, https://www.nytimes.com/2010/01/12/sports/baseball/12mcgwire.html.

6. Childs Walker, "Earl Weaver Preached Moneyball Before It Became 'Moneyball,'" *Baltimore Sun*, January 19, 2013, https://www.baltimoresun.com/sports/orioles/bal-earl-weaver-preached-moneyball-before-it-became-moneyball-20130119-story.html.

7. Michael Lewis, *Moneyball: The Art of Winning an Unfair Game* (New York: Norton, 2003).

8. "Hedge Fund Moneyball: Big Data, Sports and Finance," *Institutional Investor*, December 2013, Gale General OneFile, https://link.gale.com/apps/doc/A359346371/ITOF?u=mlin_n_umass&sid=ITOF&xid=7e731c6d.

9. Lindbergh and Miller, *The Only Rule*, 5.

10. Henry Abbott and Yaron Weitzman, "Daryl Morey, Rafael Stone, and the Exploding Rockets," TrueHoop, December 29, 2020, https://www.truehoop.com/p/daryl-morey-rafael-stone-and-the.

11. Travis Sawchik, *Big Data Baseball: Math, Miracles, and the End of a 20-Year Losing Streak* (New York: Flatiron Books, 2015).

12. "Hedge Fund and Private Equity Managers That Own Sports Teams," Little Sis, April 26, 2020, https://littlesis.org/lists/963-hedge-fund-and-private-equity -managers-that-own-sports-teams/interlocks. Little Sis presumably is a reference to the opposite of Big Brother.

13. Joe Pompeo, "The Hedge Fund Vampire That Bleeds Newspapers Dry Now Has the *Chicago Tribune* by the Throat," *Vanity Fair*, February 5, 2020, https:// www.vanityfair.com/news/2020/02/hedge-fund-vampire-alden-global-capital-that -bleeds-newspapers-dry-has-chicago-tribune-by-the-throat.

14. Joseph L. Bower and Clayton M. Christensen, "Disruptive Technologies: Catching the Wave," *Harvard Business Review*, January–February 1995.

15. "Masters of the Universe Are Taking Over Your Local Sports Teams," *Business Finance*, December 9, 2019, https://link.gale.com/apps/doc/A607979229/ITOF? u=mlin_n_umass&sid=ITOF&xid=8463164e.

16. Jared Diamond, "'Dark Arts' and 'Codebreaker': The Origins of the Houston Astros Cheating Scheme," *Wall Street Journal*, February 7, 2020, https://www.wsj .com/articles/houston-astros-cheating-scheme-dark-arts-codebreaker-11581112994.

17. Markus Adhiwiyogo, "What I Wish I Had Learned before Starting as a Consultant," Vault.com, June 19, 2017, https://www.vault.com/blogs/consult-this-con sulting-careers-news-and-views/what-i-wish-i-had-learned-before-starting-as-a -consultant.

18. Anon (Former McKinsey Consultant), "Top 5 Internal McKinsey Resources for Consultants," Working with McKinsey, November 22, 2013, http://workingwith mckinsey.blogspot.com/2013/11/Top-5-Internal-McKinsey-Resources.html.

19. Reiter, *Astroball*.

20. Ethan Raisel and Paul Friga, *The McKinsey Mind: Understanding and Implementing the Problem-Solving Tools and Management Techniques of the World's Top Strategic Consulting Firm* (New York: McGraw Hill, 2002), xv, xix, 1.

21. Mike Vorkunov, "'It Was Crazy': How a Famous Consulting Firm Contributed to the Chaos of the 2013–14 Knicks," *The Athletic*, November 25, 2019, https:// theathletic.com/1384231/2019/11/25/it-was-crazy-how-a-famous-consulting-firm -contributed-to-the-chaos-of-the-2013-14-knicks/.

22. Evan Drellich, "The Astros Opened Baseball Ops to McKinsey Consultants, From Scouting to R&D and the Farm," *The Athletic*, July 17, 2019, https://theathletic .com/1056165/2019/07/17/the-astros-opened-baseball-ops-to-mckinsey-consultants -from-scouting-to-rd-and-the-farm/.

23. Drellich, "The Astros Opened Baseball Ops."

24. Jonathan Wagner, "New York Knicks: Two Decades Since John Starks' 2-For-18," HoopsHabit, June 22, 2014, https://hoopshabit.com/2014/06/22/new-york-knicks -two-decades-since-john-starks-2-18/.

25. "NBA Salary Cap History," Basketball Reference, https://www.basketball -reference.com/contracts/salary-cap-history.html.

26. "MLB Team Payrolls," Steve O's Baseball Umpire Resources, http://www .stevetheump.com/Payrolls.htm#2011payroll.

27. Vorkunov, "It Was Crazy."

28. Drellich, "Astros Opened Baseball Ops."

29. Jason Karaian, "Dan Bricklin Invented the Spreadsheet—But Don't Hold That against Him," *Quartz*, December 22, 2015, https://qz.com/578661/dan-bricklin-invented-the-spreadsheet-but-dont-hold-that-against-him/.

30. Arno Gruen, "On Abstraction: The Reduction and Destruction of Human Experience," *Journal of Humanistic Psychology* 18, no. 1 (Winter 1978): 37–45, https://journals.sagepub.com/doi/pdf/10.1177/002216787801800105.

31. Jon Pessah, *Yogi: A Life behind the Mask* (New York: Little, Brown, 2010).

32. Ron Kroichick, "Baseball's Code of Ethics/Conduct Governed by Rules Based on Respecting the Game," *SF Gate*, August 6, 2012.

33. N. Katherine Hayles, *My Mother Was a Computer: Digital Subjects and Literary Texts* (Chicago: University of Chicago Press, 2005), 108.

34. Constance Perin, *Belonging in America: Reading Between the Lines* (Madison: University of Wisconsin Press, 1988), 228.

35. Tom M. Tango, Mitchel G. Lichtman, and Andrew E. Dolphin, *The Book: Playing the Percentages in Baseball* (Washington, DC: Potomac Books, 2007), 14–15.

36. Leo Marx, *The Machine in the Garden: Technology and the Pastoral Idea in America* (Oxford: Oxford University Press, 1964), 32.

37. David McGimpsey, *Imagining Baseball: America's Pastime and Popular Culture* (Bloomington: Indiana University Press, 2000), 68.

38. Jason Reid, "'Moneyball' Is Compelling, But Leaves Out Much of the Real Story," *Washington Post*, October 11, 2011, https://www.washingtonpost.com/sports/nationals/moneyball-is-compelling-but-leaves-out-much-of-the-real-story/2011/10/11/gIQAMA1cdL_story.html.

39. Roderick Nash, *Wilderness and the American Mind*, rev. ed. (New Haven, CT: Yale University Press, 1967), x–xi.

40. Robert Bednar, "Marking Territory: Constructing and Maintaining Boundaries Between Nature and Culture in the Western National Parks," *Snapshot Semiotics*, https://people.southwestern.edu/~bednarb/snapshotsemiotics/deconstructing.htm.

41. For a discussion of the role of horses in creating waste in the early modern city, see Ann Norton Greene, *Horses at Work* (Cambridge, MA: Harvard University Press, 2008). She notes that cars and mass transit actually improved sanitary conditions in cities.

42. For example, see Mike Ozanian, "Winning The World Series Could Boost the Value of the Washington Nationals," *Forbes*, October 31, 2019, https://www.forbes.com/sites/mikeozanian/2019/10/31/winning-world-series-could-boost-the-value-of-washington-nationals/?sh=2dc3f08065ba.

43. Reiter, *Astroball*, 158–161.

"Defendant Houston Astros":
Michael Bolsinger vs. The Houston Astros

Note: The following lawsuit was filed in California by Michael Bolsinger, a former Major League Baseball pitcher. As the lawsuit explains, Bolsinger believes he was directly affected by the Astros' sign stealing; it led to a terrible half-inning of work that led to him to be sent down to the minors soon after that game. Whether that was the main factor will be sorted out by the courts, if it ever makes it there; as of this writing, Bolsinger has not refiled the case after it was dismissed by California courts, because the action took place in California. (The text has been lightly edited for grammar and repetition.)

SUPERIOR COURT OF THE STATE OF CALIFORNIA FOR THE COUNTY OF LOS ANGELES
MICHAEL BOLSINGER, an individual;
Plaintiff,
vs.
HOUSTON ASTROS, LLC, a limited liability company; and DOES 1-300 inclusive; Defendants.
Case No.
COMPLAINT FOR DAMAGES:
1. UNFAIR BUSINESS
PRACTICES BUS. & PROF.
CODE SECTION 17200 ET SEQ.;
2. NEGLIGENCE;
3. INTENTIONAL INTERFERENCE WITH CONTRACTUAL RELATIONS;
4. INTENTIONAL INTERFERENCE WITH PROSPECTIVE ECONOMIC RELATIONS
5. NEGLIGENT INTERFERENCE WITH PROSPECTIVE ECONOMIC RELATIONS
DEMAND FOR JURY TRIAL

INTRODUCTION

1. COMES NOW Plaintiff Michael Bolsinger ("Bolsinger") who brings this action against Defendant Houston Astros LLC ("Astros") for their involvement in an elec-

tronic sign stealing scheme in 2017 resulting in the Defendant Astros winning the World Series.

2. Plaintiff Bolsinger was a professional relief pitcher with the Toronto Blue Jays who was called into the game by his team on August 4, 2017 after the prior pitchers on his team gave up several runs. In .1 innings pitched, Plaintiff Bolsinger gave up 4 runs to the Defendant Astros and was immediately terminated and cut from the team never to return to Major League Baseball again.

3. The Defendant Astros sign stealing scheme was recently discovered and involved a camera in the Defendant Astros' outfield which video recorded and decoded the signs given by a catcher to the pitcher of an opposing team which Defendant Astros then relayed to the batter by, *inter alia*, making a "bang" noise from the side of the field depending on the pitch.

4. The Defendant Astros' unlawful and tortious business practices have had consequences far beyond wins or losses and strikeouts or home runs. Indeed, the Defendant Astros have been unjustly enriched in the amount of several hundred million dollars by their illicit scheme, and went from a team controversially purchased through massive debt in 2011 to the one of the most valuable sport franchises today with a value of approximately $2 billion.

5. Plaintiff seeks two categories of damages through this lawsuit:

6. First, Plaintiff seeks the consequential and general damages he suffered and continues to suffer in the form of the Defendant Astros interfering with and harming his career.

7. Second, Plaintiff seeks restitution in the form of Defendant Astros returning the post-season bonuses earned from winning the 2017 World Series which, upon information and belief, is approximately $31 million. Plaintiff would seek to direct that this category of restitutionary damages relating to post-season bonuses be used exclusively for charitable causes focused on bettering the lives of children with an emphasis on charities in Los Angeles as well as a fund for elderly retired 4 professional baseball players in need of financial assistance.

PARTIES

8. Plaintiff Michael P. Bolsinger is a resident of Carrollton, Texas.

9. Defendant Houston Astros LLC is a limited liability company with headquarters in Houston, Texas. Upon information and belief, Defendant has member-investors who reside in Los Angeles, California and who were involved in the fraudulent conduct at issue in this action.

10. Defendant DOES 1-300 include other member-investors and affiliates of the Defendant who were involved with and/or aided and abetted the tortious conduct at issue. The names and identities of the DOES are not yet known. Upon further inquiry, investigation, and discovery their names will be added once determined.

JURISDICTION AND VENUE

11. The Court has jurisdiction over the present matter because, as delineated within this Complaint for Damages, the nature of the claims and amounts in controversy meet the requirements for unlimited jurisdiction in the Superior Court.

12. Venue is proper in this county because a significant portion of the activities giving rise to the claims in this action occurred in the County of Los Angeles. Specifically, (a) Los Angeles is the situs where the Defendant Astros fraudulently won the 2017 World Series; (b) upon information and belief, Defendant has member-investors involved in the fraudulent scheme who reside in Los Angeles, California; and (c) the impact and damages caused within the County of Los Angeles exceeds all other jurisdictions and substantial tortious conduct was directed at Los Angeles.

FACTUAL BACKGROUND

The Purchase of the Houston Astros

13. The roots of the Defendant Astros malicious conduct find its origins in the massive debt and peculiar ownership structure used to acquire the team in 2011.

14. In 2011 the Astros sold to a large investor group led by Jim Crane for approximately $680 million. The deal was the source of substantial scrutiny and controversy based on certain past conduct by the acquiring party and by the massive debt—approximately $300 million—used in the acquisition.

15. From the outset, the Defendant Astros were motivated to pay down its substantial debt, refinance, and avoid costs such as the luxury tax. Ultimately, this was done by any means necessary. Indeed, the annualized percent increase in the value of the Astros following the 2017 World Series Season was approximately 17 percent or $300 million with the team now worth approximately $2 billion—a 200 percent increase in the value of the team since its acquisition seven years earlier. This massive financial windfall was the direct result of the sign-stealing scheme.

Michael Bolsinger

16. After three successful seasons as a starting pitcher at the University of Arkansas, Plaintiff Mike Bolsinger began his professional baseball career in 2010, when he was selected by the Arizona Diamondbacks in the 2010 MLB Players Draft.

17. For the next four years, Plaintiff Bolsinger found success as a starting pitcher at each level of the minor leagues and was promoted the following year of each season.

18. In the beginning of the 2014 minor league season in Triple A, Plaintiff Bolsinger pitched a dominant first two games and was then called up following his second start. As many rookies find in their first year in the MLB, Plaintiff Bolsinger found himself getting sent up and down throughout the season while still performing well at the minor league level and showing promise in the MLB. At the end of the season, his contract was purchased by the Los Angeles Dodgers that November.

19. In 2015, Plaintiff Bolsinger was called up in late April to make a start where he did very well but was sent down after the game. Plaintiff was called up again in early May, where in that month he won the Dodgers' pitcher of the month at the MLB level. Plaintiff continued to have huge success, and he was sent down to the minors at the beginning of August due to trades within the organization. He then got called back up on September 1st to the MLB for September call-ups and finished the year with a 3.62 ERA.

20. In 2016 by the end of Spring Training, Plaintiff Bolsinger had made the opening day roster with the Dodgers as one of the five starting pitchers, but unfortunately,

an oblique injury sidelined him right before the season started. From there, Plaintiff Bolsinger rehabbed in Triple A and was called up to the MLB on May 18th for six starts that were tainted by the lingering injury. Plaintiff Bolsinger was sent back to Triple A one month later with the thought of transitioning into a long relief role. Shortly thereafter, he was traded to the Toronto Blue Jays as a starting pitcher where he spent the rest of 2016 in Triple A readjusting once again to his new role.

21. Plaintiff Bolsinger remained with the Toronto Blue Jays for the 2017 season where he finished spring training and was designated to Triple A to start the year. After a successful start to the year in Triple A, Plaintiff was called up as a starting pitcher for three weeks in May to then be designated to Triple A on May 31st. From there, it was determined that Plaintiff Bolsinger could have extreme success as a reliever, so he spent the next month of June transitioning to this new role in Triple A.

22. On July 3rd, Plaintiff was called up to MLB to begin his new journey as a reliever for the Toronto Blue Jays. After five optimistic outings of relief, Plaintiff would enter his 6th and final outing of relief against the Defendant Astros in Houston.

23. On August 4th, Plaintiff Bolsinger only saw .1 innings against the Astros. Plaintiff Bolsinger gave up four runs due to the Houston Astros' sign stealing scheme. This ultimately cost him his job, as he was immediately sent down to Triple A after the game never to be called up again.

24. At the time, the Blue Jays believed that as a result of the disastrous inning, that Plaintiff Bolsinger was not capable of being a relief pitcher and other MLB scouts shared that view. For a journeyman pitcher in the MLB like Plaintiff, a disastrous inning, such as was what took place in Houston on August 4th, could and did prove to be the death knell to Plaintiff's career in the MLB.

25. Due to the inning against the Houston Astros, Plaintiff Bolsinger was no longer seen as a successful relief pitcher that could be trusted in this role and was not picked up by the Blue Jays for the following year.

26. After being demoted by the Blue Jays, Mr. Bolsinger continued to dominate in Triple A where he finished the year with a 1.70 ERA.

27. Plaintiff Bolsinger could not secure a role in the United States after this, so he opted to take a job in Japan with the Chiba Lotte Marines, a team in the Japanese professional baseball league, where he was considered one of the top pitchers in all of Japan for 2018. Plaintiff Bolsinger was selected to play in the All-Star game that year and received the highest winning percentage award for the year.

28. Plaintiff Bolsinger remained with the Chiba Lotte Marines to finish out his contract for 2019 and is currently a free agent hoping to secure a job in the United States for the 2020 season.

The Astros' Unfair Business Practices—Electronic Sign Stealing

29. Ironically, the 2017 Defendant Astros were widely praised at the time for their purported unprecedented technological innovations and analytic and algorithmic approach to baseball which they touted to mask their illicit sign stealing.

30. Before the sign stealing scheme was uncovered, copious news articles and even full books were written about the 2017 Defendant Astros and their data-based approach to the game.

31. By way of example, a November 2, 2017 article in the *New Yorker* entitled "Long Wait, Great Win," stated, "This Astros championship began with fresh ownership

and management after 2013 and 2014, when the team suffered more-than-a-hundred loss seasons. Brilliant draft picks and front-office algorithm strategizing brought us this case of thrilling newcomers."

32. The bestselling book *Astroball: The New Way to Win It All* by Brett Reiter proclaimed to be a "story of the next wave of thinking in baseball and beyond, at once a remarkable underdog story and a fascinating look at the cutting edge of evaluating and optimizing human potential. . . . *Astroball* is the inside story of how a gang of outsiders went beyond the stats to find a new way to win—and not just in baseball."

33. As it turned out, the "new way to win" the Defendant Astros utilized was the duplicitous and tortious scheme of sign-stealing which was uncovered in November 2019.

34. On or around November 2019, Evan Drellich and Ken Rosenthal of *The Athletic* published an article detailing how the Houston Astros electronically stole signs during their 2017 season. Current Oakland Athletics pitcher Mike Fiers, who spent three seasons with the Defendant Astros, went on the record and admitted that his former team had a tech-fueled sign-stealing scheme in 2017.

35. Shortly after the article came out, MLB launched an investigation. Major League Baseball Commissioner Rob Manfred released his findings on Jan 13, 2020 and confirmed that the Defendant Astros engaged in the sign-stealing scheme throughout the 2017 regular season and postseason and in early 2018. Defendant Astros' Manager A. J. Hinch was suspended and fired as was Defendant Astros' General Manager Jeff Luhnow. Subsequently, the New York Mets fired their Manager Carlos Beltrán, a member of the Defendant Astros 2017 team, and the Boston Red Sox fired their Manager Alex Cora, the bench coach for the Defendant Astros when they illicitly stole signs.

36. The Defendant Astros' sign stealing scheme involved the use of a camera positioned in center field to steal signs. Team personnel from the Defendant Astros would watch the feed in a hallway between the clubhouse and dugout and would relay what was coming to the hitter by hitting a garbage can. A "bang" usually meant that an off-speed pitch was coming, and the Defendant Astros personnel did not make any noise when a fastball was coming.

37. *The Athletic* published an article on January 31, 2020 where it conducted a deep statistical dive into the 2017 Astros revealing the historically unprecedented nature of how the team improved at making contact. It found the reduction in team strikeouts by 365 was by the far the most in the live-ball era (since 1920). *The Athletic* wrote that the Defendant Astros' "strikeout rate at home took a plunge . . . unlike anything we've seen in the last century. . . . They went from punching out 1,452 times in 2016 to a mere 1,087 in 2017, which meant they transformed themselves from a team that was striking out at one of the highest rates in history to a team that struck out less than any team in baseball that season."

38. Further, a recent report prepared by graphic designer and web developer Tony Adams diligently documented every instance of trash can banging he could find by writing a web application to sync up the data with video footage of Defendant's plate appearances from all of the Astros' 2017 home games. The findings have been shocking and disturbing.

39. In the more than 8,200 pitches tracked, more than 1,100 trash can "bangs" were detected. According to the data, after the Defendant Astros appeared to experiment with the banging technique early in the 2017 season, it was in full effect by late May.

The data detected 28 bangs in a May 28 game against Baltimore, an 8–4 Houston win, and then the sign stealing scheme accelerated in the summer with banging on an average of about 30 pitches per game.

40. The most bangs used by the Defendant Astros in the 2017 season took place on August 4, 2017, the game when Plaintiff Bolsinger was called in as a relief pitcher. In that game, there were 54 bangs documented with bangs on 12 of the 29 pitches or 41 percent of pitches thrown by Plaintiff Bolsinger in the .1 innings of play. Based on the data, the Defendant Astros had decoded and stolen the sign for essentially every pitch thrown by Plaintiff and transmitted it to the Astros' batters. As a direct result of his poor performance that game, the Toronto Blue Jays cut Plaintiff from their roster. Plaintiff was viewed by the Blue Jays and MLB scouts as not having the ability perform as a relief pitcher. Plaintiff has never played in the MLB again.

41. Following the August 4, 2017 game, members of the Defendant Astros spoke with the media about their performance that evening—of course concealing their sign stealing and bragging about their "talented offense." Defendant's manager A. J. Hinch told the media, "First and foremost we have a really good offense . . . it is not unusual for us to have big nights when we put good at-bats together."

Fraudulent Concealment

42. Defendant Astros fraudulently concealed their sign stealing scheme until it was preliminarily exposed on or around November 2019 and confirmed through the Commissioner's findings on January 13, 2020. Defendant Astros not only deceitfully concealed their unfair business practices, but they promoted and encouraged fraudulent statements such as those made to the media on or around August 4, 2017 regarding the performance of their offense.

43. Plaintiff could not have known of the Defendant's tortious conduct at issue here and had no way of ascertaining information to otherwise place him on notice of Defendant's conduct, until such time as the fraudulent conduct was exposed and officially confirmed on January 13, 2020.

44. As a result of the fraudulent concealment of the conduct at issue, the running of any potentially pertinent statute of limitations would commence January 13, 2020.

FIRST CAUSE OF ACTION

Unfair Business Practices, Bus. & Prof. Code Section 17200 et seq.
(Plaintiff Against Houston Astros LLC and DOES 1-300)

45. Plaintiff realleges and incorporates by reference each and every allegation contained in the preceding paragraphs as if fully set forth herein.

46. Defendant Astros' sign stealing scheme constitutes unfair or fraudulent business practice or act pursuant to Business & Professions Code Section 17200 *et seq.*

47. California Business and Professions Code section 17200, *et seq.* prohibits unfair competition including "any unlawful, unfair or fraudulent business act or practice."

48. The unlawful conduct described herein resulted in economic harm to Plaintiff, including the loss of his job as a MLB pitcher with the Toronto Blue Jays and other potential opportunities at the Major League level.

49. Plaintiff Bolsinger is entitled to restitution for his losses in an amount to be determined and other general and special damages permitted by law.

SECOND CAUSE OF ACTION

Negligence (Plaintiff Against Houston Astros LLC and DOES 1-300)

50. Plaintiff realleges and incorporates by reference each and every allegation contained in the preceding paragraphs as if fully set forth herein.
51. Defendants owed a duty of care to Plaintiff Bolsinger to supervise and operate Houston Astros LLC so as to avoid causing unreasonable risks of harm to Plaintiff Bolsinger.
52. Defendants breached their duty by failing to properly supervise their employees working for Houston Astros LLC. Defendants failed to adequately train their employees and supervise their work so as to avoid any harm to Plaintiff Bolsinger. Defendants made and/or aided and abetted a cheating scheme which involved the use of a camera positioned in the center field to steal signs. Team personnel from the Defendant Astros would watch the feed in a hallway between the clubhouse and dugout and would relay what was coming to the hitter by hitting a garbage can. A "bang" usually meant that an off-speed pitch was coming, and the Defendant Astros' personnel did not make any noise when a fastball was coming.
53. Had Defendants properly hired, trained, and supervised its employees, Plaintiff Bolsinger would not have been harmed. Instead, Plaintiff Bolsinger was terminated from his role on the Toronto Blue Jays and never returned to play baseball professionally at the Major League level, all as a result of the negligent acts of Defendants.
54. Defendants' negligence was the direct cause and a substantial factor in Plaintiff Bolsinger's damages.
55. As a direct and proximate result of the conduct alleged herein, Mr. Bolsinger has suffered past and future general and special damages in an amount to be determined at trial.

THIRD CAUSE OF ACTION

Intentional Interference with Contractual Relations
(Plaintiff Against Houston Astros LLC and DOES 1-300)

56. Plaintiff realleges and incorporates by reference each and every allegation contained in the preceding paragraphs as if fully set forth herein.
57. Defendants were aware of the contractual relationships Plaintiff Bolsinger had entered and/or intended to enter, including the contract between Plaintiff Bolsinger and the Toro.
58. Defendants made or aided and abetted a cheating scheme with the intent to interfere and cause harm to existing and prospective contracts entered by Plaintiff Bolsinger, to which Defendants knew that disruption in the contractual relations was certain or substantially certain to occur. The Defendant Astros' sign stealing scheme involved the use of a camera positioned in the center field to steal signs. Team per-

sonnel from the Defendant Astros would watch the feed in a hallway between the clubhouse and dugout and would relay what was coming to the hitter by hitting a garbage can. A "bang" usually meant that an off-speed pitch was coming, and the Defendant Astros' personnel did not make any noise when a fastball was coming.

59. Plaintiff Bolsinger was damaged in the disruption of his contractual relationships, including the termination of his position as a MLB pitcher for the Toronto Blue Jays.

60. Defendants were a substantial factor in causing Plaintiff Bolsinger's harm.

61. Plaintiff suffered contractual damages and general and special damages as a result of Defendants' conduct in an amount to be determined at trial.

62. Defendants' conduct was malicious, fraudulent, oppressive, and/or done with a reckless disregard for the rights of Plaintiff Bolsinger, thus giving rise to punitive damages.

FOURTH CAUSE OF ACTION

Intentional Interference with Prospective Economic Relations
(Plaintiff Against Houston Astros LLC and DOES 1-300)

63. Plaintiff realleges and incorporates by reference each and every allegation contained in the preceding paragraphs as if fully set forth herein.

64. Plaintiff Bolsinger was in a prospective economic relationship with third parties, including the Toronto Blue Jays and other MLB teams, that would have resulted in future economic benefit to Plaintiff Bolsinger in the form of further employment as a Major League Baseball player.

65. Defendants were aware of the economic relationships Plaintiff Bolsinger had entered and/or intended to enter, including the relationship between Plaintiff Bolsinger and the Toronto Blue Jays.

66. Defendants made or aided and abetted a cheating scheme with the intent to interfere and cause harm to prospective contracts entered by Plaintiff Bolsinger, to which Defendants knew that disruption in the contractual relations was certain or substantially certain to occur. The Defendant Astros' sign stealing scheme involved the use of a camera positioned in the center field to steal signs. Team personnel from the Defendant Astros would watch the feed in a hallway between the clubhouse and dugout and would relay what was coming to the hitter by hitting a garbage can. A "bang" usually meant that an off-speed pitch was coming, and the Defendant Astros' did not make any noise when a fastball was coming.

67. Plaintiff Bolsinger was damaged in the disruption of his contractual relationships, including the termination of his position as a MLB pitcher for the Toronto Blue Jays and the subsequent lost opportunity to continue to play at the Major League level.

68. Defendants were a substantial factor in causing Plaintiff Bolsinger's harm.

69. Plaintiff suffered consequential, general, and special damages as a result of Defendants' conduct.

70. Defendants' conduct was malicious, fraudulent, oppressive, and/or done with a reckless disregard for the rights of Plaintiff Bolsinger, thus giving rise to punitive damages.

FIFTH CAUSE OF ACTION

Negligent Interference with Prospective Economic Relations
(Plaintiff Against Houston Astros LLC and DOES 1-300)

71. Plaintiff realleges and incorporates by reference each and every allegation contained in the preceding paragraphs as if fully set forth herein.

72. Plaintiff Bolsinger was in a prospective economic relationship with third parties, including the Toronto Blue Jays, that would have resulted in a future economic benefit to Plaintiff Bolsinger in the form of employment as a professional baseball player.

73. Defendants knew or should have known of the existence of Plaintiff Bolsinger's economic relationships, including his relationship with the Toronto Blue Jays.

74. Defendants knew or should have known that Plaintiff Bolsinger's economic relationships, including his relationship with the Toronto Blue Jays, would have been disrupted if they failed to act with reasonable care.

75. Defendants failed to act with reasonable care through actions including, but not limited to failing to supervise and train their employees and by engaging in a cheating scheme. The Defendant Astros' sign stealing scheme involved the use of a camera positioned in center field to steal signs. Team personnel from the Defendant Astros would watch the feed in a hallway between the clubhouse and dugout and would relay what was coming to the hitter by hitting a garbage can. A "bang" usually meant that an off-speed pitch was coming, and the Defendant Astros' personnel did not make any noise when a fastball was coming.

76. As a direct and proximate result of Defendants' wrongful conduct, Plaintiff Bolsinger's prospective economic relationships, including his relationship with the Toronto Blue Jays, was disrupted, and Plaintiff Bolsinger incurred special and general damages in an amount to be proven at trial.

PRAYER FOR RELIEF

WHEREFORE, Plaintiff prays for judgment as follows:

1. For past and future general damages in an amount to be determined by proof at trial;

2. For past and future special damages in an amount to be determined by proof at trial;

3. For punitive and exemplary damages against the Defendants;

4. For costs of suit;

5. For reasonable attorney's fees and costs as provided by statute; and

6. For such other and further relief as the Court deems just and proper.

DEMAND FOR JURY TRIAL

Attorneys for Plaintiff Michael Bolsinger
Plaintiff Michael Bolsinger hereby demands a jury trial.
DATED: February 10, 2020

Contributors

TONY ADAMS was voted as the winner of the Contemporary Baseball Analysis Award of the Society for Advanced Baseball Research for his research and analysis at SignStealingScandal.com, published on January 29, 2020. Adams is a Houston-based graphic designer and web developer who spent more than sixty hours writing an application to analyze video and audio footage of the 2017 Houston Astros' sign-stealing operation.

RICHARD CREPEAU is a professor emeritus of history at the University of Central Florida, where he taught courses in sport history and twentieth-century American history. He has written extensively about sport history, including books on Major League Baseball and the National Football League. He has written articles in academic publications and newspapers, as well as columns for the Sport Literature Association that have appeared in the *Huffington Post.*

EVAN DRELLICH broke the story of the Astros' cheating with his colleague at *The Athletic*, Ken Rosenthal. Drellich's book *Winning Fixes Everything* will be published in 2023 by HarperCollins. The book examines the scandal, the management culture of the Astros, and the efficiency evolution of the sport in the last decade.

STEVEN GIETSCHIER has been a sport historian since 1986, when he joined the staff of the *Sporting News* to create and manage its research center. In 2008, he took an academic position and began teaching courses in American history, sport history, and baseball history. In 2021, he rejoined the *Sporting News* as a historical consultant. He lives in Florissant, Missouri.

GEORGE GMELCH is a professor of anthropology at the University of San Francisco and Union College. He is the author of sixteen books, four of which relate to professional baseball. He has done ethnographic research in Ireland, England, Canada, Barbados, Alaska, and California, as well as studying the culture of professional baseball. His book *In the Field: Life and Work of Cultural Anthropology* (2019) was the inspiration for an ethnographic film, *A Year in the Field.*

MICHAEL HINDS is an associate professor in the School of English at Dublin City University. From 1996 to 1999, he was a visiting lecturer at the University of Tokyo and retains an interest in the culture of Japan, as well as its representation elsewhere. His main interest lies in American literature. He is the coauthor of *Johnny Cash International: How and Why Fans Love the Man in Black* (2020).

MATTHEW KLUGMAN is a research fellow at the Institute for Health and Sport, Victoria University. His research examines those who love and hate sport, along with the intersecting histories of emotions, sports, race, gender, sexuality, medicine, science, migration, the visual, and bodies. His most recent book is *Black and Proud: The Story of an Iconic AFL Photo* (2014), coauthored with Gary Osmond.

WILL LEITCH is the author of five books, including the novel *How Lucky* (2021). He is also a contributing editor at *New York Magazine* and writes weekly for that magazine, *Intelligencer*, and *Vulture*. He also writes regularly for NBC News, the *New York Times*, the *Washington Post*, Medium, and MLB.com and is the founder of the late sports website Deadspin. He lives in Athens, Georgia, with his wife and two sons.

ALLISON R. LEVIN has a JD from Washington University in St. Louis and a master's degree in applied communication from Southern Illinois University–Edwardsville. She currently works at the School of Communications and Journalism at Webster University. She serves on the board of directors for the Society for American Baseball Research (SABR). Her research primarily explores the intersection of popular culture, sports, and social media on traditional communication methods. She lives in St. Louis, Missouri, and is a born-and-raised Cardinals fan.

KATHERINE MURRAY is a freelance writer and PhD candidate in literature at the University of California, San Diego. She specializes in critical gender studies and is writing her dissertation on nineteenth-century gender and sport. Presenting her research at the Baseball Hall of Fame was one of her top five favorite days of being alive.

EILEEN NARCOTTA-WELP is an associate professor of sport management at the University of Wisconsin–La Crosse. Her research interests include the intersections of race, class, gender, and sexuality in regard to high-performance women's sport. Her work has appeared in the *Journal of Sport History, Sport and Society, Soccer and Society, Team Performance Manual*, and in several edited volumes.

MITCHELL NATHANSON is the author of *Bouton: The Life of a Baseball Original* (2020) and *God Almighty Hisself: The Life and Legacy of Dick Allen* (2019).

ROBERTA J. NEWMAN, a longtime baseball scholar, focuses on the intersections between baseball and other forms of popular culture, most particularly advertising and comics. Her book *Here's the Pitch: The Amazing, True, New, and Improved Story of Baseball and Advertising* won the 2020 SABR Research Award. She is also coauthor of *Black Baseball, Black Business: Race Enterprise and the Fate of the Segregated Dollar*, a study of the business of the Negro Leagues in its cultural context. She is a clinical professor of liberal studies at New York University.

JOSEPH RIVERA is a tenured assistant professor of philosophy and theology at Dublin City University. He is the author of three books: *Phenomenology and the Horizon of Experience: Spiritual Themes in Henry, Marion, and Lacoste* (2021), *Political Theology and Pluralism: Renewing Public Dialogue* (2018), and *The Contemplative Self after Michel Henry: A Phenomenological Theology* (2015).

JONATHAN SILVERMAN is a professor and chair of English at UMass Lowell. He is the coauthor, with Michael Hinds, of *Johnny Cash International: How and Why the World Loves the Man in Black* (2020) and author of *Nine Choices: Johnny Cash and American Culture* (2010). He has served as the Fulbright Roving Scholar in Norway (2007–2008) and was a John H. Daniels fellow at the National Sporting Library (2013–2014).

MATTHEW STAKER was a member of the baseball team at Webster University, where earned a BA with a minor in sports communication and a master's degree in management and leadership. Born and raised in San Diego, California, he is a die-hard Red Sox fan.

ERIN C. TARVER specializes in feminist philosophy, American pragmatism, and the philosophy of sport. She has particular interests in the relationship between popular culture and the self. She has written on a range of topics, including politics, sports, William James, and Michel Foucault. Beyond philosophy, she loves sports, cooking, and south Louisiana, where she was born and raised.

DAIN TEPOEL is an assistant professor of sport management and coordinator of the sport management graduate program at Lock Haven University. His work has appeared in *Sport in Society, Journal of Sport History, International Journal of the History of Sport, Sport History Review*, and *Nine: A Journal of Baseball History and Culture*. Before starting his career in higher education, he worked with the Northwoods League, the St. Paul Saints Baseball Club, and the Minnesota Timberwolves.

Index